W9-AUO-666

GUINEVERE

OTHER BOOKS BY
NORMA LORRE GOODRICH

King Arthur
Merlin
Priestesses
Medieval Myths
Ancient Myths

GUINEVERE

NORMA LORRE GOODRICH
KDO KTJ, FSA Scot.

HarperCollins*Publishers*

FIRST EDITION

Designed by Cassandra J. Pappas

Library of Congress Cataloging-in-Publication Data

Goodrich, Norma Lorre.
    Guinevere / Norma Lorre Goodrich.—1st ed.
    p. cm.
    Includes bibliographical references (p.) and index.
    ISBN 0-06-016442-5 (cloth)
    1. Guinevere, Queen (Legendary character)—Romances—History and
criticism. 2. Arthurian romances—History and criticism.   I. Title
PN57.G85G66   1991
809'.93351—dc20   89–46530

91 92 93 94 95 CC/RRD 10 9 8 7 6 5 4 3 2 1

To

Barbara Paul Fanshier,
chief of commissioners of the
Clan Mackay Society of the United States of America,
with gratitude, love, and admiration
from the author

CONTENTS

LIST OF ILLUSTRATIONS

*Figures and Map by Michael R. Cap de Ville,
California State University, Long Beach*

ACKNOWLEDGMENTS

THANKS TO MY HUSBAND, JOHN HEREFORD HOWARD, WHOSE GENEROSITY and unflagging support remain unequaled. Thanks to son Jean Joseph Lorre for technical assistance and data recovery. Thanks to Jana Seely for library, research, and manuscript assistance, and for her knowledge of Scriptures.

Thanks to former editor Kent Oswald, to Senior Editor Craig Nelson, and Assistant Editor Jenna Hull, as to my friend and agent Harold Schmidt. My debt to my colleague Ruth Palmer of the Interlibrary Loan Office, Honnold Library, Claremont Colleges is great. I am also grateful to my most distinguished colleagues, Professor A. Robert Bell and the artist Michael Cap de Ville of California State University at Long Beach.

Special thanks are offered to my former graduate student at the University of Southern California, Dr. Joan Milliman, for her discussions with me concerning the last ballet of Sergey Proko-fiev, *The Stone Flower:* Kirov State Theatre of Opera and Ballet, Leningrad, July 6, 1958; Metropolitan Opera House, New York City, May 4, 1959. The prima ballerina portrays the Mistress of the Copper Mountain.

Special thanks are offered to another former student, Katie

Spies Mueller, for her continued interest in comparative literature.

Many persons were kind enough to walk me through this book, and to offer encouragement and information from their own archives. Among these were Dr. William Douglas Bookwalter, Mr. D. S. Bell-Irving, Clan President Willis L. Cunning, Professor Willard A. Downie, Professor Barry Fell, Miss Eleanor Greenan, Mr. Ronald A. Hecker, Esq., Mrs. Laurence M. Marks, Mr. J. P. Morgan, Colonel J. Ross Oborne, Miss Nadia Sawyn, Clan Chief John Shaw of Tordarroch, Mr. William S. Stinson, Mr. Niall R. Thomson, Mrs. Gladys Thompson, Mr. Gregory M. Thompson, Mr. Allen Thompson, Mr. Wesley R. Tilden, and Mr. Frank C. Tribbe, Esq. My thanks to these persons and especially to those who are, like editors Barry Fell and Frank C. Tribbe, authors whom I much admire.

My admiration is great for two scholars who by their work on Chrétien de Troyes have revolutionized Arthurian studies: R.L.G. Ritchie of Scotland and Eugene J. Weinraub in Israel.

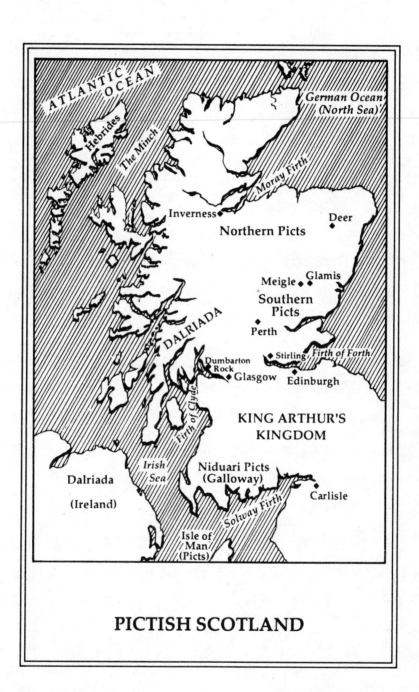

PICTISH SCOTLAND

CHAPTER I

Guinevere

Death may end a life, but it doesn't end a relationship.

—JOHN WHITE,
The Meeting of Science and Spirit

QUEEN GUINEVERE DIED IN SCOTLAND, BEFORE THE DAWN OF HISTORY there. She did not long survive King Arthur's passing, around 542, and she had been his wife for thirty or forty years. Neither his nor her death ended that relationship. The mystery of their lives has only deepened as the Dark Ages try to slide down the ramp of time, deeper and deeper, into total obscurity.

But this primary human mystery, even today, is clearer than the other black envelope that shuts her and her champion Lancelot into their secret, star-crossed love affair. Somewhere in that dark north land their phantoms must still stretch out a helping hand to the beloved.

By name and fame, by stature and ill-repute, Queen Guinevere may well be the world's most glamorous woman. She reportedly walked in queenliness and incomparable beauty. Her beloved, the forever youthful Lancelot, stood by her side, swore she was innocent of all charges against her, laid down his tartan, drew his naked sword, and offered to die for her if he could not kill all her accusers. He killed them all, and swore to her again a deathless love.

Was it her beauty or her majesty that raised her posthumously to such heights of glamour? Or was it her crimes, and especially this adulterous liaison with Lancelot?

This queen's black-hearted adultery, it is still falsely charged, was what caused the collapse of King Arthur's golden kingdom. Thus wretchedly ended his gallant life and paradisal rule. Tar with a full brush, says the adage, and slap it on her; some calumny will stick, no matter how many times the queen protested and how fiercely Lancelot denied it. Not even judicial trials by combat could stop the slanderers' mouths. They said she caused King Arthur's final, deathly battle at a place called Camlan, which was very probably the Camboglanna Roman fort on Hadrian's Wall. There on high land north of the deep river bend King Arthur met his last young nephew Modred in a terrible battle. The two died, or slew each other. What tragedy!

Despite the deaths of Arthur and Modred there at Camlan, wildly untrue and unreconciled rumors remain: Queen Guinevere had remarried Modred; Modred had escorted her to safety in the Highlands. Queen Guinevere was drawn and quartered by horses; she escorted King Arthur to the Grail Castle where he died. She caused his kingdom to collapse; she died of grief in England. She entered a monastery, where King Arthur visited her and forgave her. The queen was Lancelot's unrepentant lover in the triangular relationship: Arthur, Lancelot, and Guinevere. Queen Guinevere was barren. Her grave is in Meigle, Scotland; her grave is in Glastonbury, England. She had three fathers; she was a twin (or a triplet); King Arthur had three wives, all three named Guinevere.

None of these false charges and countercharges, scandalous rumors and accusations, has been subjected either to evidence or to the corroboration of reason. With a cool head, in an American place, safe from the special pleadings of impassioned British nationalism, religious prejudice, and racial rancor, a foreign historian now offers to reexamine the Guinevere question.

In the old days an old notion of woman prevailed. Nobody

has as yet argued in Guinevere's case that she seems to have been a warrior queen. Would that not throw a different light on her character and personality? Nobody has as yet argued that she was King Arthur's archivist in a land where neither he nor any other warrior except Merlin the Archbishop was literate. Does not her higher education throw a more flattering light on this illustrious queen? Why did it not occur to the chroniclers, who mention her only as an adjunct to Arthur, Gawain, Merlin, and Lancelot, that she may have been a native and, therefore, a foreign princess caught in cross fire between invading Irish Scots on the west coast of Britain and conquering Anglo-Saxons on the east coast?

Nowadays scholars in Scotland particularly have taken to walking the terrain to measure the land, to search for landmarks described in Arthurian manuscripts, and to argue time and distance. They have also succeeded in locating ancient sites, cities (*civitates*), and hill forts. They are currently sifting with spoons Arthur's old battlefields. Wars have passed over these northern parts of Great Britain between the Roman walls, Hadrianic and Antonine, and been settled at these same fords, these same reconstructed strongholds, these same pleasant meadows; across the very same bogs, waterways, and mosses. Today as a result we locate Salisbury in Edinburgh rather than in England, Arthur's Camelot number one as Carlisle near the Solway Firth, and Guinevere's birthplace even farther north where lived Pictish natives, who were to be absorbed by Scots, Angles, and English. Guinevere was probably one such foreigner—a native Pict.

Today again we may wish to approach the problem of love, which was Guinevere's and Lancelot's private relationship, with more caution than has as yet been exercised. Early in our century such famous authors as Simone de Beauvoir in France and Denis de Rougemont, whose English editor was T. S. Eliot, in Switzerland launched long attacks against the notion of passionate love synonymous, they said, with the longing for death first developed by medieval authors of Arthurian texts. However that may be, we should be willing to look hard at those Arthurian manuscripts, which supposedly propose adulterous love, a madly passionate love (*fin amor*) as the relationship of Lancelot and the queen. What if only one text so represented the situation—and by error in translation? Was Guinevere being calumniated or was the French lady commissioner of the text, by way of Guinevere, being tarred?

Truly one cannot find in Denis de Rougemont (Paris, 1939), who blamed the Guinevere-Arthur-Lancelot triangle of adultery, and/or in the Isolde-Isolde-Tristan triangle any evidence of deep scholarship in medieval texts. Idem, for Simone de Beauvoir. Either readily accepts inherited translation and received opinion. Thus, an attempt at an investigative biography of Queen Guinevere must be undertaken. We are in our century, observed the Parisian barrister, Madame Nathalie Sarraute (Paris, 1956), entered on an Age of Suspicion. Today we ask for evidence and proof. We would prefer a record set straighter.

Guinevere's story and her life descend to us in bits and pieces from the Dark Ages, which was a period of invasion and unparalleled demolition of homes, fortresses, and hill forts with an attendant destruction of most written records. In such cataclysms, under repeated floods of invaders on all coasts from all northern seas, does it seem likely on the face of it that Guinevere and Lancelot indulged in love games decade in and decade out? Planned defense, personal courage, excellent physical training, eloquence in oratory, daring escapes would have served—and did serve—Guinevere, Arthur, and Lancelot better in the Dark Ages. Parlor games, divorce, and betrayal more became the eighteenth century with its powdered wigs, lice, bare bosoms, and monstrous palaces without plumbing or running water. Guinevere's home lay beside a bank of the Forth River in eastern Scotland. She could go boating and get washed at least.

Guinevere's biography will not be endebted either to Denis de Rougemont or Simone de Beauvoir, much less to any so-called medieval cult of deathly, passionate love, but rather to Arthurian writers and scholars from every country of the Western world, chiefly from America to Scotland and Germany via Ireland and France. Her story will draw on history, archives, ancient voices, and such modern authors versed in mythology as Heinrich Zimmer and his editor Joseph Campbell. Eschewed will be all soap operas, especially the Victorian, where Tennyson's queen grovels wickedly at Arthur's feet, rolls her eyes, and cries out her remorse. To us in the twentieth century she did no such thing, for in Guinevere's day, as we know, adultery was immediately punished by death. Neither appeal nor rank would have saved Guinevere for one minute. Hers would have been the bonfire if Lancelot ever failed to prove her innocence. He could not fail, he said, because *she was innocent.*

If heroical epics had ever been written about women heroines, or if epics had ever even portrayed a heroic woman, then that sort of biography would have suited Queen Guinevere. But alas, epic heroes are always male sacrificial victims expendable for the good of the community. That was far from Guinevere's case. Gawain died in combat. So did Lancelot. Modred, who was Arthur's heir, died in combat either beside or against his Uncle Arthur. Perceval, Galahad, and Lohengrin disappeared, or went as pilgrims to Jerusalem. Guinevere was the sole survivor of them all. But she seems much more an epic figure than a sob sister in some Victorian hole-and-closet romance. Much less suited is she to the stock opinion: that Lancelot jumped on her bed, made love to Arthur's queen, and caused her sheets to be bloody. How distasteful are dirty books of any century.

Nor will tragedy suit Guinevere's story, for even if she were put to death by being torn apart by horses, that would make her only a wretched figure, but not a grandly tragic heroine defiant to the end but bowed in disgrace *through no fault of her own.* So she fits no literary genre, and the same is true for Lancelot. Both he and Gawain die in battle and according to the fortunes of war. Both had in peacetime gone guarantee for Guinevere whom both cherished as their true and lawful sovereign.

Lancelot was certainly Guinevere's love. It is far from certain that he ever became her lover. And yet ladies the world over adore him before Arthur. Why is that? What is there about Lancelot that sends the heart to beating, which caused young ladies in his days to diet madly for weeks before he was to appear before them and they before him?

In 1948 the German scholar Heinrich Zimmer put his finger on Lancelot. Zimmer's editor Joseph Campbell recorded this new interpretation of the Guinevere-Lancelot love affair not as adul-

tery but as love-to-the-death between liege and sovereign, perhaps something like Benjamin Disraeli's reverence for and adoration of Queen Victoria. Lancelot was no epic hero either, decided
Zimmer. No less a tragic hero fallen like Oedipus from a great
estate to ignominy:

> Lancelot is an incarnation of the ideal for manhood
> that exists, not in the world of masculine social ac-
> tion, but in the hopes and fancies of the feminine
> imagination (from "Four Romances," in Zimmer,
> 1948–68, p. 133).

Reflecting upon Zimmer's conclusion, one must ask another obvious question: Whose feminine imagination did he think created Lancelot? We know that Arthurian manuscripts originated
like the German *Lanzelet* in Carlisle, as in Melrose (both then in
Scotland). Then who besides Merlin could have been the recorder of Lancelot's deeds? Several texts specify in so many
words that when Lancelot returned from time to time to Arthur's
Court, he had his adventures written. By whom? By what "feminine imagination," if not that of Queen Guinevere? Merlin employed his own full-time scribe, or bard, named Blaise. Guinevere was Arthur's full-time scribe, or bard; and Ireland boasted
many such who were royal women and also fine poets.

The vast Arthurian corpus, or literature—which is, in fact,
the largest in the world—did not accumulate around an unin-
spired nucleus. It required over the centuries patient and talented
recorders who were trained writers and probably also avid readers themselves. While impossible to prove today, because *Northern Annals* are still missing, one may at least ponder Zimmer's
original suggestion and extend it to a logical corollary that
Guinevere herself, like Queen Elizabeth I after her and like the
probably royal Arthurian poet Marie de France, was this Lancelot's original author. In fact, her wedding contract so stipulated
that the new queen would act as court recorder. Thus this hero
Lancelot who over succeeding ages has so appealed to women,
young and elderly alike, may have been a projection of Queen
Guinevere's ideal man. He was, if so, truly her beloved. No

Arthurian text has missed that last point, which is their relationship.

The French writers of the Middle Ages have always claimed Lancelot as a native son, thought him native French because of his elegance and his French-sounding name, its three syllables easily pronounceable in Old or in modern French. Only recently was the etymology discerned, making *Lancelot* merely a translation into French of the Latin name *Anguselus*. Therefore Lancelot was not a native of continental France, but a royal clan chieftain of the Gael, or Celts, whose name in modern English would be "the Angus" (i.e., Latin, *Anguselus;* Old French, *L'Ancelot*).

This Lancelot, who was held to be of both royal and saintly lineage, was a revered son of two dead, departed kings also named Lancelot. Their gravestones he guarded and moved to safer repositories as Arthur's wars appeared to be worsening. Lancelot was clearly portrayed as a gorgeous hero and a royal prince before whose passage maidens and ladies queued up, before whom everybody bowed and gasped in adulation, doubtless with streaming eyes.

The charge of adultery was not leveled at Lancelot by the Oxford don Geoffrey of Monmouth nor, in fact, by any clergyman in Britain. That allegation, which also comprised all the nastier details of bloodied bedding, came from eastern France circa 1172. It took only some thirty-five years for the immense popularity of Geoffrey's *History of the Kings of Britain* (1136) to inspire an Old French work centered entirely about the personage of this royal Lancelot.

The paid continental author Chrétien de Troyes, from Troyes in Champagne, who wrote the *Lancelot* of 1172, has never been referred to as less than a genius in bloom. France has a tradition centuries older than England's, and older than the English language itself, of respecting authors who like Geoffrey and Chrétien were literary men of genius. Chrétien is always granted the benefit of the doubt, unqualified praise, despite the fact that his Arthurian texts cannot compare, either in historical stature, in lofty impartiality, or in sheer beauty of language to Geoffrey's much more popular and successful *History of the Kings of Britain* (composed originally in Latin).

After Chrétien's *Lancelot*, Queen Guinevere is suddenly and widely branded an adulteress whose supposed crime supposedly distanced Lancelot from his military duties to King Arthur. Some later authors go so far as to make Lancelot leave Britain altogether and desert Arthur's side and Guinevere's. Such treatments have not gone unprotested by historians of Scotland, for both Scotland and England claim Lancelot and Guinevere. Geography cannot allow the latter, however. The Scots must now be heard. They have other explanations for Lancelot and Guinevere, which understandings surface in the massive Old French volumes of the *Prose Lancelot* (written in 1220–1230). They come in French, of course, from Scotland and the days when the French were still governing Britain.

Guinevere and Lancelot today, then, still stand at the apex of controversy, the late English texts blaming them, the earliest Latin text of Geoffrey at Oxford, England, exonerating them. Paradoxically, the earliest French text of Chrétien rises to world fame by dwelling on the immorality of these royal British personages and the inevitable catastrophes that ensued: no less than the expulsion from Paradise of the loathsome female Guinevere before the dissolution of the paradise that had been King Arthur's peaceful reign of some long years, or even decades.

Possibly none of this alleged adultery may have been taken seriously, until modern critics such as Geoffrey Ashe commenced considering these royal personages as historical. While Guinevere sobs out her guilt at a convent in Amesbury, England, as per Sir Thomas Malory's *Le Morte d'Arthur* of the fifteenth century and Alfred, Lord Tennyson's *Idylls of the King* in the nineteenth century, readers may nod complacently at her. Adulterous women are no longer burned at the stake or stoned to death in England or France. Adultery nowadays is perhaps even condoned. Guinevere foresaw her terrible reputation, Tennyson wrote, and dreamed that she would ever be maligned. It came to her in an "awful dream," or was she perhaps a priestess?

But when we confront the possibility that after all these fifteen hundred years since Arthur's death circa 542 our characters in Malory's exquisite prose and Tennyson's unforgettable poetry may have been historical, then we must look deeper into the allegations. History does not condone adultery, and certainly not in queens. Nor was Guinevere guilty.

This attempt at a biography of Guinevere amounts to a second look at her situation in history and Lancelot's. Principally, who was this Guinevere? Where did she hail from? Why her great reputation for grace and beauty? What was her military expertise, which even Sir Thomas Malory accepted? Through what testings did she earn her homage for extraordinary courage and heroism in mortal peril? What was this powerful woman who brought home to Carlisle (Camelot) two wounded warriors by leading their horse, on which she had loaded them, through the perilous forest? How to explain her longevity when all about her had died? If she was escorted to safety in Scotland, then where in Scotland did she go? Where in Scotland was she sheltered, and why? And why Guinevere? Can anyone seriously believe Scots ever sheltered an adulterous queen of Britain?

The Scot historian Boethius in the sixteenth century, studying history then at the University of Paris, proclaimed Guinevere's honorable interment in Scotland. Not only that, he personally *had seen her funeral monument inside Scotland,* which was not only a tall gravestone but also a marvel of the sculptor's chisel, a work of art. According to historians of Scotland, Modred was no traitor and no abductor of Queen Guinevere, but a prince of Scotland and King Arthur's duly named heir. Quite clearly, Guinevere's case needs a second look and much more study.

The mysteries dancing attendance on Queen Guinevere are those that shroud every human personality and particularly women's because women are taught to be closed and secretive. Perhaps the lady Guinevere belongs royally and rightfully, by birth, by marriage, and by longevity to the most royal of sovereigns like the queens Elizabeth, Victoria, and Boudicca of the ancient Iceni in England. Because of her notoriety, Guinevere belongs perhaps also with Cleopatra and Catherine the Great. But her case is still more special than even Malory or Tennyson guessed when they rose to the supreme heights of literature in their holy treatments of dear Arthur's coming and passing from this world.

The mystery of Guinevere thus depends on several vexed

questions. The most important points remain to be solved. Her most profound secrets all demand to be unveiled, for she is still so unhappily shrouded. Everything about this ancient queen, whose history in the *Prose Lancelot* fills page after page, volume after volume, must be reevaluated.

While the world remains moonstruck before her, as it were, and totally absorbed in puzzling over her adultery, it lets the queen slide peripherally away from our vision. Obsessed with sex and her lack of morality, the modern world has ceased to note the more perplexing problems her situation raises. Meanwhile we have neglected another reading of the kindly, much more voluminous sources such as the *Prose Lancelot.* These later texts pay closer attention to facts and details such as her marriage contract, her betrothal ceremony, her wedding night, her twin sister or double, and her reactions whenever she stood in danger of her life during more than one emergency. These later authors are not infatuated with sex, or with the various ancient queens of Britain as Geoffrey of Monmouth was infatuated. These *Prose Lancelot* authors have rid themselves of the stringencies of poetry; they write cool prose, the prime purpose of which is to share information. They write loftily, above any bee in the bonnet concerning sin, like noble clergymen well aware of the human condition and how to deal even with heinous lapses. In their wake we, too, have a less-passionate view of ancient royalty.

In any event, given the nature of the human personality, Guinevere will never allow us to lose our sense of mystery before her or our desire to know her better. Even if we journey again and again to Scotland and lay our hand on her gravestone there, which towers over us, and even if we then have tears in our eyes, they will not be tears of sorrow for Queen Guinevere, but tears of gratitude that so much of our commonly shared ancient past is recoverable. All we shall ever know comes from experience, all of which lies in the past. It is worth weeping over, by the long road into the Highlands.

In touching her rosy and beautiful gravestone, which ever since Boethius wrote about it in Paris five hundred years ago many have journeyed to Scotland to see and touch, we actually do lay our hands on Guinevere, as on her past. Her case is much unlike Arthur's, for whom, say the *Annals of Wales,* recently edited by Rachel Bromwich at Cardiff University, there never was a grave. It is true that the late Nora Chadwick (also of Cardiff University in Wales) pointed to a site twenty miles from Carlisle (Camelot) at a parish named Arthuret as a site peculiarly connected to King Arthur because it was named after him: "Arthuret." But it is only a lone parish church and overgrown, ancient *graveyard.* It may be Arthur's grave, however.

In Guinevere's case we do have her real grave, beside a village church, in an isolated area of Scotland. Nowadays her gravestone has been moved. It now stands inside a Woman's Museum to which admission is open and free if one can find the caretaker. Furthermore, distinguished visitors have over the last few centuries visited this site and given us the benefit of their expertise and experience. (It was one of them who looked at her sculptured stone memorial and concluded falsely that Guinevere was evil in life, that she was drawn and quartered by horses— and richly deserved it, for the crime of adultery.)

If asked for an opinion, a modern reader of Arthurian texts from the High Middle Ages would have to reply that Queen Guinevere strangely resembled several of her contemporaries. Because of her extraordinary courage and presence of mind, she resembles the Geneviève who became the patron saint of Paris (Luxembourg Gardens). When from the city wall she saw the army of Huns approaching, Geneviève advised her fellow countrymen to hide in perfect silence behind the ramparts. Believing the city looted and abandoned, Attila and his army withdrew. The ancient Guinevere also much resembles the brave Mary of the Gael who set a new standard for women worldwide when she chose virginity and joined the Church, eventually meriting the honor of being interred beside Saint Patrick, not in Glastonbury, England, but in Ireland at Downpatrick. The evidence that Queen Guinevere still wore the antique green of a holy Druidess raised and educated on the Isle of Man, Irish Sea, comes as the most stunning of surprises.

Queen Guinevere will not be what we expected to find. She and Lancelot alone knew the way at low tide to the Grail Castle, on Saint Patrick's islet, facing Ireland. After he survived a painful initiation, Lancelot termed the place paradise: "Isle of Joy." The queen also, but earlier than Lancelot, was educated on that same Isle of Maidens (priestesses) where commissions were being received for King Arthur's sculptured sarcophagus and where Lancelot actually raised the lid on the tomb where all too soon he, too, would lie ceremoniously in death.

Because Merlin was then High-Priest in Britain, he must have known Guinevere while she was still a pupil of Merlin's chosen lady teacher for Lancelot and his cousin Bors. The Lady of the Lake may also have superintended Guinevere's formal instruction, for it had included not only the symbols used in Pictish sculptures such as standing Celtic crosses but also the calligraphy used on parchment (manuscripts), or handwritten texts. It was the Lady of the Lake Niniane/Vivian, her name reading one way in Scotland and another in Wales.

The German Wolfram, author of *Parzival,* which belongs among the earliest of Arthurian texts, claimed that "Grail Maidens" educated by the Lady of the Lake were sent "out," or home, at the end of their school days so that they could wed equally royal youths. Such were Guinevere and Arthur: royal Roman by birth, because born in the Roman Empire.

Of course, we are to recall that Britain, even including parts of what is now Scotland, had been ruled by Rome for five hundred years before Arthur and Guinevere were born. This Roman world with its Roman structures they saw every day of their lives. By the time of Merlin's archiepiscopal rule, and King Arthur's assumption of royal sovereignty, these isles had been Christianized. Saint Patrick had led the way, having become the first Christian Bishop of Man and the southern isles some three decades before Merlin was born. Without her long training by royal and Christian teachers, Queen Guinevere could never have become King Arthur's archivist.

Finally, any biography of Guinevere depends almost wholly on ancient sources as rewritten in the Middle Ages. It is necessary to translate proper names from Old French back into Celtic. Familiar personal names will be let stand during the following narratives, which will eventually allow final corrections into some original form, such as:

English	Latin
Merlin	Dubricius (*Sanctus*)
Arthur	Arturus (*Rex*)
Lancelot	Anguselus (*Ille*)
Guinevere	Guanhumara (*Regina*)

(*Sanctus,* "saint"; *Rex,* "king"; *Ille,* "the famous"; *Regina,* "queen")

The kind of biography Guinevere will acquire in these following pages depends on Old French, Welsh, and Old German original translations of lost sources from Britain, which France was governing in the Middle Ages. It may be assumed that all our authors, even those prominent scholars who wrote the *Prose Lancelot* and preferred dignified anonymity, almost certainly knew each other and most certainly collaborated. One can only imagine with what naked greed these medieval writers searched for manuscripts and haggled over borrowing and lending just as do our Inter-Library Loan Offices in American universities today.

Even Geoffrey of Monmouth probably had read and also had met his follower and alter ego, Chrétien de Troyes, according to Eugene J. Weinraub (1975), recently of Bar-Ilan University, Israel. If that is so, and it truly seems so, then Chrétien would also have had professional and perhaps also political reasons for contradicting Geoffrey with pleasure and for chuckling over the result. The measure of Chrétien's success as an author rests today directly proportionate to Geoffrey's early and late abysmal disgrace.

Nobody must fall off the chair at the likelihood that Queen Guinevere and Lady Macbeth shared a common heritage, birthright, and somewhat similar first names. Any slight understanding of Pictish real estate law opens the door to realizing why Guinevere was personally so sought after as bride and persecuted to the point of being kidnapped after marriage. How be sure the pretender to her body had her and not her double if the real heiress was not tattooed? The location of Guinevere's dowry would alone have dictated her supreme position in Merlin's eyes, in Arthur's, in Gawain's, in Galehaut's—but probably not in Lancelot's.

Only Lancelot had learned as a child to love Guinevere, according to German writers. She had been an older sister, Wolfram von Eschenbach believed, to Lancelot when he was a baby forlorn, alone, cold, orphaned, motherless, half-drowned, and pulled out of the lake barely in time to save his life. That childhood danger alone would make Guinevere's anguish clear as years later and in daily danger of her own execution she saw Lancelot again at his maturity. The ties that bound these two far surpassed the hidden pleasures of any passing sex.

A woman reading the scene of their first meeting as adults feels Guinevere's repressed emotion at the sight of the child Lancelot grown into a splendid man. It was the never-forgotten love of the small girl for the even smaller boy (cousin?) playmate. As a woman Guinevere certainly never forgot this special, tender, protective love of the older girl for the younger male child who is more vulnerable, who must be watched over and helped through his tests. For all the while she knows that he is alive only for a day. His birth requires him to die young in battle on some foreign field that will in all likelihood be her own property. And she herself will live to learn of it, perhaps will have to view the site where he fell on the bloody ground.

Even after the Lancelot-Guinevere relationship is viewed thus alternately, a far greater mystery remains. Something characteristic of Guinevere is still missing. Who was she really? Was she only an heiress-become-queen at Arthur's Court? It would appear that so far our sources have failed to alert us plainly to Queen Guinevere's prime functions. Money alone and property, immense though her real holdings doubtless were, would guarantee not much more than her marriage. After that day everything she owned would be administered by King Arthur, before whom she too constituted mere personal property. Rather than sink gracefully into second place, Guinevere continued to rise and still rises or looms, veiled probably, green clad certainly, bejeweled and bedecked in another majesty, superior by far.

So we must turn to those whom we consider superior authors from the Middle Ages and for long moments shunt both

Geoffrey of Monmouth and Chrétien de Troyes onto an unused siding. Authors on the main line will have to be newly interrogated, for they claim certain advantages such as anonymity, distance, open-mindedness, lack of bias, worldliness, stature, sympathy, high birth, leisure, and superior knowledge. The essential ancient material they had to have at hand was twofold: *bardic paeons* of praise, and a clear understanding of symbols.

The Bards of Arthur's day had been prepared over long years to celebrate fittingly the lives and great deeds of their royals. Consequently, they wrote set pieces appropriate to each great occasion. For this reason we are able to see Guinevere first as she acted publicly: her reception of visitors, her betrothal, her wedding, her coronation, her testings at Arthur's Court, her trials, her presence at judicial combats, her leadership at ceremonies, and her stops along journeys. Aside from such occasions, we have some knowledge of her background, her contracts, her functions, and her feelings.

What we must unfortunately learn for ourselves, each one of us separately, is the meaning of those symbols that more than any other body of information, even more than language, reveal the hidden Guinevere to us. It is generally understood today that certain symbols occur as our common property in four areas: folklore, tales, art, and religion. Fortunately for the world, each area contributes immediately to our understanding of Guinevere: art precisely through the Pictish carvings in eastern Scotland and, specifically in her case, the sculptured standing stone that is her rose-colored memorial. She is also a heroine of folklore because of the colors she wears, because of her jewels, because of that particular metal that surrounds her on special occasions, because of her human conditions of fiancée, confederate, bride, wife, sister, and queen among others. We note that both tales and folklore, her written and ancient material that is the basis of history, come from literature itself. Every symbol mentioned thus far is also the property of myth, ergo of religion. All ancient myths were once in some way and to some degree liturgy.

Let us prepare by looking in paraphrase now at certain of the lesser symbols that characterize Guinevere: crown, dove, pillar(s), fountain, and blood.

In Guinevere's case her two crowns symbolized her aura, an aureole, plus a token of majesty and royal authority, which resembled and brought vaguely to mind the bridal crown of Venus, for example, or a godly crown in which the Holy Grail gleamed like a fiery ruby, some crown of Wisdom, a crown of Christian love, a crown of the spring flowers of Flora, and the red heart encircled by Christ's Crown of Thorns. Ultimately free association leads each allusion back to religion, both to Satan and to Christ.

The four doves carried before Guinevere at her coronation are recognizable as descending from heaven at the baptism of Jesus, or as the Holy Ghost. Only Perceval, who was to be crowned last king at the Grail Castle, and Guinevere herself are allowed white doves as cognizance. Flocks of doves also attended olden priestesses in Asian oracular shrines. Ancient tombs were, therefore, called "dovecotes" in honor of priestesses of the dead. The dove also brings to mind the superior elevation of the priestess's soul (*anima, psyche, alma*). Guinevere's *four* doves resemble the four nails of Christ, the four rivers of Paradise, and the four-leafed clover, which is prophylactic. Because of Noah's dove, hers also become tokens of the sea, suggesting Guinevere herself was a foreigner from across the sea; the Irish would have called her "Fomorian."

When Lancelot lurched unexpectedly toward a goddess figure inside a domed, gilded temple, he saw Guinevere standing between two gemstone pillars. That day he must have recognized her. It was, indeed, Guinevere, but clad in ceremonial vestments. All ancient temples were entered, like Solomon's Temple in Jerusalem, by passing between twin pillars. Freemasonry knows this, and the twin pillars could have suggested those that upheld the poles. Women were called "pillars" of the early Christian churches. There were two solid gold pillars at Tyre. Guinevere also was a twin.

Guinevere's adventures grow more and more arcane from her halt at the (Irish) fountain such as the one where Gawain received the gift of eternal youth. Nearby or subsequent to the fountain of spring water the heroine herself performed the Celtic cauldron-regeneration ceremony, which must have come down from the pagan god Fons of the Fountain. Close by it loomed the black entrance to Purgatory where everyone brave enough descended to be purged and made pure.

The most fearsome of elemental symbols associated with her is blood (water) because it belongs with flesh (earth), breath (air), and fire (heat), all curative powers. Because blood is a powerful healing agent, the hero Lancelot will become a donor by means of a phlebotomy. From her cauldron or cup or Grail the priestess will let Lancelot drink before he descends into hell and the Irish Land-below-the-Waves. Then we sense that he is fated to die within the year, which knowledge freed his mind by releasing it from fear. Blinded as he arose by the red gem surmounting the Holy Grail, he prepared to kill Guinevere's enemy Meleagant next day.

A blood ceremony is called in Christian teaching the doctrine of transubstantiation.*

Other similar symbols are also called "things composed of two." They are said, as here in Guinevere's case, to light the way to eternity, to foreshadow the future, to link past to present, to confront the reader with the unknown, and to deepen awareness of the universe.

The Irish priestess sings:

> There is a distant isle,
> Around which sea-horses glisten:
> A fair course against the white-swelling surge—
> Four pedestals uphold it.
>
> •   •   •
>
> Colours of every shade glisten
> Throughout the gentle-voiced plains:
> Joy is known, ranked around music,
> In Silver-cloud Plain to the southward.†

*But see also HarperCollins's new and superbly illustrated *Woman's Dictionary of Symbols & Sacred Objects* by Barbara G. Walker (New York, 1988).

†"Isles of the Happy," from *Selections from Ancient Irish Poetry,* translated by Kuno Meyer (London, 1911).

Symbols preceded all written language. Considered as profound as any other kind of instant communication, symbols picture for us hitherto unsuspected reality midway between ignorance and understanding, day and night, the human and the divine. They alone reveal Guinevere during her journey to Purgatory and Paradise. There she stands clad in her true qualifications, performing at the Grail Castle rites thought to have been celebrated before her time by Christ and the Virgin Mary.

Such symbols light the way to eternity. The Romans knew this was a holy ceremony performed by the Celts. They called it "journey to Paradise": *iter ad paradisum.* The Romans well knew from experience that when they fought Celts, they warred until the bitter end—all the way to death. The Celts, said the Romans, go gladly to war after this particular pardon ceremony. They fight fearlessly, said the Romans, who were defeated at least twice in northeastern and Pictish Scotland, under the dreadful flying Red Dragon of Death. Merlin Pendragon? King Arthur Pendragon? Guinevere Pendragon?

Guinevere was a queen of the death-defying Celts. Her life story starts in the middest. The Romans called it *in medias res.*

CHAPTER II

The Wedding of Guinevere

He [Arthur] now led his army to Moray, where
the Scots and Picts were under siege.
—GEOFFREY OF MONMOUTH,
The History of the Kings of Britain

GUINEVERE ENTERS THE PAGES OF HISTORY IN THE MIDST OF THE ANGLO-Saxon invasions of Britain. She enters history at this time of massive panic because she is a famous princess whose presence and assistance are needed by King Arthur and his allies. The allied defenders need this girl because she is an heiress of vast, landed estates and because her father is a chieftain and warrior whose support they also require, immediately. King Arthur and his governor Merlin will attempt to take for the young king a bride whose father and whose property are the most coveted conquests inside Britain.

The best source for this story of Guinevere is the voluminous *Prose Lancelot* manuscript written in Old French during the French or Angevin or Plantagenet rule of Britain. The Old French manuscripts were by and large commissioned and paid for by these royals either inside Britain or in their vast Angevin Empire on the Continent. We should understand that there is an attempt on the authors' parts to please their patrons, persons like King Henry II and his Queen, Eleanor of Aquitaine. Of course, the authors enjoy this high drama of invasion and defense. They are vastly amused at King Arthur's problems of defending Britain against the Anglo-Saxons. Nothing in the *Prose Lancelot* comes very close to Guinevere's real life, marriage, betrothal, and alliance. Our medieval authors have, in fact, no more serious problem than to please and entertain some great medieval lady like the former Queen of France Eleanor, now the beautiful Queen of England and mother of seven beautiful children.

Their account reads pretty much tongue in cheek, like this, and it begins in the middest or middle or *in medias res:*

Each time they were defeated by the newly elected Arthur, eleven rebellious kings withdrew to headquarters of their ringleader King Urien of Wales and the Isle of Man. There they were reenrolled, counted, and provisioned by his nephew Bademagus. No sooner settled in from their latest trouncing than they heard the worst possible news.

"Saxons" were landing in force this time on two fronts simultaneously, they were told, one party on the south coast, or Rhinns of Galloway, and the second, on the east coast, or Firth of Forth. How could eleven exhausted kings defend their homelands in Galloway and along the Firth of Forth shores and still rebel against "King" Arthur? How could they still oppose his claim to be their sovereign?

The rebellious kings and their bands finally elected to disperse. They chose to fade away separately, each to his own stronghold, hole up inside, walled in. Even so, they felt unsafe. All had heard about the Saxon chieftain's dread sister, who was the Druid priestess named Camille. This fearsome pagan had already arrived to direct the invasions in person. The young King Arthur was still brideless, ergo, impoverished, which is to say, possessed of no real estate.

Merlin directing, Arthur set out alone for the great fortress of Carmelide. His royal and closest allies, kings Ban and Bohors, accompanied him. King Leodagan of Carmelide was still shut in this chief fortress, still under siege by fierce Saxons. The notorious King Urien also claimed he now wanted Leodagan's beard for his collection. He had already been joined by boatloads of villainous "Giants" from Norway, Denmark, probably Iceland, points west, and points east. Anyway, Urien already boasted twenty-nine royal beards stitched inside his imperial mantle. So maybe he would be satisfied with Leodagan's golden fleece.

Merlin advised Arthur that he doubtless now desired to call up the first or oldest contingent of his royal nephews. Arthur agreed.

No sooner had King Leodagan accepted the services of these anonymous volunteers, who were Merlin, Arthur, his nephews, and the two kings, than King Urien and foreign Giants attacked: Saxons, Danes, Slavs, and Lithuanians too. They took King Leodagan prisoner.

From the curtain wall his daughter Guinevere, who watched attended by her ladies-in-waiting, saw huge pagans surround her poor father and sweep him away. At the sight she almost died of grief. Fortunately, Merlin was looking out for King Leodagan. He ordered his personal escort to bar the way and surround the pagans. In a flash they were slain and the king freed. Everywhere Merlin's flaming dragon pennant brought relief that day to the defenders.

Below the young princess the battle also raged along the shore where the Forth River bathed the castle ramparts and then swept eastward into the great Firth and the North Sea. She strained to see warriors and to identify them. Many foreign champions had come to her father's rescue, from Carlisle in the south, somebody told her. They were led by a young king and his prime minister, Merlin.

Her unknown hero was Arthur. He performed so many marvels this day that everyone, whether on the walls or on the riverbank, stopped to watch him. King Leodagan's daughter and her damsels raised their hands to heaven and prayed the Lord that the young hero be kept safe from peril and death. They burst into tears to see his efforts and his cost. They could not understand how so young a prince could endure so much pain and strife.

Arthur struck right and left that day with Excalibur, cutting off arms, heads, feet, and legs, lifting helmets from heads, shields from shoulders, felling warriors and their mounts. He fought so near the outer rampart that a stone falling from the wall would have bounced off his helmet.

As soon as each noble, unknown champion had been relieved of his combat gear and weapons, he was thanked personally by King Leodagan. Then his beautiful daughter Guinevere, dressed in robes of costly fabrics, entered bringing warm water in silver ewers. Arthur refused her services, but kings Ban and Bohors accepted them when King Leodagan prayed them to yield. The princess herself washed their hands, their necks, and their faces, and then dried them with towels of finest linen.

A second beautiful princess, also named Guinevere, the daughter of the seneschal, performed the same services for the less-noble victorious warriors.

It is well known that King Leodagan's dead, departed queen had been a great lady of huge estates and high birth, but it was less well known that she always kept at Carmelide fortress, beside her, a noble maiden only a little less beautiful, only slightly less well bred than herself. This attendant married King Leodagan's seneschal, or standard bearer, which guaranteed her position at court.

During the night that Guinevere was conceived, as soon as her mother the queen left the chamber to prepare morning services in the chapel, King Leodagan awoke from sleep and forced the seneschal's wife. In other words, he raped the lady-in-waiting. Nine months later, and during the same first hours after midnight, both ladies bore a baby girl. Both babies were perfectly beautiful. And both were named Guinevere.

The royal Guinevere might not be told from her illegitimate half-sister except that the former had a birthmark shaped like a crown above one hip. In addition, her color was usually higher than her sister's, and her hair, more luxuriant. Then, too, her speech was much more fluent, that of a royal personage yielding to none in public eloquence and reasoning. It was well understood that the second baby *was not a twin,* but really the child of the seneschal's wife. No queen of Carmelide could have given birth to such a monstrosity as a twin! King Leodagan had only one royal daughter, let it be understood, was the word.

As soon as they were seated at the table, the guests watched the princess fill a golden goblet and step first to Arthur, who had been seated between kings Bors and Bohors. Kneeling before him, she offered the goblet to Arthur first. He looked down at her. He could not help again admiring her beauty.

The Princess Guinevere was in her day generally considered the most beautiful girl in the world. Her face was entirely unveiled that evening as she knelt before Arthur. She wore a wreath of gold leaves on her hair, which fell in long tresses across her shoulders, and down to the small of her back. Her raven hair shone more golden in the sun and more lustrous than the purest gold. Her cheeks alone were tinged with color. Hers was a white-and-cherry face. She held her slender shoulders straight, but they were pliant as a reed. Her body, too, was slender and curved like a willow. Her arms were round and long. Her limbs were straight and polished. Her sides were slender, and her hips were low. Her naked feet were white and round; her fingers, long and soft. Everything about her was beautiful. She was an image of brightness, high birth, great worth, honor, presence, and courage. She would always be remembered in malachite green and gold.

Arthur looked at her with pleasure, following the movement of her small breasts that looked like little apples. He saw how black her hair really was, how white her skin was, like new fallen snow, and he knew how soft her flesh about her body must be. He completely forgot to eat or drink.

"Take this cup, Sir," she told him, "and kindly forgive me if I do not address you by your name, for I do not know it. If you please, do not hesitate to eat and drink as freely as you wage war on our behalf. Then you were watched by crowds of people who also did not know your name."

"Many thanks," Arthur told her, "my beautiful maiden, for your royal service. May God grant me the strength and courage to acquit myself toward you."

When the tablecloths had been removed, King Ban casually remarked to their host, "I am amazed that you have not considered marriage for your daughter." King Leodagan had already guessed what the price would be. He countered by objecting the war. He rehearsed the dangers, the perils he had faced. He had been too busy, he said, to think of his daughter's marriage.

During a strategy session in his great hall King Leodagan openly again asked Merlin and his allies to reveal their names. When the men hesitated and looked to Merlin for a signal, Leodagan burst into tears. He could not utter another word, but fell humbly to the ground at their feet. Arthur raised him.

"So," said Merlin, "you desire to know our names and why we travel across this land seeking adventures. It is our hope to meet a powerful baron who will consent to give us his daughter in marriage."

"Well, well," cried Leodagan. "Why search any longer? Mine is the most beautiful girl on earth, the most intelligent, and the best trained in this century. Neither her parentage nor her dowry diminishes her value in the least; if such is your pleasure, I give her to you as wife, and all my lands after my death, for I have no other heir than her."

"Assuredly," said Merlin, "you have made refusal impossible."

Leodagan himself went at once to notify his daughter that she was the price of their deliverance. He advised her how to dress now in her very richest vestments. He took her hand and led her to the hall where the four royal persons awaited her. Then entered also from their side the highest persons of that kingdom, including the members of the Round Table. In a loud voice Leodagan addressed the assembly. "Sire," he began, "you whose name I cannot name, pray come forward to receive my beautiful and mannerly daughter, with the gift, after my death, of all honors, lands, and estates dependent upon me. I could not give her to a greater hero."

Arthur stepped forward, and said, "Many thanks." Taking his right hand, Leodagan placed it in his daughter's hands. Then the bishop of Carmelide citadel pronounced them betrothed.

Merlin then warmly advised Leodagan and his subordinates to swear due homage immediately to their new lawfully crowned lord. "Here is King Arthur," he told them. This done, the allies prepared to continue the war as Merlin commanded, against the "bearded" King Urien, his rebellious confederates, the Saxons, and their various foreign allies. Then Guinevere knelt again before Arthur to fasten his spurs. Then with Merlin's permission she gladly allowed Arthur to kiss her and to embrace her publicly, and for the first time.

The streets of Leodagan's citadel had been carpeted with foliage, the bare earth covered with sweet herbs. Ladies, servants, and maidens danced and caroled as King Arthur rode past. Youngsters were gaming and breaking lances as best they could in his honor. Inside the great hall, where Leodagan escorted the groom and his party, Guinevere waited. She rushed to Arthur with open arms. In full view of all present, she kissed him on the lips. Then they joined hands and climbed up to the fortress itself. There a sumptuous festival awaited them.

Next morning Leodagan asked Arthur if he was not ready to conclude the marriage. "I desire it more than you do," he replied, "but I believe I shall await Merlin's return. My good friend promised me to arrive in time. I think he will not keep us waiting longer than eight more days."

By the time Merlin appeared, he found everything ready for the lordly ceremony. As Merlin made it his business to know everything that went on in the kingdom, he realized how impatient Arthur was to see him, but he also understood that certain other arrangements had already been made by persons intending no good either to Arthur's party or to Leodagan's. Probably the latter would have to be put away.

Relatives of the cuckolded seneschal had secretly sworn vengeance on Leodagan, and this in accordance with their ancient, ancestral custom of the Picts. When dishonor struck one person, it struck every other member of this Pictish royal family. Leodagan had raped the seneschal's wife, and the seneschal had quietly endured the injury. In revenge for this shame, his relatives undertook now to suborn the matron who governed Arthur's bride-to-be by having her assist them in introducing the False, or second Guinevere, who was Leodagan's bastard by the seneschal's wife, into Arthur's nuptial bed.

The conspirators planned to wait in the dark garden for

Princess Guinevere to come down there alone to attend to her private needs. Then they intended to abduct her and carry her to a ship they had tied up alongside the citadel. Meanwhile the False Guinevere would be handed over to the faithless matron. "Let us see how such treachery succeeds!" cried the authors of the *Prose Lancelot* manuscript.

Early next morning Merlin and Arthur climbed up the eastern access road to the fortress. Leodagan ordered his daughter dressed in her most magnificent malachite robes, gold pieces, and gorgeous apparel. One could only admire her beauty the better, the more inestimably rich was the heiress's attire.

Then the Court adjourned to the minster of Saint Stephen the Martyr. With measured steps kings Arthur and Leodagan led the procession. They were followed by all the noblemen of the region in order of importance: Gawain and Merlin processed first followed by Arthur's personal bodyguard and ending with his foster father Antor and his foster brother Kay. Then processed the high-born heiress herself escorted on either side by kings Ban and Bohors.

Guinevere's face that day was again unveiled. Her gold chaplet rose over her glossy head. She wore a gown of beaten green silk sprinkled with emeralds and other precious stones, with a long train that flowed behind her.

After Guinevere came the seneschal's daughter on the arm of a minor nobleman, then the newly ordained warriors, then the members of the Round Table Order, the barons and lesser nobility of Carmelide, and, finally, the noble ladies from outlying estates and those from inside the town or citadel.

The wedding processants were received at the church door by Merlin, who was King Arthur's Archbishop Dubricius; but it was Leodagan's master chaplain who blessed the bride and groom and who performed the final marriage rite. The offering that day was huge and very rich. Once services were completed, the party returned from church to the fortress lawns through a crowd of women jugglers and minstrels. The festivities lasted until the wedding dinner began and recommenced as the guests left the tables.

Inside the fortress, after vespers had been sung, and as soon as everyone began to think of sleep, the ten relatives of the seneschal armed themselves with swords and stole into the garden. They had with them the second, or False Guinevere.

Meanwhile the bride's matron had no sooner observed the guests taking leave of the kings than she ordered Guinevere to take off her shoes and to undress so she could get into bed. Before tucking her in, she escorted the bride into the garden so she could urinate. The two had barely reached the bottom of the steps when ten traitors leapt forth. They seized the royal Guinevere and, handing over the False Guinevere to the governess, they transported their precious hostage to the seaway nearest the eastern base of the cliff fort. She had fainted. They prepared to haul her on board.

But Merlin had secretly warned two of Arthur's champions to arm themselves fully and await his signal. Like rolling thunder they fell on the kidnappers, killed some, and forced the others to let their bound, bundled, and half-suffocated hostage go. They carried out Merlin's plan so expertly that having hurled the guilty matron from fortress cliffs into the waters below, they carried Guinevere home to the castle.

This account of King Arthur's wedding to Guinevere is found in the *Prose Lancelot,* our manuscript in Old French. One of the most beautiful illustrated copies of this text may be seen in the J. Pierpont Morgan Library in New York City. The copy usually printed is Ms. fr. (French Manuscript) lodged in the Bibliothèque Nationale in Paris, France (numbered 747 and beginning at f. 178, v.). The famous illustrated copy in New York City was written about 1310.

The wedding story of Guinevere may read like pleasant legend; but it is not entirely amusing or entirely legend. The tale of Guinevere's wedding to King Arthur repeats another grim and brutal history typical of marriage practices common in the fifth and sixth centuries. Pictish brides fairly regularly failed to survive nine months of marriage, for at the birth of a first child the father's estates fell by matriarchal law to that child. The greater the heiress, the sooner she died. That Guinevere survived at all testifies to some other characteristic. If she had been endowed with real estate alone, she would not have survived. Pregnant, she would not have survived any more than did her lost mother.

Whoever has reflected on the real customs and real laws of the Dark Ages in northeastern Britain, which was Pictish territory, will already have grasped the tension of an essentially political situation here masked behind the later medieval writers' concern to please a feminine public enamored of "courtly love." Any question of love in the preceding nuptial arrangements would have been not only inaccurate, but actually unthinkable.

Merlin and Arthur had found themselves faced with domestic rebellion linked to foreign invasions on western and eastern coastlines. Those landings were taking place at military sites that must be held at all costs: Carlisle and the Solway Firth, which affords entrance to the Britons' chief fortress at Dumbarton Rock on the west, and the Firth of Forth on the east. The eastern and western firths, Clyde and Forth, must be held, or the defenders would have no alternative but surrender. Both deep waterways into the interior of what is now Scotland must, therefore, be held *at all costs.* Any and all sacrifice must be accepted at once, without demur, without argument. And the unknown northern Picts must be courted above all others, for it was they, and they alone, who had stopped the Roman advance into the far north.

Faced with such overwhelming needs, Merlin and Arthur had to place first measures first. Which one fortress must absolutely be saved? They stood face-to-face with the terror of history—one irreversible catastrophe.

Only the loss of what we now know as Stirling Castle on the north shore of the Firth of Forth would cut the island and, therefore, cause the immediate fall of Britain. This stronghold garrisoned through the ages—in fact, from time immemorial—is known as the Key to Scotland. Throughout history the fleets of Britain and her allies have mustered there. Furthermore, the single crossing of the Forth estuary lay below the gray cliffs of Stirling. These mosses of the Forth River barred the route otherwise from the Lowlands of Scotland into the remote Highlands and homelands of the warlike Picts. This wide swamp was totally undrained in Arthur's day and thus virtually impassable. Even today it remains so, for the grasslands that look stable really lie over deep, waterlogged clay that clings to shoe and hoof until person or mount is halted by its mass and weight. Had Stirling fallen, neither Arthur nor Merlin could have saved even their own lives. Nor could they have found another place of retreat if they lost the passage to the unconquered, northern Picts.

Our text has informed us indirectly, even though the first, thirteenth-century redactors of the *Prose Lancelot* would neither have known nor cared to know, that Arthur's nephew Gawain and his brothers were themselves Picts. The males were identifiable as such because of a remarkable racial characteristic: their rising and falling strength. But King Loth of Lothian, in southeastern Scotland, who is Gawain's father, figures among the hostile or eleven rebellious kings. Therefore, once King Leodagan has been delivered from besiegers, he pays the necessary price. Next Gawain turns on his own kin and captures his insurgent father. Faced with instant death at his eldest son's hand and sword, King Loth then also consents to swear allegiance to King Arthur. Thus Merlin and Arthur have ensured, by two close strokes of diplomacy, the south and north shores of the Firth of Forth. King Loth's hill-fort was Traprain Law near the present town of Haddington, Scotland.

The French writers, even if their noble public was still keenly interested in a Britain they had been governing since 1066, would not even have taken seriously the question of this long-since vanished people called "Picts," whose two states in Scotland had collapsed by the ninth century. Thus, the history of "Scotland" always commences at this collapse, after which the Picts themselves, despite their waning and rising strength, disappeared from the published pages of acceptable history.

The royal French lords and ladies who paid for the *Prose Lancelot* were primarily interested in King Arthur as lover of Guinevere and as the perfect husband who made her the best-beloved royal lady of ancient Britain (their real estate also). Understandably, the wedding story at the forefront gratifies their notion of ideal love. Their Arthur is incomparably victorious, strong and silent, recognizably royal, every lady's idle dream of a spouse.

Guinevere rises to the forefront because of her royal birth, which is still the Old World's prime criterion and *sine qua non* of excellence, followed by breeding, beauty, and the one desirable accomplishment dear to all Celts, the gift of what they called gab.

Merlin rings true, being in all versions of the Arthurian corpus, the prime mover, prime minister, and prime diplomat. Our authors come close to a slip when they have Merlin process up to the church door where he could have met himself garbed suddenly as an archbishop named Dubricius. Even though the French authors of the *Prose Lancelot* have no reason to suspect that Merlin and Dubricius (his clan name) are one and the same dignitary, they still have not presented his unofficial and official persona together, face-to-face. The authors of the *Prose Lancelot*'s wedding of Arthur and Guinevere were not paid to explain Merlin's role. Nor were they curious.

Terrifying history breaks through all this aura of perfect love if the reader asks questions such as: Why are Arthur and Merlin anonymous? Why do they continue to withhold their names, especially from Leodagan? Even Lancelot's often repeated reason, that he does not know his name and that he will not learn it until he has avenged the death of his father and/or successfully earned back his, or his wives', real estate. Once he has set himself up in the world and conquered enough dowries to match his royal aspirations, he introduces himself: Lancelot or Anguselus or King Angus of "Scotland," historically speaking, Pictland (Pentland).

Merlin and Arthur, or Arthur at Merlin's bidding, remain silent as to their identities because they are attempting to establish Arthur as legal sovereign. Merlin has already demonstrated the young hero's heaven-sent eligibility by having him draw the sword magically from the Stone. Stones generally, and especially the coronation Stone of Scone in Pictland (now in Westminster Abbey), have been revered as objects of deepest veneration from remote antiquity, as from the building of Stonehenge (c. 1750 B.C.). Even so, disbelievers in Arthur moved to open war against him, and they were led by eleven rebellious kings. Merlin and Arthur were fighting and winning an uphill battle, one calculated step at a time.

Merlin, therefore, finally admits only that he and Arthur are in actuality seeking a bride. By the way the chosen bride, or victim, is then manhandled on her wedding night, it would appear that what they are really seeking is her property. No tourist from the United States today can travel over Britain or fly over it without seeing the many large holdings, all prime real estate. King Arthur, no less than the future Lancelot, must first become a royal man of large property.

Arthur and Merlin are descended from the virtually prehistoric Celtic royal lines of Cunedda and Brychan, and both had proven this descent precisely from nine generations of forefathers. Arthur's claim to kingship and kingly succession came through the oblique line, by the daughter of Cunedda and by his wife, Gwen, and, unfortunately, not through primogeniture. The name Arthur comes to us directly both from the Latin *Arturus* of Geoffrey of Monmouth and also from the Anglo-Saxon monk Layamon's (Wace and Layamon, 1977) paraphrase of Geoffrey of Monmouth's *History of the Kings of Britain.* Layamon spells it phonetically: *Ar d'ur.* But the Anglo-Saxon name itself (*Ardur*) also means "father" to the young, says Layamon (1977, v. 19, 936): " 3 ungen for fader." The name *Arthur* appeared three times in the seventh century, or within a hundred years of King Arthur's death—all three times in Scotland. It also appeared twice in the oldest Harleian Annals manuscript of Wales (#3859), opposite the years 516 and 537.

The early Christian Father Tertullian spoke of ancient peoples harbored in "Abraham's bosom," a phrase that William Shakespeare (*Henry V* 2.3) revised to designate the diverse peoples of Great Britain itself, all of them safe in "Arthur's bosom."

Merlin's name in ancient Celtic would have been *merch llian* (son of the woman or child of the nun), which meant that he was fatherless as well as designating him as enrolled early in academics, already engaged in the long training for the priesthood. His royal and Celtic priestly name, Saint Dubricius, referred back to his illustrious and royal progenitor Brychan. Thereby, Merlin was Arthur's older cousin.

The French redactors of these *Prose Lancelot* passages are talking nonsense when they inform us that Leodagan will at his death bequeath all his real estate to the heiress Guinevere. Ancient, non-Salic laws prove them misinformed. Real estate by most ancient, matriarchal law belonged by right of birth to daughters only. All Arthur had to do to acquire it was consummate the marriage.

Readers of Arthurian texts must always have wondered at the murders of brides so early in their marriage. Equally striking is the general absence of mothers. The first Christian "saints" (prelates) set about protecting heiresses. In northern Britain or in Wales they claimed to be able to put the severed heads of young brides back on their bodies. In Ireland and France they received young brides, even wedded queens of France, and virginal princesses of Ireland, into the sanctuary of the Church. It seems fairly obvious today that the bride was utterly expendable as soon as she bore a daughter, during whose minority up to age thirteen and the onset of her menstruation, the father ruled her domain.

Thus, Arthur and Merlin remain silent, we are to assume, as to their identities until they have placed Leodagan so deeply in Arthur's debt that he transmits "his" estates when he hands over his nubile daughter to Arthur. Merlin had chosen her for two reasons, first of all, because she had begun to menstruate, which the French ladies dreaming of "love" should have known; France too was once divided into the large estates of landed aristocrats.

Their second reason for remaining silent is the clouded nature of Arthur's birth. At best, he was illegitimate. At worst, he was a fostered son, with only Merlin's word to the contrary. And Merlin was, at best, if Arthur was the son of Uther Pendragon, Arthur's first cousin. Merlin had no father. The births of both Merlin and Arthur were, therefore, shrouded in mystery; both emerged from under a cloud. If they were Picts, however, and not noble Romans as they claimed, they were not illegitimate. In any matriarchal society, which many scholars still say the Pictish was, there could be no such person as an illegitimate child. All male children were sons of the mother, i.e., "merlins."

Ancient Pictish laws may have suited the Picts very well, but they could not suit, or even be countenanced, by Christain prelates. Some married Pictish ladies openly practiced, and defended, a system of husbands in common. They did not view adultery as a crime, but as their privilege. Not so, the Anglo-Saxons. And not so, the Christian Church. Consequently, Merlin and Arthur trod carefully and dropped no names until Leodagan was deeply endebted to them. Then they sprung the trap: They had really come for Guinevere.

Thus, we have the nightmarish scene of the helpless maiden's abduction. Doubtless wrapped in blankets like a condemned vestal virgin, her cries muffled, and herself half-suffocated, she was hauled down the cliff to the water's edge. Thence she would have been cast adrift. Such was the fate of Saint Mungo's mother, who only miraculously floated ashore on a sandy beach whence she was rescued and assisted in childbirth.

Then we are asked to believe that Guinevere was rescued from her ten captors by only two men. Then she was put to bed? Although still bathed in tears, she was examined visually by her father so that he could thereafter testify that he had fulfilled his part of the bargain. What really happened to Guinevere was the age-old practice of marriage by capture.

Our texts leave her there for the nonce, mumbling unclearly about other dangers to befall her. We are to recall that the False Guinevere is still alive and residing at no great distance. Only Leodagan saw the bride's birthmark. Did Arthur see it? Did Merlin see it? But why was Guinevere in such mortal peril? What was there about Guinevere that presaged treachery and death to her particularly?

History has the ugly answer, if the Arthurian corpus is now really examined and pondered in its light. Guinevere was heir to that one prime section of real estate that could sink or crown King Arthur and, if acquired, immortalize both him and Merlin.

"Carmelide" is a French alternate spelling for Arthur's great, necessary eastern fortress, the Key to Scotland: Camelot. Her dowry in modern terms was Stirlingshire, Key to the unconquered eastern Highlands.

Even the Anglo-Saxon monk Layamon knew that Guinevere's dowry was the most valuable because it was the most strategic property in Britain and that the property was also called "the Round Table."

CHAPTER III

Coronation

Of the other party, the archbishops and pontiffs
led the Queen, crowned with laurel and wearing
her own ensigns, unto the church of the virgins
dedicate.

—GEOFFREY OF MONMOUTH,
History of the Kings of Britain

ONE CUSTOM APPEARS TO HAVE BEEN PRACTICED WIDELY IN THE INDO-
European world of long ago: Ambitious sovereigns became en-
tranced with glamorous, foreign brides. They pored over minia-
tures of exotic princesses from some mysterious, impossibly
distant land. They purchased her and awaited her arrival or
breathlessly engineered her capture. This usage especially became the newer warrior lords such as Arthur, who were perforce
intent on binding together warbands and establishing rights. But
shahs of Persia also chose, bid on, and ordered brides from
China. Siegfried operated differently, somewhere overcoming
the foreign warrior maiden Brunhilde for his King Gunther.
Similarly, Tristan fetched the virginal Isolde from Ireland and
lived to regret it. King Pepin of the Franks ordered, as if by mail
catalog, his Finno-Ugric bride Bertha from Hungary. A Danish
king, in whose antlered castle Beowulf fought Grendel, proudly
displayed a foreign, submissive Queen Wealtheow, much resem-

bling the kneeling Guinevere, but a queen whose name and origin have escaped us, as has Guinevere's.

Guinevere's name and origin have so far escaped definition, it is true; but she seems, even at first glance, to have been another such gorgeous, foreign treasure. Knowing as we do that she was born in the east of what is now Scotland, we are moved to quarrel again with the *Prose Lancelot.* If she was foreign, as seems clear, what about their story of a dowry? If Arthur demanded and received her dowry, which was real estate, what does that indicate? What foreign peoples ignored the custom of dowering brides, and which people demanded payment along with person? In what society were daughters tied to real property?

By the Pictish law of the most ancient eastern lands, daughters alone inherited real estate, and by Celtic custom long sanctioned as practiced, dowries were expected with brides. Thus, Guinevere seems, even this early in her history, to have been a foreign princess of this unknown Highland people, the eastern Picts. If so, then the Pictish crown on her royal hip was probably not a birthmark, but a tattoo. The Picts were said by the Romans—and Guinevere was also "Roman"—to be the "painted" or tattooed ones. Because he received a dowry, Arthur himself was a Celt, and most probably a Gael. Were Guinevere to die without a daughter, her property would likely pass to her half-sister, the False Guinevere. Thus, this latter remains a personage of great account.

We shall expect more news from this "illegitimate" (according to our laws), or False Guinevere. In a matriarchal society such as the Pictish, there would have been no "False" Guinevere, because by matriarchal law there were no illegitimate children. And we know how loudly and scornfully modern British historians deny any taint of matriarchy for the Celts (Scots) in western Scotland. Thus by her marriage, even if it was not by capture, Guinevere entered a foreign and Celtic culture probably excessively hostile to women and violently opposed to ideas related to matriarchy and its laws.

This one mark or tattoo on the princess's hip should probably also be recognized as a religious practice sanctioned by long custom not only in eastern Scotland, but elsewhere in the ancient world. For example, at the Asian temple of Hieropolis where the ceilings and walls were plated with pure gold, all worshipers purchased a tattoo for hand or neck. This permanent mark indicated their religious affiliation. To hear of such an identifying sign, and to realize that the authors of the *Prose Lancelot* passed it on to the reader, must give pause. It is a first indication that Guinevere is also some sort of holy personage. The second hint is the mention of her feet, as if she were to be considered what the Gaels would have recognized as *Argento-coxa,* a priestess called White Foot, because her feet also had been anointed. King Arthur and Merlin were by this marriage in effect saving "Scotland" from Anglo-Saxon rule and Anglo-Saxon paganism. It doubtless was essential to crown the royal, "Roman" Guinevere whose nationality, wealth, royalty, and perhaps sacred person guaranteed Arthur's realm. No one could forget that the Picts north of Hadrian's Wall, like the Germans east of the Rhine River, permanently stopped the Roman advance. Those handsome Romans who liked the country, or who were chosen by Pictish ladies, had intermarried with the Picts.

Several authors have claimed with assurance that Guinevere was crowned, that she was queen of Arthur's realm, which honor would have raised her political status immeasurably. Others probably thought it more politic, considering her generally bad reputation later at Arthur's Court, to leave her uncrowned and thus freer to commit ensuing adultery. The Pictish ladies bestowed their favors at will, it was charged by the vanished Romans. The procoronation advocates probably argued that a coronation, with magnificent pageantry plus booty, free food, drinks, lodging, and entertainment for victorious warriors would endear their leader to them. The coronation of Arthur and Guinevere should belong to history, however, as much as his battles and the problem of her dowry. A proper coronation as detailed still bears witness to us of a human experience perhaps shared by multitudes of people around the turn of the sixth century. The procoronation advocates actually record either fact, popular memory, or patriotic kitsch. Values from an almost lost age resurface for a few moments here. Best of all, Guinevere's coronation accounts turn out to be immensely mysterious, the closer we scrutinize the text.

Four prominent writers, or colleges of writers, recorded a coronation for both King Arthur and Queen Guinevere. First and foremost among this company stands Geoffrey of Monmouth who in his *History of the Kings of Britain* (1136) wrote the longest, most-detailed version. He remains to this day the most popular writer of the Middle Ages although, among the English and Welsh, by far the most hated. Geoffrey claimed that both sovereigns—Arthur and Guinevere—were noble Romans, which is to say, patricians. Robert de Boron,* the earliest French author of *Merlin,* in his last verses corroborated Geoffrey: Guinevere was crowned and, therefore, became a queen in Celtic Britain. The *Prose Lancelot* specifically and on several occasions excoriated Queen Guinevere for adultery, sadly pointing out that she *had been anointed* during her coronation ceremony "on the hair," "on the palms" (of her hands), "and on the cheeks" (of her face). These authors were endorsed in the closing years of the Middle Ages by Sir Thomas Malory's (1961) eight hundred or so pages in English called *Le Morte d'Arthur,* or *Death of Arthur.* This last work inaugurated English as a major prose language, just as the *Prose Lancelot* two hundred years earlier had inaugurated French as one of the world's major literary languages for prose.

These prose writers, it must be said in their defense, have not left many recoverable records of sources; but this has created, but should no longer create, an insurmountable difficulty. Their sources were bardic. The Bards of Celtic Britain (that is, the noble Bardic Order) were trained during many years of strictest isolation techniques to record for posterity the great ceremonies of their world. Most medieval authors speak of having actually heard Bards recite such coronation material. Among them were the Celtic Bards whose order unbelievably did not become extinct in Scotland until a mere hundred or so years ago. Their Bards were trained to write what could be called "set pieces," in the way poets write sonnets, epics, and odes. The Bards, therefore, had been severely disciplined by years of deprivation, dark-

---

*Robert de Boron (Borron) is perhaps a pen name.

ness, hunger, and almost daily practice to record the conquests of just such warlords as King Arthur, the weddings of just such heiresses of an entire people as Guinevere, the coronations of such a king and queen (*rex* and *regina*), their battles, their deaths, and their funerals. They certainly also celebrated the foreign queen's superb beauty, for such other set pieces recur frequently and verbatim inside medieval Arthurian texts. And no Greek ever celebrated female beauty as did the Celts of Britain and France. The Bards of the Celts adored Guinevere, as they adored all "king's daughters." Royalty impresses.

Geoffrey (see p. 54, bk. IX, 13) says, "omnibus . . . congregatis," after all had congregated for this high and ceremonious occasion, which was the coronation of Arthur and Guinevere, the holy offices commenced and archbishops officiated, chief of whom was Saint Dubricius (Merlin) because this (Stirlingshire) was his diocese. Arthur was escorted by four kings (*quator autem reges*) of *Albania, Cornubia, Demetia,* and *Venedocia* (Albania or northern Scotland; Cornwall, which here means southern Scotland or the Rhinns of Galloway; plus South Wales; and North Wales). He also gives us further glimpses of the history and geography of Dark Age Britain.

There is, then, in Guinevere's day a kingdom called Albania, which is ruled by "Anguselus"; and we translate "Scotland north of the Firth of Forth" with a "Lancelot" as ruler. There is also a kingdom called Lothian, which is near Edinburgh, as we already knew, with Gawain's father, Loth, as ruler. There is a King Urien, whom we met at Guinevere's Camelot, and he rules the lands of the "Murefensium," says Geoffrey, whose spelling of "peoples of Murray" here refers us to Old Irish for this place name *Murray,* which is now spelled "Moray" in Welsh and English. The ubiquitous Urien is generally also called some such title as "Lord of the Isles." If in his younger days, as hero, he ruled northcentral Scotland adjacent to the Moray Firth, then he could conceivably have dropped down the east coast to war on Leodagan's territory.

Although Geoffrey knows these virtually unknown but credible localities in northern Scotland, he speaks less convincingly when he then says that kings of both Demetia (South Wales) and Venedotia (North Wales) attended Arthur this day or, even less credibly, ruled by his permission. If Geoffrey was educated in Wales, on the other hand, or born at Monmouth, Wales, then he may have yielded to pressure there. One could have wished these two attendant kings to have been Damnonians and not Demetians, Venicones and not Venedotians. Damnonians would have given us central Scotland (Edinburgh to Glasgow) and Venedotians would have placed Arthur's last liege in the ancient Kingdom of Fife, next to Angus's *Albania.* In any case, Murray is the same place name as Moray, the spellings alternating in Scotland at least through the year 1332 in the case of Thomas Randolph, first Earl of Moray, or Murray.

Arthur's birth on the Rhinns of Galloway would also place him as related to the royal tribe of Votadini, for which reason he naturally was mentioned in their Dark Age epic poem, the Scottish *Gododdin,* or history of the Votadini. King Loth and his wife, sometimes called Anna, who was Arthur's half-sister, and her five sons—from the oldest, Gawain, to the youngest, Modred—are all not only close relatives of Arthur, but also members of this very royal tribe. In his book about his uncle Agricola, the last great Roman General to penetrate the Highlands of Scotland, the Roman historian Tacitus situates these tribes in these same ancient lands in the first and second century A.D.

The two highest dignitaries attached personally to Arthur and Guinevere have left famous names and famous adventures for generations of readers over the many centuries since Arthur's passing in 542: the Standard Bearer Kay and the ceremonial cupbearer at the wedding feast Bedevere. The former, known anachronistically in English as "Sir" Kay, is Arthur's foster brother. He will "go bad," say the old male gossips, because his foster mother nursed Arthur in preference to her own son, Kay. The case of Bedevere, who tradition claims attended the dying Arthur and consented finally to return Excalibur to the Lady of the Lake, seems to have been Guinevere's brother. He is contested, however, and claimed by both Welsh and Danes as a prince of their native blood.

Everybody in Britain who was anybody, it would seem, rushed to attend this coronation, the largest contingent coming from the Lowlands of Scotland, between the two Roman Walls.

The indigenous Pictish tribes were well represented as were Welsh, and Gaels from Ireland. The Romans too were extremely well represented, for Geoffrey's Norman-French translator Wace again insists that not only Arthur but also Guinevere was of Roman extraction. These connections are worth accepting, for Arthur proudly claimed descent from Emperor Constantine; Guinevere was presumably born at Stirling, which Agricola crossed as he set up his forts in the eastern lands of Scotland and born, therefore, where his auxiliary Roman fleet also called as they shadowed their commander's march overland. Traces of temporary Roman camps, stations, forts, and cemeteries have been found all along eastern Scotland. Their defeat by the native Pictish tribesmen, or Caledonians north of Stirling, actually caused the Romans to withdraw from the Highlands forever. The Picts under Calgacus (The Sworded), says Tacitus, suffered horrendous losses, but, say bellicose Scots today, they permanently defeated Rome. Agricola was recalled home to Rome, and was never, despite what he called his decisive victory, given another command.*

Wace also says Guinevere was crowned in a superb rite at which Dubricius officiated, that the festivities lasted four days, and that the heiress was crowned (a childless) queen. Wace translated Geoffrey while the Norman-French were still governing Britain and while French was still the language of the Scottish Court. What he had learned was once common knowledge, and among the ancient dukes of Normandie, kings of England.

The Anglo-Saxon redactor of Geoffrey, an ignorant, ugly English monk called Layamon, said first of all that the bride's name was not Guinevere, which is a Welsh spelling, but Wenhaver. In Arthur's days, he added, people ate at a board. It is called "the Round Table." He also said, with relish, of Wenhaver that Arthur dreamed of killing her, that he planned to kill her, and that Gawain planned to draw and quarter her with horses. That was why she hid in a nunnery. She survived Arthur, Modred, Gawain, and Lancelot, however, he admitted.

*In my opinion "Calgacus" is a title meaning commander-in-chief. The warrior drew forth the Sword of Command just as Theseus and Arthur drew forth the Sword from the Stone, signifying that he took charge, to wield the sword and to die by the sword.

On the other hand Sir Thomas Malory loved Guinevere, whom he honored with the title dame, as in "dame of the British Empire." He agreed with Geoffrey that Guinevere was crowned at Camelot, or Arthur's western fortress at Carlisle. There she was attended not only by her brother Bedevere but by one hundred mounted warriors whom her father provided to ensure her safe conduct. Her name was "Guenever" and "ever after" Arthur "loved her." The Victorian poet laureate Tennyson caught the young Guinevere on the road to Carlisle:

> She seem'd a part of joyous spring:
> A gown of grass-green silk she wore,
> Buckled with golden clasps before;
> A light-green tuft of plumes she bore
> Closed in a golden ring
> ("Sir Lancelot and Queen Guinevere").

A full description of an ancient parliamentary ceremony performed in (Pictish) Edinburgh between Monday, December 31 and Tuesday, January 8, 1661, as recorded by Mercurius Caledonius, differs very little from Geoffrey of Monmouth's Coronation Scene. In 1661 the "Honours of Scotland" were not four gold crowns, as per Geoffrey, but a Crown, a Scepter, and a Sword. The later ceremony also began with a procession of noblemen: Earl Marshall followed by four hundred Gentlemen, the "Honours of the Kingdom" borne by the Lord Commissioner, the Crown by the Earl Marshall, the Scepter by Col. George Keith, and the Sword by Sir John Keith. The Honours were laid on a Table, under the Cloth of State "then conform to the Ancient Custom of our Nation." The King at Arms, who would have been Arthur's Sir Kay, ranged the Nobility: Commissioners of the Burghs, Barons and their Lackeys, Lords in their Robes and each with three Lackeys, Badges of Honour on back and breast as in all Solemnities, Viscounts and Lackeys, Earls with four Lackeys apiece, six Trumpets uncovered, Twelve Heralds with their Coats of Arms, and two Sergeants with Maces. Then came the greatest Peers: the Lord Lyon King at Arms in his glorious Coat; the Earl of Mar carrying the Sword of

Honor and a Mace on each hand; the Earl of Sutherland with the "Royall Crown," the Lord Ramsay, Duke Hamilton, and the Marquis of Montrose with their hats on. At their arrival at the Parliament Yard, they were received by the Lord High Constable of Scotland. The Earl of Atholl fulfilled Bedevere's function of Cupbearer.

Geoffrey has no further notion of Guinevere's ceremony except to say that the ancient, Trojan (Celtic?) custom required ladies to enter one church and the men, another. Four queens, each carrying a white dove, preceded Guinevere. The doves seem at first to tell us very little, being open-ended symbols indicating femininity itself, breasts, love goddess Venus, or Christian souls. In ancient Babylon Semiramis was a priestess called "dove."

But the serpent and the dove *are the very tokens of Celtic royalty.* They prove Guinevere a queen. As for her attire, if tartan is as old as many think, and if it was neither Gaulish nor Scandinavian in origin, then hers may have been woven in Scotland by ancient Picts. The Gauls had paraded it in Rome centuries before Guinevere was born, and great weavers that they were, may have introduced it as they fled into Scotland. Curiously, the very Scottish attire that one would have chosen to represent Guinevere as a seaside Pict (Fomorian) is the Murray (King Urien's) with the Clan Badge showing a mermaid holding a mirror and a comb. "The powerful clan" (of Murray), says Robert Bain (1968), who wrote *Clans and Tartans of Scotland,* "had its origin in one of the ancient tribes [Picts] of the Province of Moray." The Crest Badge of the Clan Livingstone also recalls quite vividly Gawain's anger when he grasped a branch of a tree and flailed about him; their badge shows a naked, half-savage (Pictish) warrior holding a club, and the motto in French: "If I can." French specialists in armorial bearings have worked out a complete system of heraldry for Arthur and all his allies and opponents, giving the king not the four gold crowns Geoffrey allotted him at his coronation, but a total of thirteen.

If one continues, as here, to speak seriously of Guinevere's coronation that was reportedly witnessed by scores of dignitaries, then certain facets about queenship in Scotland, a strictly traditional land, must be subsumed. First of all, say historians of protocol, an ancient queen there functioned as both *priestess* and *judge,* which should give us the suffix *mara* to her name. Eastern Celts had such a queen: the Galatian Chiomara. The same suffix *mara* occurs routinely among the Gaels miles away, in far western Ireland. As queen theoretically in one of the seven ancient kingdoms of prehistoric Alba or Albania (now Scotland), Guinevere was bound by this anointing to eschew any function of a polluting nature. She, therefore, chose a delegate to act as her secular arm. The theory went that deeds of a polluting nature would drain Her Majesty of sacred energy. To safeguard her purity, she avoided defilement, such as bloodletting, which would render her unfit for this highest office of the land. She would delegate to her surrogate and secular arm, who will be Lancelot, the bloody work of her kingdom: the bearing of arms, warfare, judicial combat to decide innocence or guilt of an accused third party, and executions. The shedding of blood was a taboo for the queen whose head was taboo, as were her anointed body parts. Nor could the queen even touch base metals such as iron and bronze, but only those "purest" metals: gold, silver, and copper. (Copper is Guinevere's principal symbol.)

This reverence for copper, for it was a copper belt alone that girdled the loins of the holiest Druid priestess, should prove a likely thread. The unwinding of this employment of copper might lead us to one, last identification, a mystery that still puzzles everyone: Who were the Picts? What was their origin? What people were they?

Copper in Arthur's world held together the planks of his ships. It was also the major structural and decorative feature of the doubly mysterious Grail Castle on the Isle of Man. Gold was used for magnificent breastplates and/or torques worn by sacred, royal personages, and by sacred priestesses. Silver has always made the Clan Badges, worn universally by Scots and by persons proud of Scottish descent.

As Arthur's anointed queen, Guinevere was immediately empowered to select from among all champions presenting themselves for service at her Court, one male delegate. On this choice hung her future as ruler, as queen, as sovereign, and as woman. This delegate—Lancelot, in French, or Anguselus, in

Latin—would henceforth enforce her doom; reply with his life to all imputations made against her; answer in single combat all heavy charges laid against her; rescue her, if she was assaulted; search for her, if she was lost; rescue her, if she was captured; stand beside her whenever she was being tested; avenge her when she was insulted, humiliated, or tortured; ransom her, if she was ever taken prisoner; post bail for her; and swear to love, honor, and obey her without question and without hesitation, so long as he lived.

Looking at such a choice with the eyes of a modern woman, one will perhaps agree with Queen Guinevere that Arthur's oldest nephew Gawain would have been a poor choice. Brave as he was, powerful superabundantly as he doubtless was, Gawain would still have proven a sorry delegate. He won his distinctions too much by brute strength rather than by intelligence. He gave way to rage whenever threatened. He lacked that last surge of cool staying power that sets the jaw until a person turns the tide of battle and saves his or her life in direst emergency. Gawain had also failed to honor his father, which is a black presage of fundamental immorality in a person. He was more than once accused of rape, which certainly demonstrated not only sexual malfunction but also a probably incurable, irreversible hatred of womankind. And Merlin, who knew everything, had once roundly chastised Gawain for cowardice.

Queen Guinevere, therefore, probably turned for advice here to the one woman in her world preeminently suited to offer it: the Lady of the Lake. High-Priestess of the Manx world, as Saint Bridget at her holy fires of Kildare was High-Priestess of Ireland, only the Lady of the Lake would have been able to recommend a male delegate to Queen Guinevere.

In even older days doubtless the choice would have been made by the impersonal forces of nature: stars, moon, wind, wave, light, flight of birds, eclipse, and oak trees (*Kildare* or *Kildarroch*, "Temple of the Oaks"). Either astronomy or astrology could have afforded a means to determine eligibility and predict worth. Very probably the ancient stone circles (also called *Kil*, or "Temple") were used for such purposes. Ancient astrology would have alleged electromagnetic forces, in other terms, and predictably mutant female genes. The spirits of the wind, it was thought, would have carried his name to her.

The ancient belief of the Celts would have persuaded them to rely on the easiest, most readily available authority when gravest questions needed settling. That ultimate authority in their world, as it had been in ancient Asia Minor, Egypt, Greece, Troy, Rome, Africa, Scandinavia, Germany, and Gaul, was Woman. Women, the Celts also believed, possess an especially extraordinary power, which is foresight. Women, more than men, foresee consequences. Women, more than men, sense oncoming events. Therefore, rather than allow an observatory such as Merlin's to draw up a horoscope of the most suitable male who would probably be the best risk, Queen Guinevere deferred to the resident High-Priestess of the Grail Castle. She was the Lady of the Lake; the only personage who, we are sure, at her ritual of conferment had been anointed on the bare feet.

Queen Guinevere was anointed on the hair of her head, so deputized, as were ancient kings of the world. Royal personages always wore their tresses long, and Celts especially were inordinately fond of lustrous, long hair. Guinevere's hair was, by traditions long maintained in Great Britain, extraordinarily beautiful; and it was also said, but incorrectly, to have been blond as was the uncut hair of the Lady of the Lake. Both ladies, then, resembled physically a later ideal Scandinavian beauty. The cutting of hair removed power from the person; even more seriously, in Roman times it also reduced the person to bondage. Only chattels and slaves wore short haircuts. The comb for long hair and the mirror thus indicated royalty, and appear together on almost all Pictish carvings from northeastern Scotland: Stirling to the Moray Firth and farther east, almost to Aberdeen.

The Merovingian princesses and queens of the Franks, who were Arthur's and Guinevere's contemporaries across the North Sea, also wore their luxuriant locks long and uncut, even after the loss of virginity. In upper-class France today a young lady may receive her first haircut only after her wedding night and may wear her first seductive dress or bathing suit thereafter.

If one youth of proper age and suitable military might possessed, in addition to all superior qualities of body and mind, a birth that set him above all other such youths, he would be offered as the queen's man by the Lady of the Lake. She might love and treasure one such beautiful young man, and immeasurably so, if his genealogy proved him of both royal and holy blood. This most rare personage, on whom royalty and holiness were conferred by birth, possessed what the British Celts and the Merovingian kings would also unquestionably recognize as absolute legitimacy.

Her delegate would represent an absolute sacrifice in the service of Queen Guinevere. By sacrifice he would instantly understand the performance of any act, without expectation of reward. His would be a strength without ambition or passion. He would have so unbound his bond with greed that he would stand apart, as if inviolate. He would bear pain painlessly and die to rid Guinevere of the threat of danger. Because of his safeguarding, the queen would remain guiltless of breaking the taboos laid on her at her coronation: no shedding of blood, no wearing of hot colors (only white or green allowed henceforth), no touching of base metals, no permitting of any person to touch her head or anointed parts, no cutting of the hair.

The *Prose Lancelot* has it that Queen Guinevere took office at Carlisle at the Feast of the Virgin, in August. That day she wore her crown. Warriors ("knights") filed past her, each swearing allegiance. Then Arthur assigned the queen her functions at Court: to act as his treasurer and to hire four professionals to write their Annals. They then heard that the "Anglo-Saxon" King Urien (who previously had been called Danish) trod once more the warpath.

The prime authority on the heroic legends of Denmark has had a good deal to say here about such British, royal personages as Queen Guinevere and company. First of all, Axel Olrik (1976) listed the aspersions already cast at her, which were no less, of course, than the charge of treason once leveled at King Arthur's mother. Both Guinevere and the ill-nursed Kay had automatically acquired the accusation of "evil by nature," she, because of her descent from a foreign race of "Gnomes," or "Giants." Each had, by infancy, a supernatural and troubled heritage. As everyone knew from the Bards, the Norn hero Starkath the Ugly was the son of a woman raped by a Giant. Queen Oda had been ravished; she bore the elvish Hogni of the Nibelungs. One of the Merovingian queens had also been raped—by a sea monster. At Guinevere's home were sung historical legends of the blond rulers of Norway: Kingmother Gunnhild of Orkney and Harold Hairfair's son by Sniofrith. Thus, people then also knew that King Arthur's association with the bear was propitious, like his and Merlin's association with dragons. They knew of the Russian hero Volga, who was like Arthur a dragon's son. Both bear and dragon were ancient, tutelary deities.

Axel Olrik pointed out that persons who fail to accept Arthurian manuscripts as containing age-old material certainly err. Antiquity of material can be determined absolutely by myths delineating social customs and beliefs held before the dawn of history. These aspersions cast on British royalty stem from a prehistoric belief once widely credited: that the parents of Arthur and company were no less than progenitors of the gods, and offspring of Gnomes and Giants. This is also Guinevere's case. In other words, Arthur has wed and crowned the most royal of foreign heiresses, whom Welsh scholarship today (*Companion to the Literature of Wales,* Oxford University Press, 1986) suggests is Sovereignty Herself: "Sovereignty is represented as a beautiful woman whose marriage to the hero symbolizes his union with the kingdom."

Knowing no less, Sir Walter Scott so understood any marriage of hero and Sovereignty, writing in "The Lady of the Lake" of Camelot's king (Camelot was called Snowdoun by the French, or *Senaudone*): "And Snowdoun's knight is Scotland's king" (stanza XXVI). Arthur became king by virtue of his acquisition by marriage of Guinevere. Her inherited ownership of "the Round Table," which included Stirling, made him king thereof.

> It [Snowdoun] was probably derived from the romantic legend which connected Stirling with King Arthur, to which the mention of the Round Table gives countenance. The ring within which justs were formerly practised, in the castle park, is still called the Round Table ("The Lady of the Lakes" app.).

The French compilers of the *Prose Lancelot* have Gallicized the father's name: Leodagan. Earlier than them, the Welsh carefully spelled it Gogyrvran and added Gawr (the Great), which is the same as the modern Welsh spelling: Ogrfran Gawr. Translators have made of this in English whatever they chose, such as Ogre Bran (King Ogre) or Ogre Vran (King Raven), or Ocur Vran (Evil Raven). In any case, Guinevere is the slant-eyed daughter of a king who was not native to "Cameliard," but a foreigner from a land of Gnomes and Giants.

Aspersions cast on Arthur and family prove their long and close association with a foreign, pre-Christian culture. Olrik points the finger at Gawain and Modred, both sons of Arthur by a sister, said the reprovers. And so was Roland said to be son of Charlemagne by his sister, which is far worse; for they lived in 800, well within Christian and Catholic France.

Why is incest practiced by Arthurian royalty? Olrik suggests genetically engineered heredity, which was the hope of doubling certain traits considered hereditary: intelligence, for instance, or courage or physique or beauty. Thus, Sinfiotli was son of Queen Signy by her heroic brother Sigmund. Although the offspring's strength was so extraordinary as to have been believed doubled, he lived nonetheless under the pagan curse of his birth. His mother, like Merlin's mother and Guinevere's, conveniently expired during or soon after childbirth. The child is the thing, of course. The mother is always expendable.

Curiously such customs and hideous beliefs are recoverable from the Arthurian corpus even though the written texts we have today stem from the High Middle Ages, beginning with Geoffrey of Monmouth in 1136. But he was very shortly followed by many learned Franco-Scottish poets and compilers, who remain anonymous, and by the Norman monks across the Channel.

Looking back at fragments of ancient genealogy, we recover not only Guinevere and the lordly Giant who was her father, but also now from the Welsh "Song of the Graves" her brother Bedevere, still alive after Arthur's last battle Camlan: "The tomb of the son of Osvran [Leodagan] is in Camlan. . . . The tomb of Bedwyr [Bedevere] is on the hill . . ." Danish scholarship challenges Wales here and claims foreign, or Anglian (Danish) origins for Bedevere.

The final problem of Guinevere's dowry was solved only incidentally by a Scot, the textual scholar John Stuart, who in 1869 was editing *The Book of Deer* for the Spalding Club in Scotland. Because Deer (Deare, in Moray) was one of the oldest monasteries in Scotland and was personally founded by St. Columba, Stuart minutely studied the names of those persons (alive only thirty years after Arthur and Guinevere) who granted lands to the new foundation. A Pictish Queen Gruoch, for example, who was wife to a Pictish King Macbeth, granted lands to Deer. Stuart also found that Arthur's O'on, which was a Roman rotunda (*rotonda*) in Stirlingshire, was also chartered land. The rotunda was very remarkable, said Stuart (p. cli), because stone "houses" were rare in ancient northern lands. Most buildings in Scotland then, as in Norway then, were built of wood. Because Arthur's O'on was so rare a landmark, it gave its name to a baronial estate, a barony, in Scotland.

Now, Arthur's O'on was the Round Table, a tabled rotunda, a rotunda constructed on a stone table or foundation. Therefore Guinevere's barony, which centuries later appears in the land charters of Scotland as "Stenhouse (stone house) in Stirlingshire" was also called the Round Table. It was later identified legally as "Scottish house" (*domus Scoticana*), adds Stuart, when in 1461 it was deeded ("granted") by Alexandre de Broys de Stanehouse.

In *A Journey from Edinburgh* (1802) Alexander Campbell saw this Roman monument called "Arthur's O'on" or "Little Pantheon," he said, "a work of the Romans." "This singular monument of Roman antiquity was nearly entire till the year 1742." (Campbell 1809, vol. I, 39).

Thus, Queen Guinevere brought in marriage to King Arthur "the Round Table," which was Wace's original phrase that passed into the language of all future authors, composers, editors, mythographers, and the rare historian interested in Dark Age Scotland. In short, her dowry was, in fact, Stirlingshire.

CHAPTER IV

The Three Fathers

Arthur had three wives all named Gwenhwyvar,
but no poet has ever availed himself of all three;
that would have spoiled his plot.
　　　　　　　—Sir John Rhŷs,
　　　　　　　　Studies in the Arthurian Legend

Ancient triadic lore—directly from Wales in Guinevere's case, but also generally from classical antiquity—has longed to believe that there were not one but three Guineveres, either all three alive at the one time, or one at a time alive and wedded to King Arthur. Welsh patriarchs in Arthur's day boasted several wives. Such persistent associations with Queen Guinevere can only underline her native, supernatural presence in King Arthur's Court. There was one Queen Guinevere. Three Guineveres are only mythological, a sign of the ancient reverence of the number three.

The number three in northern Scotland still designates "the Bride," however, for whom triangular cakes were ritually baked at Halloween. Three-cornered cakes would especially compliment a divinely beautiful queen if she were herself as fragrant as the fleur-de-lis, or as triple as the shamrock.

Like the three fairy sisters or the three Weird Sisters met by Macbeth near the Moray Firth or the Three Graces of Greece and

Rome, Guinevere also floated in magic. Doves suited her royalty as they had escorted both the Greek Aphrodite and the Jewish Virgin Mary. The triple colors of religion—black, white, and red—allowed each glorious lady to choose her raiment. She was in a sense triple, like body, mind, and soul.

So tripled, Guinevere will have to prove to us now that she was a priestess, like the thousands such attendant on the Greek and Roman Mother Goddess, the Triple Hecate, who sat threateningly at the junction of three roads.

A last association leads directly not only to the triple Guinevere's identification as a supernatural princess to be revered and dreaded: the color green, the carbonate of copper, which is the green gem malachite. This mineral was long used as a local anesthetic, as protection against the evil eye, and as stimulant able to arouse extrasensory powers. Its magnetizing green color evoked the peacock feathers of the Roman love Goddess Juno. It is no wonder Guinevere has proven unforgettable.

When one consults the ancient *Triads* of Britain, as recently edited by Rachel Bromwich in Cardiff, Wales, one reads only from this one ancient source that Guinevere had three fathers. The first of them was the Pictish King Leodagan or Ogyrvran the Giant or Ocur Vran, Evil Raven. Charles Squire in his *Myth and Legend* (1905), which is now titled *Celtic Myth and Legend,* seconded John Hill Burton: Guinevere had three fathers, all three mythological. Ogyrvran was Satan or Vulcan, but in any case a Lord of the Underworld. The second father, Gwyrd Gwent, is still only a name (p. 331), and the third father Welsh mythographers know as some god leading in the night sky overhead, the Hounds of Hell. This third father, who is named Gwythur ap Greidawl (son of Greidawl), is also an ancient British god who struggles with Gwyn, the god of hell, for possession of the bride. In other words, Guinevere's fathers number 2 and number 3 are pagan gods from Greek and Roman religions. Only Guinevere's mother is prominently absent, but we are to suppose her the grieving mother Earth who weeps and searches for the Maiden named Summer during the ice of Winter. Ancient Celts, too, usually represented Hell as one hundred thousand miles of frozen ice.

Their daughter Summer was once fought over during annual
May Day celebrations.

Nowadays it is generally agreed that Guinevere's Pictish
father alone is at least quasi-historical and also that Old French
names and place-names in continental manuscripts are so superior as to be generally relied on.

These mythical fathers solve a mystery by connecting
Guinevere with Glastonbury, because the royal St. Collen of
Glastonbury personally fought Gwyn ap Nudd, a Guinevere god
and father, for possession of the Maiden every May Day. In
other words, Christianity fought paganism at Glastonbury.

The ancient *Triads* also claim that there were three Guineveres, that Arthur married all three, or that Arthur also took
three mistresses.

Early critics and even eyewitnesses in the Middle Ages
struggled to prove that the second Guinevere of the three was
really the one buried in Glastonbury. Such a search has seemed
futile after such Irish scholars as Patrick Weston Joyce (1920) of
Trinity College, Dublin, proved that the abduction of Summer
by her male sweetheart named Hell was an old Irish fairy tale of
King Airem, Queen Etain, and Lord Mider of Hell.

These Welsh *Triads* are not only real history, but mythology
from classical Greek, asserted the French critic Arbois de Jubainville in 1899. Three is the Indo-European divine number: father,
mother, and child. Three squared gives us the Muses. Hera swore
on three gods: Zeus, Poseidon, and Pluto (Earth, Water, and
Hell). All Druidical maxims were triadic: "Honor the gods, do no
evil, act bravely." The Greeks failed thrice in their attempts to
enter Troy. In Gothic fiction the hero fails thrice in his attempt
to penetrate the square castle. Thus we have had enough of three
mythological Guineveres, three fathers, three wives, three mistresses. The Irish hero Cuchulain may settle the question; he
received the requisite three gifts at birth: sight, understanding,
and calculation.

But Sir John Rhŷs, who is one of the most brilliant of Arthurian scholars in our century, still chose the mythological view of
Arthur and Guinevere. It is true that this view was current and
very fashionable in his day. He concluded in his charming and

prestigious book of mythology called *Studies in Arthurian Legend* (1891):

> On the one hand we have the man Arthur, whose position we have tried to define (warrior, emperor), and on the other a greater Arthur, a more colossal figure, of which we have, so to speak, but a *torso* rescued from the wreck of the Celtic pantheon.

King Arthur, he concluded, was the Roman god Mercury euhemerized, and so made immortal in legend. His name came from the Latin word-family of farmer, cultivator, plowman, i.e., *artor, arator*. The name Guinevere is also a Welsh translation, Rhŷs explained: *Gwen* (white) plus *hwyfar* (phantom, ghost). But, of course, Guinevere has as many spellings to her name as any ancient goddess had names, and to such a degree that at least one of Rhŷs's collaborators (Rhŷs and Jones 1900) declared that Guinevere and her people were probably not even Indo-European, much less Welsh, much less Gaels, much less Scots!

Sir John Rhŷs of Oxford University was hugely seconded in the 1920s by another mythologist, Roger Sherman Loomis, and students from Columbia University, who with massive charm and scholarship held and maintained two general theories: (1) the mythological origin of Arthurian literature and (2) the Breton transmission, from Brittany on the Continent, of these "stories," which are, he claimed, the body of Arthurian "romance." Arthur's "knights," Loomis also asserted, are nothing but Irish gods (*Celtic Myth and Arthurian Romance,* pp. 3-51). He concluded (p. 24): "The most significant impulses" of pagan story and pagan pattern arose in *pre-Christian Ireland.* "There lies the chief fountainhead of all these streams." We have in the Arthurian corpus, he said, "the ritual and myths of pre-Christian Ireland." It all comes from paganism, which is the "schools of the druids" (p. 31). Guinevere's abduction in particular was lifted directly from an Irish fairy tale, "The Wooing of Etain," where Guinevere's first husband, who was the god of the Underworld, took her back to his wintry realm. The Irish King Mider of the Underworld was so godly, so beautiful in his purple tunic with his long, golden

hair over his shoulders, and his lustrous, gray eyes, that Guinevere must have gone to him willingly. Loomis provisionally concluded in 1927 that the problem solved by Arthurian writers
was an

> elucidation of . . . primitive culture of the western
> isles whose resurgence in the romances of the Round
> Table supplied to medieval Europe . . . [the] same
> . . . imaginative stimulus . . . [as] Homeric tradition
> . . . to the Hellenic world two thousand years before.

The Grail heroes were young sun gods, he added. The names of
pagan Irish and Welsh gods are interchangeable with those of
Guinevere, Arthur, and all his heroes, and so are the Greek gods
and also the figures of the Zodiac. As Sagittarius Arthur won
back his bride from the Underworld's god and took her home
after a long war, so Etain was carried home to Tara by King
Eochaid Airem.

While the theories of Rhŷs and Loomis continue to delight,
with many believing today that Arthur and Guinevere were
mythological only, and cheering along with the archaeologists
who proudly announce from time to time that Arthur was never
here or there because they found here and there no trace whatsoever of his presence, or that mythology is impervious to archae-
ology, other persistent persons chip and chip away at their pro-
nouncements. One of the first doubters was a James Logan (of
Glasgow, presumably) who around 1830, or before Loomis's tenure at Columbia University, tried a new approach: sociology.
Would it be possible to authenticate the ancient personages of
the fifth and sixth centuries by their manners? Or are the customs and manners of King Arthur and his "knights" truly ancient? We are not allowed even to whisper that King Arthur
might be historic, scholars said then to themselves as they continue today; for otherwise, we will lose our tenure. But, then,
why do we not zero in on the Picts? What about them and their
manners? The Picts were certainly historical.

Logan's (n.d., 21ff.) book is well worth studying for the
inferences it is possible to draw from his inquiring mind. Guine-

vere's name Guanhumara meant "white" because the Celts, Gauls, and Galicians, to whom *C* and *G* were interchangeable, were an aboriginal, primitive race of "Gealta," white or whitened men and women. The *Pictish Chronicle* so stipulated: the Picts called themselves *Albani* of *Alba* because they were white and white haired, or flaxen haired. As the historian Appian wrote, they were Celts or Gauls or Cimbrians. Plutarch added, "No man knew what they were, or whence they came." The Picts were either Giants in size, everyone reported, or Gnomes who lived in the mountains. Formations of their warriors trod over everyone, with the queerest music you ever heard and hideous yells. Their women with bare, white arms reached out and ripped the shields off Roman legionaries. They were called Hyperboreans from the North, who inhabited opposite Gaul an island that was as large as Sicily.

When the Romans left Britain around 446, thirty years before the birth of Arthur, there were still sixteen tribes of dreadful Picts in the Highlands, north of the Antonine Wall, or the Clyde-Forth line (Dumbarton and Glasgow to Edinburgh and Stirling). There were also five dreaded tribes of Romanized Picts south of that line—in the Lowlands, between Hadrian's Wall and the Antonine Wall. Up north they hid from time to time in their impenetrable or "horrida" Caledonian Forest ("silva").

Logan went on, in the first four chapters, to describe the customs of the Gaels who had intermarried with Picts during Arthur's lifetime (475–542). The Celt usually married late in life, he said, and his bride was chosen to match his own prowess and size. If the king could vault over six horses, then so could she, like Brunhilde, match his feat. If he survived three days under the stone slab at initiation, so did she. The chiefs were not only the tallest men in the land but able to make the greatest strides and having freest gait. Their skins were as white as snow. They took great pride in their ability to survive cold weather naked and even greater pride in fancy dress, finery, beautiful hair, and adornment. The Picts all bore tattoos as identification and as ornament. They wore their hair, which was as red as gold, combed off the forehead and drawn up to the crown of the head. Arthurian texts rave about the beauty of Perceval's auburn hair and that of his father. Their best lassies, said Logan, had white linen locks and blue eyes, as Guinevere was described early in the *Prose Lancelot.* Their women's eyebrows and lips were small, delicate, and very chiseled. Logan quotes Athenaeus: *"Celtae pulcherrimas habent uxores"*—"The Celts have the most beautiful wives." For this reason also, the Celts were notoriously insolent, remarked the Romans; they were all unpardonably arrogant and especially contemptuous of shorter, lesser folk.

Logan quoted Tacitus to the effect that among these mixed northern peoples (some tall and some short), the chief was chosen for "splendor of descent," that Arthur was king, it is reasonable to believe, by Celtic right of primogeniture. The chief named his heir, ergo, Modred, by law of tanistry. Being next highest in blood and name, and by Pictish law the rightful heir as sister's son, Modred, and not Kay, was the "tanist," or "second" person. At Arthur's death Modred would have become, says Logan, "captain of the clan," and "first, royal person." Three women had become governing chieftains of a Celtic people: Velleda, Boudicca, and Cartismandua.

The Clan Chief entered his governing council by standing on a cairn shaped like a pyramid or by standing on a coronation stone. A person (Merlin) gave him (Arthur) a sword and a white wand, and he recited the chief's pedigree, also a practice of great antiquity. This place of ceremony was called by the Gaels a *moid* and was the later "Moot" Hill of Scone (*super montem de Scone*), from 850 to 1306.

Both Scot and Pict venerated the head. The Picts embalmed the heads of their enemies in cedar oil and carried them about. Even by Arthur's time, however, such manners, tartan dress, and customs as Logan detailed could still be found scattered all throughout Western Europe:

> That the Franks and Saxons retained, for a long time,
> the manufacture of their Celtic ancestors, has been
> shown. Charlemagne (c. 800), adhering to the primi-
> tive costume, dressed like the Scots Highlanders;
> and, from Windichind's description of a Saxon, he
> closely resembled a Caledonian (p. 183). (Logan drew
> from Camden's *Britannia.*)

Interesting and learned as it certainly is, Logan's book and, in fact, this sociological study of ancient Gaels and Picts, did not convince anyone that Arthur and Guinevere really lived outside the mythology of Ireland and Wales. The problem has intrigued scholars.

If sociology could not even decide who the Picts were, then perhaps linguistics could oblige. For Transactions of the Buchan Field Club of ancient Pictland (Feb. 9, 1894) John Gray studied personal and place-names in the *Book of Deer*, considered a vehicle for deciphering the ethnology of the prehistoric Picts of northern Scotland. This book is an historical document "of the greatest value" since the Monastery of Deer (Deare) was founded by St. Columba in 580 A.D., less than fifty years after the deaths of Guinevere and Arthur. The northern Picts, due to their remote homelands safely beyond the Caledonian Forest, retained, to a late period, their race, their language, and their institutions, more or less unchanged by contact with others. "The law of succession through the female, for instance, survived into the thirteenth century" there, although perhaps not among immigrant Picts of Galloway, Ulster, and Munster. The Pictish place-names in the *Book* "are usually of far greater antiquity than the oldest historical documents" and add much to the "meagre outline pictures of prehistoric peoples drawn for us by the archaeologists."

Place-names found in the *Book of Deer* are older than the Irish (Scot) invasions of the fifth century and could even be non-Celtic, said Gray. If so, *Basque* or *Iberian* should be found and is found among these remnants of names of the northeastern aborigines. These Picts were survivors who lost their kingship only in 844 to Kenneth Macalpin.

The peoples of Buchan were *Taxali*. The geographer Ptolemy had listed their tribe in A.D. 125. Their Pictish inscriptions also show a postfixed, rather than a prefixed, definite article (the) and a genitive (possessive) in *an* (*en*) precisely as does the Basque language Gray found to his delight.

Gray then proceeded to list the personal and place-names of this holy *Book* so very close to Arthur and Guinevere in both *time and place*. Of particular interest are the totems he discovered in local Pictish names, such as Macbeth: *Mac Beth*, "Son (of a) Dog" (tribe with the dog as totem). The *Prose Lancelot* supports this finding, because as a small boy Lancelot in a terrible rage slew his tutor for beating a dog. *Morcunn* meant "seadog." *Bracklawmor* was "Great Wolf's Tomb." *Matain* meant "Dog Whelp." *Malbrigte* meant "Wolf's Slave." *Dobarchon* meant "Water Dog." *Turbruad* meant "(King) Brude's Tower" (Inverness). *Comgell* meant "Foreign Dog." *Brucklay* meant "Tomb of the Badger." *Broccin* meant "Person of the Badger Tribe."

A weakness of John Gray's system appears finally in his own admission (p. 17): "These Taixali probably spoke a Pictish or Basque language, with a large admixture of Brythonic words." In any case, Guinevere's first real father, as proferred by an excellent linguist of the dawning twentieth century, was to have been Basque, or Celto-Iberian. As late as Helen Hill Miller's book on Arthur (1969, 19), one hears of the Picts as "the Ibero-Celts of Brittany." Many Scots have found Celto-Iberian ancestors.

One needs no more than a claim such as John Gray intended—that Arthur, Guinevere, and Picts were Basques—to raise the hackles of Celtic scholars resident in Britain. Roger Sherman Loomis and Sir John Rhŷs were supported by Stuart Glennie who in 1869 had listed Arthurian place-names in Britain and had *proven Scotland was by far the most prominent Arthurian locale.* The scholar and editor William Forbes Skene overpowered all others with his *Celtic Scotland* (1956) and other celebrated works. W. Douglas Simpson, librarian and geographer of Stirlingshire, supported military historians, who also realized the strategic importance of that area.

The most influential scholar of all has been O.G.S. Crawford of Glasgow, who patronized and encouraged the American antiquarian P. K. Johnstone, and others, to begin Arthur research all over again, text by text, site by site, from the ground up. And despite his immense labors founding and editing *Antiquity* magazine while it was published in Glasgow, Crawford walked the hills searching for Arthur and measured and hoped and would not bow down to pagan mythology. Crawford proved Arthur historical.

Those who know Arthur really lived and that he was a Celt rely also on the old, familiar tool of genealogy, commonly treasured by the Scots of today as verification of life and as each person's contact from an ancient past to a future. Thus, King Arthur appears prominently in pedigrees of Scotland, Ireland, and Wales. Irish genealogists derive him personally from King Feargus Leathdearg and give him the son born in Dumbarton, precisely where Lancelot and Guinevere delivered Arthur from a Saxon, or an Irish, prison. This son also figures today in Irish genealogical records as Mervie or Smorlie.

The august historian of the Campbells, the Duke of Argyle, recorded that Arthur's second wife was daughter to a king of the Franks, who bore him this son also called Smerviemore (Great Smervie), who died at age twenty-four. Born in Dumbartonshire, Smervie did not succeed to a throne, claims this record; he preferred hunting alone in the forest. Because of this choice, he acquired the nickname "Fool of the Forest." He married and sired a son of his own, which is attested to as during the lifetime of St. Columba, *"anno 570"* (Duke of Argyle 1983, 10–11). Annals of Ireland give the line of descent: Constantine, Ambrosius, Uther (Pendragon), Arthur, and Smorlie.

A current alternate or Welsh genealogical theory now accepts all Arthurian personages as historical and treats the general situation of King Arthur's life as spent in war inside what is now Wales, between North Wales and South Wales, Goidelic Celts versus Brythonic Celts, dark men versus fair-complected men, ending at Arthur's Battle of Camlan in a *cam-lan* (crooked glen) near Dollgellau in North Wales, c. 470. Arthur is here considered "Emperor" and in the Roman Imperial style, *"Pontifex,"* or High Priest also. He is still considered Patriarch, Chief, and Father of his Country. The various Welsh Arthurs cited are Arthwyr (Arthrwys), Artorius (Antonius), Anhun, Artmail, Arthvael, and Arthfael. The ruler named Arthrwys is also the *Prince Arthur* of lengthy verse (see *Prince Arthur: An Heroick Poem in Ten Books,* by Richard Blackmore, M.D.). Blackmore's tedious verses are a trial to read, but the author was a contemporary of the great narrative poets Spenser and Milton, the latter of whom had projected an Arthurian epic. No Welsh chieftain is an Arthur, however.

The *Prose Lancelot* would tend to confirm only King Arthur's errant son born in Dumbarton, which refuge it treats at great length during Arthur's "War in Scotland." The "Saxons," claims the text, had taken Dumbarton Rock, Geoffrey of Monmouth's *Alclut*, Fortress on the Clyde River. This astonishing place was, and is, a tremendous lava rock mountain with double red cones rising nowadays on the right bank, or Loch Lomond side, of the Clyde River.

> 'The king's forces,' a damsel told Lancelot and the warriors, 'is a dozen leagues away from us, before the *Saxons' Rock.'*
>
> That was a fortress constructed during the lifetime of the old King Vortigern who had married the Saxon princess. She was Hengist's sister.
>
> Now the beautiful [sorceress] Camille resided there. She was the sister of the Saxon King Hargoda [Hargodabran]. Camille was as learned in the arts of enchantment as were Arthur's Morgan and Merlin's Vivian [the Lady of the Lake]. Through her conjurations Arthur had fallen madly in love with Camille. For her part she did not despair of seducing him (*Le Livre de Lancelot del Lac,* vol. III, 405ff.).

The enchantress Camille invited Arthur to spend the night in her arms, a proposition he joyfully accepted. In the morning he found himself surrounded by enemy warriors who shut him up securely in an iron-barred dungeon.

Queen Guinevere had meanwhile set up her command post on the south bank of the Clyde River and proceeded to direct the following battles, which eventually, thanks again to the personal heroism of Lancelot, freed the emprisoned but passionate king.

The names *Camille* and *Mervie* have probably encouraged the theorists who believe that these foes who imprisoned Arthur and the enchantress who bore his son were Franks, even members of the Merovingian dynasty. This may have been the case. But their king's name of Hardogobran is more reminiscent of the Danish King Hardegan, hero of the oldest Scandinavian historical poem, the *Biarkamal.* If that is what the *Prose Lancelot* relied on here for the "Saxons" who were planning to transport Arthur into Ireland where they, rather than Merovingians, had sea bases, then the lady magician's name was more like *Krimhild* than the Vergilian *Camilla.*

According to Sir Walter Scott, who was a poet as well as one of the most influential of modern novelists, since he invented historical fiction in prose, it was not Guinevere who had three fathers anyway but Arthur who fathered three children. In his lovely poem "The Bridal of Triermain" Scott wrote an interpolation called "The Druid's Tale":

> The mystic tale by bard and sage
> Is handed down from Merlin's age (can. I, ix).

One day King Arthur, says the Druid, journeyed via Penrith into Cumberland, and past huge Mt. Saddleback (Glaramara). The king adjudged this land to be "a theatre" created by Nature for "high achievements." He preferred it to "Dame Guenever's" bower. He came to a castle in a vale, rode round it three times, heard no sound, and thought it

> Of wizard stern, or goblin grim,
> Or pagan of gigantic limb,
> The tyrant of the wold.

He blew a blast on his gold-tipped horn. The castle fell open to him and to his sword Caliburn. Inside the castle Arthur found a band of one hundred damsels. They played at undressing him. Arthur yielded perforce.

> Where lives the man that has not tried
> How mirth can into folly glide
> And folly into sin?

The queen of damsels was Guendolen. Arthur dallied with her (cans. II, III).

> Her lovers bartered fair esteem,
> Faith, fame, and honor, for a dream.

. . . .

> Another day, another day,
> And yet another, glides away!
> The Saxon stern, the pagan Dane,
> Maraud on Britain's shores again.
> Arthur, of Christendom the flower,
> Lies loitering in a lady's bower; . . .

for the three months of summer in her garden of delight.

Arthur swore to Guendolen that if she bore him a son, he would inherit a kingdom, and if, a daughter, she would have a suitable husband. Then dressing in "Persian" fabrics Arthur mounted his "Libyan" stallion and passed out the gate. There he met Guendolen dressed as a huntress, holding a golden cup. She pledged him a drink from a recipe passed down by her fairy ancestors.

Arthur accepted the cup and bent his head to drink; but as he did so, one drop of liquid fell on his horse like "liquid fire from hell." The horse jumped two feet in the air. "Peasants" still show how his hoof cut the flint. Arthur couldn't stop his horse until it reached a hilltop. Then when Arthur turned to look behind him, he could not find Guendolen's castle. It had disappeared. There was no castle in the middle of the vale—nothing down there but rocky crags.

Fifteen years later, after Arthur had wiped out the Saxons, the Picts, and the Romans, he held Court at Caerleon, says Scott, laughing, or at Camelot, or at Carlisle (cans. II, XIII). Into the king's presence came the same huntress from Cumbria: eagle feathered, bare ankled, sandal footed. He almost said, "Guendolen"; but he recognized his own royal blood in time.

> And in the forehead's haughty grace
> The lines of Britain's royal race,
> Pendragon's you might ken (can. II, xiv).

Queen Guinevere (Guenever) looked mildly on at this scene of human frailty, continues the Druid. The huntress was Arthur's daughter Gyneth. Arthur gave her Strathclyde, Reged, and

Carlisle's fortress and town as her dowry. In the following tournament, when her father told her to stop the fight before all his warriors died, Gyneth refused to obey him. Taught to obey only her mother, she let the warriors die, gasp, and stain her sandals red. Then the earth quaked

> And from the gulf-tremendous birth!
> The form of Merlin rose.

"Stop, madmen," he cried. It was Merlin who condemned Gyneth to sleep alone in her Vale until she was awakened. Eventually all adventurers ceased searching for her. So she sleeps until the trumpet of doom, which is how Scott's Druid ends his fairy tale.*

The genealogist Lucinda Boyd (1908) makes a much stronger claim for the Nith River (*Niduari*) Picts of Arthur's generation when she writes in her introduction:

> Gwallon's [Gawain's] sister, Thenelis, was the mother of the celebrated Kentigern, or St. Mungo, whose name is retained by a Dumfriesshire parish. Marken or Marcus [King Mark], brother of Loth, had a son named Kinder; to him belonged the district which now forms the parish of Newabbey, and which was at first called after him, Loch Kinder. A son of Kinder, Yrien or Yrvin, owned lands in Eskdale which bore his name; and to him it is that the prolific family of the Irvings, who, ages afterwards, flourished in Annandale, and often held civic rule in Dumfriesshire, owe their origin.

In his history David Irving (1861) argued from Edinburgh that because river names, and the names of the mountains, villages, towns, and castles, of Scotland are Celtic, the Picts themselves must have been Celts. (He later reconsidered when he saw

*A correspondent from Cumberland writes to tell me how solid the traditions concerning Arthur still remain there. He is called "Raven" there, she says (from "bran" or "vran," king confused with Raven?).

evidence to the contrary.) Joseph Anderson held, also in Edinburgh, in 1881, that the Picts were already Christian at least by the years A.D. 586–597, or forty-two years after Arthur's death when their King Garnard built a Christian church. Garnard succeeded the King Brude who reigned over the Northern Picts at Inverness immediately following the Battle of Camlan (542) where Arthur was fatally wounded. And St. Columba needed an interpreter to speak about religion to King Brude and Pictish courtiers. Clergymen and local historians named Cameron, Macbain, and Kennedy, writing from Inverness in 1892, made no mention of Picts at all, but declared there were three elements in ancient Scotland: Gaelic, which was the largest; British, which was the older substratum; and Norse, from the foreigners who after Arthur's day settled the western isles.

It is interesting to see that the English chronicler Raphael Holinshed (d. 1577) was, on the contrary, very knowledgeable about the Picts, naming their various territories, some of which have already occurred prominently in Guinevere's life: Angus (Lancelot), Perth, Stirling, Lothian, the Carron River and Round Table, and the ancient Roman fortress of Camelon, which was on the Roman road from York to Stirling. These Picts intermarried with Britons, Holinshed said, and had a round stone temple "not farre from" the Carron River, "which remained in some perfection untill the reigne of our King Edward called the first after the conquest, by whom it was subuerted: but the monument thereof remaineth to this daie."

The Britons, Holinshed assures us in his usual voice of authority, ordained their own thirteen kings from the year 447:

1. Vortigern	8. Vortiporius
2. Vortimer	9. Maglocunus
3. Aurelius Ambrosius	10. Caretius
4. Uther	11. Cadwan
5. Arthur	12. Cadwallon
6. Constantine	13. Cadwallader
7. Aurelius Conans	

As far as Arthur's century is concerned, the only person who should have been, or who could have been a chronicler is St. Gildas, born in Dumbarton c. 500 or, as he says, at the date of the great victory of Mt. Badon, which one has assumed means Dumbarton. Scholars publishing in *Antiquity* magazine have tracked Gildas to Arthur's war on Man and have claimed that Gildas was himself a Pict. Gildas manages to say only that the Picts were "from the north," that they were "worms" and "foul hordes" who were plunderers and pirates with "oars like wings" to their ships. He also says both Picts and Scots were an "overseas people." "On the seas" would seem to translate the fierce and gigantic invaders of Ireland of that name, "Fomorians." Patrick Weston Joyce, who was one of Ireland's most learned and kindly scholars, gives us the etymology: *Fo*, "on" plus *Muir*, "the sea." The Fomorians were "Gnomes" or "Giants" from Scandinavia, or from Scythia. Their most notorious king in Ireland was Balor of the Isles. His giantism, royalty, and preferred dwelling on the coast at Tory Island make one think of Guinevere's ogre-father Leodagan.

If Guinevere's father was a Dane from Lochlann, then we turn to the most admirable and authoritative of early chroniclers such as lack in Scotland: Saxo Grammaticus (c. 1150–1220). As John Hill Burton (1905) remarked in 1873, one should look to Denmark for invasion points; it lies a scant two hundred sea miles from northern Scotland and the Orkneys. Invaders from Roskilde Fjord in west Copenhagen had only to sail due west. That native British chronicler who, by every standard literature can apply, was Saxo Grammaticus's equal and contemporary was Geoffrey of Monmouth. Geoffrey's *History of the Kings of Britain* goes Saxo one better, for it still stands after eight centuries among the world's masterpieces. Although nobody in Britain gives Geoffrey house room, foreigners, and especially French historians, praise him to the skies.

Without blinking an eye, Saxo Grammaticus adopts not only Guinevere as Scandinavian but the whole company of Arthur and his companions—and proves them all Scandinavian by comparative literature. The heroes are admired for their physiques and for the beauty of eyes, hair, and stature. They matured at age twelve, or soon thereafter. They decorated their wooden stockades with the severed heads of their enemies. They died in snake pits. Good wives died with their husbands. Adulterous women were stoned to death and/or had their noses and cheeks amputated. The winning warrior decapitated the loser. Trial by judicial combat was legal. The white horse or "October equus" was sacred to royalty. The sight of a hobby horse, which doubtless reminded people of the October sacrifice of the horse, caused extreme terror. Silence was the proper remedy, to still palpitations. The heroes' swords were named. Their hosts floated superb banners like Uther's Dragon pennant. Principal totems were the bear (Arthur), boar, lion (Galehaut), leopard (Lancelot), and dog. Shield maidens graced the battlefields in Ireland as in Scandinavia. Women were captains of warrior bands. Giants haunted seaports, coves, and mountains. Great champions (Gwydion, Arthur) stole beasts from the Underworld (Ireland). The bridge to the Underworld in Britain, as in Scandinavia, was a Sword Bridge or Bridge of Blades. Heroes and sisters of heroes were frequently bled to death by priestesses. Heroes often accepted combat with Giants. They were also commonly sent to fetch a bride, who was a princess (Isolde) for their chieftain. In summary, say scholars of Scandinavian sagas, their material appears commonly in areas dominated by a Celtic population. King Arthur left the world by ship for Avalon. As did the Lady of Escalat. The Scandinavian eponymous hero Scyld arrived from the sea, as did Modred. The *Voluspa* and other sagas were known and adopted in Ireland, Scotland, Brittany, the Rhine and Rhône deltas, and in Iceland. In all these areas priestesses like Guanhumara still stood at the pinnacle of fame and respect.

Arthur's day, noted the contemporary Danish scholar Axel Olrik (1976), saw a period of migrations concurrent with the rebirth of the Teutonic race searching for new lands, novel experiences, glamorous brides, and a higher degree of civilization. Great warriors usually create new empires, he decided. This was also a period of lustrous celebration in Norse poetry as we know from the *Eddas* and *Beowulf.* The subject of this poetry was identical to the Arthurian: in Olrik's *Heroic Legends of Denmark* great kings emerge and vanish (see p. 42):

1. Ermanric's hall was as famous as Arthur's Camelot.
2. Attila's obsequies were as lavish as Beowulf's.
3. Theodoric's courage during exile was as great as Lancelot's.
4. The loves of Gunther and Brunhilde equaled in intensity those of Guinevere and Lancelot and Tristan and Isolde.
5. King Thorismund of the Visigoths won a battle on the Catalaunian Plains, which equals the fame of Camlan.
6. The kings of the Merovingians stand at the pinnacle of their world as the British kings, at theirs.
7. King Halfdan of Denmark stood a mountain strong, with a life, deeds, and battles corresponding in many details to Arthur's (p. 234).
8. Boduar Berki, the Scandinavian champion, was Queen Guinevere's brother, Bedevere.

This does not complete Olrik's list of close comparisons. He had five more points of comparison that proved to him that much of the Arthurian legend was Scandinavian, which leads scholars to Guinevere's next-to-last father and the theory that the Picts, whom Arthur and Merlin conquered at Cameliard, were northerners from Scandinavia and that their Giant King Leodagan, who disappeared even before Guinevere's wedding in Carlisle, was either Norwegian, Finnish, or Danish:

9. Geoffrey of Monmouth knew a Beduerus as Arthur's cupbearer and duke of "Norsemen" (i.e., his Normandy). His name in his own tongue was Beduwar Berki, which means "Warlike Biarki." Of exalted fame in Norway, Iceland, and Denmark, he was also listed (aside from Geoffrey's twelfth-century *History of the Kings of Britain*) in the

Liber Vitae from Durham, and there among a large number of other twelfth-century Scandinavians (Olrik, p. 256).

10. What happens to these Arthurian lords? "The race dies out with a child born of incest or out of wedlock" (p. 280), ergo, Arthur himself, plus Gawain probably, and Modred certainly. Therefore we understand the supreme emphasis in the Arthurian histories of Lancelot and Perceval, who were untainted and, thus, the *only* royal (and sainted) noblemen.

11. The Arthurian legend spread back and forth into Scandinavia: the story of Arthur's Caradoc, the story of how Seneschal Kay saved young Meriadoc, the story of how a girl Orwen married the ubiquitous "King Urien (Rion) of Scotland."

12. Contacts between Arthur and Scandinavians occurred during the king's lifetime at certain points in his world: Ireland, the Hebrides, Avalon, and Brittany. In each place of Scandinavian conquest the story of Scyld arriving safely by boat after he has—in order to test his worthiness—been set adrift recurs in the stories of St. Kentigern's pregnant and unwed mother, in that of Modred, and in that of Arthur.

13. Fingal of Ireland married the Danish king's daughter of Copenhagen. The personal names in the Scottish poetry of Ossian are largely Scandinavian. Even Fingal's grandmother was Scandinavian—a Swedish princess.

Ernst Windisch frequently supported Olrik in several common or shared points such as the stunning voyages of the dead overseas; the common armorial devices; the shared totems of bear, boar, and lion (the Boar was the ensign of Gaul, just as the Bear was of Finland); and the Island of Women such as the Grail Castle site at Avalon, or the Irish *tír nam-ban* or "land of women" or priest-esses.

This question of who were the Picts (by means of which the earlier question, who were Guinevere's fathers, has here been pursued), needs summary now before we plunge into a novel theory as yet apparently unexplored anywhere. In 1946 Thomas Francis O'Rahilly commenced making a list of historians versus mythologists in these questions of the Irish and Arthurian cycles. That subject has now led, because of Guinevere, to the underlying problem of the Picts. In the following lists dates indicate only a first or very important work, but it is understood that major scholars such as William Forbes Skene, Roger Sherman Loomis, Sir John Rhŷs, and Geoffrey Ashe have devoted—and, in the case of Geoffrey Ashe are still devoting—many admirable works to these questions.

Historical Camp	*Mythological Camp*
Geoffrey of Monmouth [1136]	Nutt 1888
Keating 1857	Rhŷs 1891
Skene 1862	Joyce 1894
Windisch 1878	Arbois de Jubainville 1899
Zimmer 1884	Weston 1901
Meyer 1911	Wentz 1911
Crawford 1949	MacCulloch 1918
Ritchie 1952	Loomis 1926
Morris 1973	Chambers [1927] 1964
Goodrich [1986] 1987, 1989, 1990	N. K. Chadwick 1932
Ashe [1960] 1987	H. M. Chadwick 1949

The above list does not necessarily mean that anyone else but Goodrich believes, champions, and endorses Geoffrey of Monmouth.

O'Rahilly presents the second problem very succinctly and

gives the most telling evidence. The Picts, he said, are thought to have been of three origins, for which reason there are three schools of thought; or as already extended to include Queen Guinevere, she had three possible fathers after all: (1) the Picts were purely Welsh and spoke a P-Celtic language like the Bretons on the Continent; (2) the Picts were Goidelic and spoke a Q-Celtic language even before the Irish left Ireland (c. 500) for Scotland—this theory has the greatest number of adherents; and (3) the Picts were not Celtic, and probably not even Indo-European—the adherents of this theory of non-Aryanism hang their hats on Saint Gildas and The Venerable Bede. We shall offer proof of this third theory.

CHAPTER V

The Love of Lancelot

Now turn we unto Sir Launcelot du Lake, that
came home two days afore the Feast of Pentecost;
and the king and all the court were passing fain
of his coming.

—SIR THOMAS MALORY,
Le Morte d'Arthur

THE SCOTTISH "ROMANCE" OF *Lancelot of the Laik* EXPRESSLY NOMINATES
Arthur for immortality even though mere kings may not hope so
much. Arthur served God, says the Scot who wrote the pane-
gyric, and, therefore His wand in the king's hand passed over the
land. Arthur chose kind judges, whose sentences he observed,
and he chose for himself wise and aged counselors. He visited
every city, province, village, and chieftain in his dominion personally. He heard the poor personally, said the Scottish eulogy,
and himself punished their oppressors justly, but with mercy. He
lighted truth in the northern land. Without familiarity, he entertained and banqueted his subjects. He rewarded them liberally,
because cheerful liberality ensures a sovereign's own safety.
After a king dies, only the memory of his virtue and honor
remains to emblazon his name. Such honor and commensurate
virtue unfortunately do not survive his queen's death.

King Arthur, and not she, remedied the shrieks of the homeless; for failing that remedy he might fear the Lord's terrible swift sword of vengeance. She watched the sword over her head every day of her life. This account from Scotland has truly portrayed Arthur's queen.

The great king stopped short of flattery. He understood that commonwealths derive their health, virtue, courage, and prosperity only from the male sovereign. His influence alone travels downward through the ranks of that society; it is a common law.

Emigrating from Ireland to the western part of (what is now) Scotland, the Scots in Arthur's day brought their Bards with them. Thus their romance of Lancelot followed the Irish literary genre of the *úrsgeul*. The prime literary form of ancient Ireland, then, was just such a romance. This form, agree Douglas Hyde and Myles Dillon, combines what we today would call epic-and-romance, or history-and-legend. Both sets belong hand in hand. Each Irish Bard had memorized 250 prototypical and prime stories about heroes, we are told, plus one hundred secondary "romances": godly, heroic, and dynastic materials memorializing also the High Kings of Ireland. The English poet and don Thomas Gray saluted such as these Irish immigrants, or Scots pouring into what is now Scotland:

> An iron race the mountain cliffs maintain . . .
>
>   What wonder if, to patient valor train'd,
> They guard with spirit what by strength they
>   gain'd: . . .
> ("Fragment on the Alliance of Education and
>   Government").

Sir Walter Scott also used to quote old Mummers' verses that continued to celebrate the heroic romances of the Scots:

> Alexander, King of Macedon [i.e., Julius Caesar]
> Who conquered all the world save Scotland alone,
> When he came to Scotland his courage grew cold,
> To see a little nation both courageous and bold.

And in her introduction to the book *Scottish Chiefs* (New York and London, 1930) Kate Douglas Wiggin taught American school-children: "The world has always needed heroes and it needs them sadly now, for the 'greatest good a hero does to the race is to be a hero and thereby inspire others to heroic living.' . . . *God armeth the patriot."* And Sir Walter Raleigh could have been speaking of heroism to King Arthur when he wrote to the Irish scholar Kuno Meyer:

> Let none carp
> If you get the biggest harp
> May the cloud on which you sit
> Fit.

If King Arthur was the biggest Scottish harp in his century, then the cloud on which he sat, averred the compilers of the *Prose Lancelot,* was the union of Queen Guinevere and her deputy Lancelot whom they called "Sir Lancelot of the Lake." The greatest of heroes had been educated secretly, or fostered per Pictish custom on the Isle of Man, where the carving for King Arthur's monuments was being done. It had been ordered by Queen Guinevere, claims this same *Prose Lancelot.* Lancelot's foster parent was the Lady of the Lake. The Lady herself, dressed in white like an abbess, escorted the youth Lancelot to King Arthur for ordination into his warrior-hero's career in arms. The Lady's white-clad and white-mounted cortege arrived on the Saturday of Saint John the Baptist's Day. The hero had, like Merlin, been dedicated to this great, holy figure.

King Arthur announced this ceremonious arrival to the queen, who was "beside herself with impatience" to see the handsome youth (*Le Livre de Lancelot del Lac,* vol. III, p. 125). The news of his coming spread through the town. People heard that the splendid white "candidate" would that day be presented at Court. Those who watched him pass solemnly along the streets said they had never before seen such a glorious youth. He rode his gorgeous white horse up to the Court and dismounted. There Yvain, who was a son of the Irish King Rion (of Galles) of the Isles, bowed, took the youth's hand, and escorted him into the royal presences.

King Arthur and Queen Guinevere rose to their feet as he approached. They even advanced to meet Lord Lancelot. They led him across the green branches, which covered the floor, and toward their seat. They, too, were dazzled by the beauty of the young aspirant. The queen sat and gazed sweetly down on him. And every time he dared, the youngster raised veiled eyes to her lovely countenance. She was so beautiful that when she bent down and took the youth's hand in her fingers he trembled at her light touch. Then he lowered his eyes again and sat quietly at her feet.

Yvain remained speechless. He could not present the youth, for he did not know his name, only that he came from *Gallia* (Galles) in the west. But the queen asked him softly: "What is your name? Where are you from?"

"I do not know," he replied, even more softly, almost in a whisper.

"He's not quite in possession of his wits," the queen said rapidly in a loud voice. She intended all to hear her plainly. "Or else," she cried with a disdainful shrug, "he has been badly brought up!"

Such unclear passages occur frequently in medieval texts, as if to say that mystery intrigues or that the old material is also cloudy or that nobody knows what is happening here. This interchange between Queen Guinevere and Lancelot has taken place in public, before a hostile audience. The queen's defense of Lancelot attempts to pass off what would appear to be complicity between the two of them. In any case the late *Merlin* texts (see *Merlin,* 1987) demonstrate a close rapport between the Lady of the Lake and Queen Guinevere. It would appear, then, that the queen was expecting Lancelot. In the light of what occurs between them later, that seems a valid assumption.

Queen Guinevere seems to have come to her deputy's aid here, and for the first time to have covered his embarrassment. Seemingly she alone understood perfectly well who this extraordinarily handsome youngster was, who had raised him, and for what purpose, where he had been secreted in tutelage, and why he had been brought specifically before her. Perhaps the queen already knew that Lancelot came for her personal service. She would have known that his Pictish name was Angus, and his Latin name, Anguselus. She would not have known that later medieval authors would give him his French name of clan chieftain: the Angus or Lancelot. Here, before her, was her secret champion.

Queen Guinevere here dissimulated. Very cleverly she spoke words for the public and exchanged looks with Lancelot that only they two understood. The only other persons who might have known what was happening would have been the Pictish princes present, and particularly Gawain, who was chief of them and the eldest.

Throughout the queen's life, two safeguards kept her alive after the transmission of her property to King Arthur: Lancelot of the Lake (which I take to be the Pictish holy refuge on the Isle of Man in the Irish Sea) and her holiness (which remains to be proven).

For his part, King Arthur was so displeased with the new aspirant Lancelot that during the succeeding ordination ceremony he omitted offering Lancelot his sword. He failed to gird it on him as custom required.

The poor youth therefore set out on his first adventures on behalf of queen and kingdom under the cloud of Arthur's displeasure and without official weapon he could wield in the king's name.

Eventually he found a way to send a message explaining his plight to the queen. Guinevere immediately dispatched a messenger bearing her own sword with which Lancelot proudly replaced his boyhood weapon.

Although scores of great ladies accepted his services thereafter, none other ever touched his heart or won his selfless adoration (Ms. fr. 773). Only for Queen Guinevere would Lancelot accept to die.

Taken literally, the scenario presented by the *Prose Lancelot* seems perfectly clear: Lancelot was Guinevere's champion. He and Arthur were never on amicable terms.

During a series of preliminary adventures Lancelot continued to ride his own white horse, dress in white as a neophyte should, and hold his own unadorned white shield before him. The Lady of the Lake had instructed him to shelter himself behind anonymity as long as he possibly could. She had knowingly sent him into a hostile environment. Preliminary tasks soon fell easily away, one after another, however, until word was brought him that King Arthur's prime champion Gawain had been captured and imprisoned in the hideous dungeons of Dolorous Gard Castle.

Worse yet, King Arthur's son Lohos (Lohot) by Lisamor of Caradigan on the Marches of Ireland (Rhinns of Galloway?) had been seized by Brandus of the Isles and was also incarcerated. Meanwhile King Arthur seemed unable to marshal his forces. Therefore Lancelot understood that the conquest of Brandus's huge castle, called Dolorous Gard, was to be his first difficult adventure. And, in fact, he soon recognized a summoner, a damsel sent by the Lady of the Lake to guide him. Under her instruction and direction Lancelot fought ten fierce champions, one by one, day after day, until all defenders of the outer ramparts had been defeated, disarmed, killed, and the prisoners released. Lancelot's immediate reward was to be allowed to proceed to the cemetery, to raise the slab from the one, certain tomb, and see his own name engraved thereon: LANCELOT OF THE LAKE. He first understood then who he was, what his lineage was, and he realized for the first time the enormity of his responsibility over a lifetime and the price he would pay for fame won across his world.

Soon thereafter he met one of the queen's own squires bearing an urgent plea for help. The queen herself, he was told, was being held inside the innermost walls of Dolorous Gard. She now called for Lancelot's assistance. "Tell her," he said, "that I will be there tonight or early tomorrow morning." In fact, he and the squire passed the postern together and rode side by side along the lighted cobblestone ways up to a heavy door. Pushing it open the squire let Lancelot enter and then banged the door behind him.

Lancelot had been tricked. He was plunged into the darkest night. All he could do was await the first ray of daylight. Then he heard a girl's voice calling.

"Sir," she cried down to him, "you are truly caught. You will have to accept our proposal and our terms of employment."

"What do you want of me?"

"That you bring permanent peace to this lamentably bedeviled castle."

"Where is the queen?"

"Faraway. She asks you to go guarantee for her. Only you can make these devilish machinations here cease."

"I accept the assignment." Lancelot was then made to swear on the relics of holy saints not to draw back from any danger. He still believed he was warring for the queen.

No sooner promised than the iron door swung out on its hinges so that Lancelot could sit down to a breakfast. "You may choose," he was further told, "whether to remain jailed inside here for forty days or attempt to solve and dissolve double-key enchantments we suffer from here."

"I prefer," said he, "the latter." After having crossed himself, Lancelot calmly picked up his weapons. He had been trained to feel no fear.

Then he stepped down into utter blackness. Even so, he advanced until he caught a glimpse of light streaming under a doorsill. He strode straight for this door and pushed it wide open only to hear a deafening crashing. Still he continued walking forward until the din reverberated so he thought the roof was falling in. Simultaneously he felt the gallery around him commence to turn on itself as did the slippery cobbles underfoot. He tried to steady himself on the nearer wall. Catching his breath, he crept along as best he could to the second barred and vaulted portal. It was defended by two monstrous warriors sheathed in shiny copper, each holding a sword it would have taken two ordinary men just to lift. They swung their swords in alternating circles, rhythmically, so as to forbid access to anyone at all. They were Pictish warriors.

Shield held high before him, the hero leapt between their blades, which slashed at his armor and cut one shoulder so deeply the blood spurted. But falling to his hands, the youth managed to crawl under their whirling weapons. His whole body screamed with shock and involuntary shivers. Even so, he raised his own sword again from the stones in front of him and continued to go forward again, shield held high before his face.

In this fashion he continued. He crept cautiously uphill until he came to a third doorway. But then he saw that he could not reach it by crawling. A deep well perhaps as much as seven feet wide by seven long lay in the dark before him. Its nasty stench made him almost retch. But the din grew worse, so loud it rocked his skull.

Then he saw that there stood before him a huge Ethiopian* blowing blasts of blue flames from his mouth while his eyes shot jets of fire as red as live coals. After Lancelot had crept closer, he watched how the monstrous guard took his two hands and lifted slowly before him a huge ax. It would be poised to fall as soon as any victim came within reach.

The queen's champion stopped to reconnoiter and estimate these obstacles, it is true; but all the time he kept repeating his last vows. Then he made his plan of attack. First he sheathed his sword. Then he got a good hold on the straps of his shield and tested its weight and balance. Suddenly he hurled it into the monster's face, catching the ax in it as it fell. The shield split, but it held the ax. Then the hero jumped the channel, or reservoir, and as he landed on its other rim brought both fists down on the back of the Ethiopian's neck. Meanwhile the monster still struggled to yank the ax from the shield.

Then the queen's champion grasped his opponent's neck and rained blows on his head with his right fist. Obliged to let go of his ax handle, the demonic warrior toppled over backward. The hero fell with him but recovering seized him by the feet and cast him into the well.

Then the queen's hero got to his feet and looked about him again. He saw ahead of him a copper mistress made all over marvelously shiny, green, with enamelwork, holding in her right hand the double-key of enchantment. To take it from her, he drew nearer to a copper pillar that rose from the center of the

---

*Whoever added this detail to the Arthurian scene must have been, I believe, a classical scholar of Greek history. The Ethiopian seems to me to be a recollection of the black warrior, slain by Apollo, who guarded the Delphic Oracle. He was killed in defense of the priestess. I therefore assume that Lancelot also is entering an oracular center.

chamber. He read the letters engraved on the metal: "The heavy key undoes the coffer. The little one coffers it."

Carefully the queen's man thrust the fat key into the pillar. Lo and behold, it swung open. But when he touched the thin key to the strongbox, it set off such a fearsome alarm that rang out more like a succession of shrill shrieks, or screams so piercing that even the copper pillar itself began to quake so strong that the hero again crossed himself, at once. Then despite bursting ear drums he opened the coffer. That set off thirty thin copper tubes to shrieking both in unison and separately, screeching and whistling, each new whistler's pitch more painful on the ear than the last. It was a dolorous castle altogether. He still did not see the queen anywhere.

That was the source, however. He had found, isolated, and lanced the very abscess that had spread its foul corruption through that formerly holy castle. All its enchantments had sprung from these fiendish whirlwinds. The black mists that often made the castle disappear came from there, plus those horrifying shrieks and groans as if all the Devils on earth were residing there in foul huddles. When he saw what Devils had really caused it all, he knew they were numerous and spawning.

All of a sudden the queen's champion felt his head swim and his strength slip from him. He fell to the stones beneath him, head beside the copper pillar. He had not found the queen. Had it all been in vain?

When Lancelot regained consciousness, he was amazed to see that the pillar, the mistress or her image made of polished copper, the well, the two giant warriors guarding portal number two—all had vanished. It had all disappeared. In fact, the whole underground passages and vaults and portals lay wide open. He walked in the quiet sea breeze freely out, holding the double-key to enchantments in his hand. He came again to the cemetery. There were no tombs there! There were no words carved there, for there were no gravestones! He saw no helmeted men-at-arms! It was daylight: greensward and the blue Irish Sea.

Lancelot returned to the chapel once more, laid the keys on the altar, and climbed up to the royal residence.

How could anyone depict the joy that shone there on the

faces of the inhabitants? They all said grace to Lancelot, thanking him for having rendered such services to them. As an ecclesiastic of lower grade and minor order he had exorcised their demons. He had by his acts of courage rejected fiends with all due solemnity. He had expelled them from the Isle of Man, kingdom of the living, and driven them away. He had charged them, bound them, abjured them to be gone. All evil spirits were now expelled from Dolorous Gard, and forever more. The realm was cleansed. The name of the castle would be changed to the Castle of the Holy Grail.

Lancelot then learned that the queen had not really been imprisoned, but that *he had been lured there* to free Dolorous Gard of evil. Therefore, he remained only overnight. Next day he bade adieu to the poor people whom demons had persecuted. Their cruel oppression had been ended by a Christian hero.

From that day forward Lancelot's initiatory castle on the coast, opposite its little island, was popularly rechristened Joyous Gard. As lord of a domain, Lancelot thereafter carried a silver shield with one black band.

The disappearing Dolorous Gard appears in this telling to be the Grail Castle before it housed the Grail. Like the future Grail Castle, Dolorous Gard is situated on the edge of the sea and opposite an islet: the Isle of Man opposite the small St. Patrick's Isle off its west coast. Both face Ireland and therefore are situated on the "Marches into Ireland"; it is the Irish Sea beside which the castle stands. Most accounts also emphasize copper as ornament and/or structural element inside the Grail Castle. Furthermore, in all accounts it is a disappearing and a lapsed castle on a disappearing, cloudy island. Queen Guinevere will again be held prisoner there, and Lancelot will once more rescue her from that Irish prison. Pagans had retaken the island whence they were chased and where many of their huge defenders were slain, as reported generally and by such Arthurian heroes as Lancelot, Gawain, and Perceval. Finally, Lancelot was there directed by a damsel attached appropriately to the Lady of the Lake herself. Her castle of maiden priestesses cannot have been far distant.

Many other accounts, however, identified Dolorous Gard

anachronistically as the present, Anglo-Saxon Bamborough on the east coast of Northumbria, particularly because most texts throw in the Humber River as a place-name, although it is also improbably associated with this adventure.

Everyone remembered Lancelot's devotion to Arthur's queen who once saved him from a useless death. He had come one day to the manor house of King Arthur, "which was situated like all his private residences along a riverbank," in this case on the left bank of the Forth River, which flows toward the sea past the western Camelot. The king's house looked across the water toward the curtain walls of that high fortress and its entrance at the tail of the Stirling crag. Catching a glimpse of Her Majesty Lancelot fell into such a deep dream that his mare waded out too far in the current. Horse and rider were being swept downstream, Lancelot in heavy armor on the mare's back. It was the queen who cried for help. Yvain de Galles rode out and towed Lancelot to the riverbank.

Lancelot's vow to the queen of eternal love and chastity came about through the wars fought against King Arthur by a greater king named Galehaut (Galahos, Galehot, Galaholt), whose name sounds like "High King of the Gaels" (Scots). If so, then Arthur, who ruled the Lowlands of Scotland, was attempting to halt masses of emigrants from Ireland. They would eventually settle and claim the Highlands: all of northwestern Scotland from Glasgow north to Sutherland, i.e., all the land west of the Grampians and including Loch Ness.

The war with this lordly Galehaut went so badly that this prince even granted Arthur a truce for a year until he could round up enough warriors to make the combat reasonably interesting. Finally Queen Guinevere was persuaded to ask her Lancelot to fight on Arthur's side, and to do it for love of her. On the other hand, Lancelot may have been persuaded to join her forces because his own Pictish tribe and tribal lands were adjacent to the queen's. In any case, Lancelot's efforts turned the tide of battles and would have won the war if Galehaut had not suddenly surrendered and quit the field. In this war Lancelot fought disguised in black armor.

At that last moment Galehaut insisted on dismounting in face of Lancelot, in giving his own horse to Lancelot, and even in acting as the latter's squire. Eventually he persuaded the lovesick Lancelot to leave Arthur's Court and journey into Galehaut's country as his honored, beloved guest.

Galehaut loved Lancelot so dearly he even had his bed made up in the same chamber. For love of Lancelot Galehaut swore allegiance to Arthur, a minor king as far as Galehaut was concerned. Galehaut and Lancelot became such close friends that the one was often mistaken for the other. Galehaut grieved when he allowed himself to be cajoled into returning to Camelot so he could present Lancelot to the queen. For her part, Queen Guinevere ardently desired to see for herself the now-famous champion in black armor. Their meeting was arranged for one evening at dusk and in an orchard. The queen was escorted by an older, noble lady and by two young ladies. Galehaut arrived first. Lancelot was then ushered in to the queen's presence by Galehaut's standard bearer.

Once arrived before the queen, the Warrior-in-Black was shaken by such emotion that he could hardly bow to her. The two knelt before her, the Black Warrior so embarrassed he could not even raise his eyes to her face. The queen knew at once which one was Lancelot. . . . After the company was seated, the queen took Lancelot by the hand, raised him, and had him sit beside her.

Our French authors now give their readers ten or so pages of direct address, where Lancelot and Guinevere meet face-to-face and tell each other of their love and devotion. However, the authors, who are writing for royal ladies and lords of the twelfth century, imagine all this as repartee in the school of courtly love. They see it as love-dove-hearts and valentines. All we need would be moon-tune-June, and we too would have the scenario of romantic love. They, therefore, loosely use one of the most troublesome words in the French language: *amis* in Old French, or *ami* in modern French, which could mean friend, lover, husband or, as in legal terminology, friend in court. Their casual wielding of the pen throws Guinevere and Lancelot into sexual fantasy, maybe into adultery—therefore, into treason—followed by the collapse of Arthur's realm. And yet, with no trouble at all, we today can read between the lines: vassalage, friend, champion, death defier, Guinevere's only true friend to the death whom the Lady of the Lake has sent her. He and he alone will die for the queen.

Reading their words in light of the desperate situation in which the young queen finds herself, we understand that Guinevere is forewarned. She suspects the worst from the foreigners around her. Lancelot has come to her from her own people. Even the medieval authors cannot say that their kiss stems from some runaway sexuality. The queen stood before Lancelot, held his chin in her hand, and kissed him.

Nor do the medieval authors realize that in this queen they are seeing an educated, literate princess wedded to an illiterate king; for Arthur could not read the lettering on the stones in the Dolorous Gard cemetery. But Guinevere ordered the writing and gave the pattern for it.

When she saw Lancelot, said the authors of the *Prose Lancelot,* the queen asked him to reassure her with his own lips that he was whom she expected. The youth looked at her and was silent. Then the two of them were alone.

When she saw that he would not or could not speak to her, the queen asked him why he was hiding. Why was he so silent? Was he not already a great warrior? All the youth would say was no. Then the queen asked him if he was not the recent hero in black armor. Again he said no. Then she asked him if he was not the warrior who had recently lost three horses under him in a pitched battle, he to whom Gawain had sent fresh horses. Lancelot stood before her, head bowed, and dumb. She tried a new tack.

By whom was he invested, she wanted to know. Then she received a response. Lancelot told her that it was she who had invested him. And not the king, she countered. He agreed, adding that whoever gives the new champion a sword empowers him to act. He said that he therefore had received his empowerment from herself, not from the king.

After she had made him admit that he was the warrior

whom she had saved from the river before Camelot, she was finally satisfied. She still wanted to know why he acted so doltishly in those days. He replied that then he had no heart in his exploits. Why not, she inquired.

Then Lancelot admitted his love for her and that he acted only for her, and on her behalf, as he had been trained to do. He told her that she herself had chosen him, that he had come to protect her, bare-armed and bare-handed. He asked God to bless her. He said to her "adieu" (I commend you to God, "A Dieu").

Then the lady told Lancelot: *"A dieu biax dols amis."* What she said was "Go with God, sweet, handsome love."

The youth then told the queen that since the day she called him "amis," the word had never left his heart. That word, he said, would make him a hero, in any adventure whatsoever would lead him into death without an instant of regret. That word alone would console him for all his wounds, cure him from all his pains, and rescue him from all dangerous straits whatsoever. The word would feed him when he was hungry and fill his purse when he was penniless.

The queen for her part demurred instantly, saying that in truth she said no more to him than to any other neophyte who presented himself before her. She said that she did not mean it so seriously as he had taken it, but only as simple courtesy. Of course, she said that she understood how well it had fallen on his ears, in that it turned him into a superior hero.

During this interview the queen was testing Lancelot. She went on to question him about his service to other persons and especially to other ladies of property. As everyone knew, Lancelot had made several successful marriages and had acquired considerable property of his own. The hero grew pale as she pinned him down to certain admissions. At one point he swayed so much that she leaned forward and held him by his hood. Even Prince Galehaut rushed over to see what the trouble was.

The queen explained to Galehaut that she had to be certain of Lancelot and that she intended to discover just how far she could trust him. Galehaut advised caution with Lancelot, who was very sensitive to the turn of the conversation.

Galehaut explained to the queen that what Lancelot came to

ask was the sealing of the bond between them. What he wished for was her request that he reserve himself for her alone and that the two of them should pledge this service like a troth. He wished the queen to accept him as her champion, who would stand ready to sacrifice his life at any time and in any place whatsoever. He would devote his life to her service and stand ready to defend her against any and all comers. He would only ask her to seal this bargain with a kiss.

The queen replied that she desired this service more than he did.

Then the queen, Lancelot, and Galehaut withdrew a certain distance from her attendants and sealed the bargain. The queen willingly told Lancelot that she accepted his service with her whole heart. She called him "Sweet, handsome love." She only asked the two of them to keep this troth a secret. She explained that her position in the world required such secrecy. She asked Galehaut to bear all responsibility for this compact, for good and for ill. She also asked Galehaut to guard Lancelot for her and to keep him at his side until and unless she called for him herself.

Then the queen said that she entrusted to Prince Galehaut her champion, and she named him: Lancelot du Lac, son of King Ban de Benoïe.

Thus, for the first time Galehaut heard the real name of his companion-in-arms. He was overcome with joy; for he had already heard the ancient Kings Ban of Benoïe spoken of as great champions, and he had also heard everyone praise the superb achievements of a certain Lancelot.

Thus took place the first private interview between the queen and Lancelot, and it was arranged and handled by Prince Galehaut. The royal persons rose from their seats at last. Night had already fallen. The full moon lighted the wide meadow. They strolled over to King Arthur's pavillion, the standard bearer forming escort to the two ladies. Galehaut instructed Lancelot to join them before departing for his own campsite, but that he Galehaut would escort the queen into the presence.

When he noticed them coming in, the king asked where they had been.

"Sire," responded Galehaut, "from those meadows where actually we were not very worthily attended."

They all sat down and conversed of this and that while both the queen and Galehaut were almost at a loss to conceal their inner delight. At last the queen rose and went to rest in the manned and reinforced arcade set aside for her safety and comfort. Galehaut commended her safekeeping to God, saying that he would henceforth share his bed and board with his beloved comrade-in-arms (*Prose Lancelot,* vol. III, 264).

CHAPTER VI

The False Guinevere

Here lies buried the renowned King Arthur, with
Guinevere his second wife, in the Isle of Avalon.
—Now discounted testimony (c. 1191)
by GERALD DE BARRY, in R. F. TREHARNE,
The Glastonbury Legends

CARLISLE

GUINEVERE'S LIFE WAS IN DANGER FROM THE NIGHT BEFORE HER WEDDING
when her first abduction took place. Her groom had only to
consummate the marriage to take legal possession of the eastern
Camelot. Now, that Camelot was and is in military terms the
"Key" to Scotland. Whoever held this one easy crossing of the
mosses of the Forth River barred the route into the North and
Pictland, always a safe refuge because of its isolation, its hordes
of native horsemen, and its rich and fertile grain fields. Just below
the Camelot (now Stirling) fortress was Pictish Lothian with
Edinburgh then, as now, the prime mustering area for the de-
fense of Britain. Lothian was held by King Loth, whose wife was
King Arthur's half-sister, and his sons, Gawain to Modred.

But what if for some reason as yet dimly grasped the marriage of Arthur and Guinevere was not consummated? How then
to gain hold of Camelot other than as the heiress's titular husband?

The French authors of the Middle Ages were well acquainted with real estate law. Guinevere's Camelot, even including the Round Table itself, was small change compared to the landed dowry that Eleanor of Aquitaine had brought to the English expatriate later returned to England as King Henry II. The medieval authors were even then watching as the English laid claim to all France south of the Loire River—a dispute that only the Hundred Years War settled centuries later, in 1453.

Even before the wedding of Guinevere her father, King Leodagan, had launched a formal investigation into her prenuptial abduction. He had convened his Court. The warriors of Carmelide called their seneschal to account for his part in the kidnapping that had occurred in the king's dark garden. Subsequently Seneschal Bertolais was summoned several times to testify. (When it came to judicial matters concerning the transmission of landed estates, the French authors of the *Prose Lancelot* felt very qualified to narrate.)

The upshot of this inquiry was that King Leodagan instructed Seneschal Bertolais to get rid of the second Guinevere, by conducting her beyond the borders of his kingdom and placing her under arrest for the rest of her life. She was also forbidden ever to return to Camelot.

The seneschal took the sentence calmly, replying that the second Guinevere was not his daughter anyway. And they all knew it. Thus Bertolais and the second Guinevere escaped. Bertolais received his orders to escort the young lady to an abbey, which stood in some uncultivated fields outside the kingdom. He took her there and left her there. Merlin still saw several loose ends, however.

Upon his return to Leodagan's Court, Bertolais was himself then, even without a corpse to prove it, accused of the second daughter's murder, tried again by a court of his peers, found guilty of that capital charge, and banished from Camelot by Merlin's order for three years. In his turn, he was ridden out of the kingdom. Because he had previously also been stripped of all his landed property, he was obliged to beg for shelter at the same abbey where he had abandoned the False Guinevere. All this

took place before the August crown wearing of Queen Guinevere.

One loose end that Merlin anticipated did not fail to dangle
before Queen Guinevere, King Arthur, and their Court. It was
Seneschal Bertolais in person, escorting the second Guinevere.
The latter accused Queen Guinevere to her face of being an
imposter, and then she presented letters of protest. This is the
way injustice was handled in the Dark Ages. Her letters follow:

The Letters

Queen Guinevere, second daughter of King Leodagan of Carmelide, salutes King Arthur, and all his
nobles and peers of the realm. King Arthur, I complain first of all to thee, next to thy peers, of great
disloyalty to me when I was perfectly loyal to thee.
A king un-kings himself when he lives out of wedlock with any woman. I was truly wedded. I was
duly consecrated spouse and queen, and this by the
Archbishop's hand. I only kept this honorable estate,
that was due me, for a single day. Whether by the
king's order, or by order of his followers, I saw my
rights trampled upon and my rightful place occupied
by a woman once my captive slave. That Guinevere,
she who passed for *Queen* in this *Court,* far from preserving my royal state as she is bound to do even at
the expense of her own, is only plotting my death
and my humiliation. I am the real Guinevere. But
Our Father, who does not forget those who beseech
Him from a faithful heart, has rescued me from her
traps, with the aid of those persons whose fidelity to
me I can never sufficiently reward. I managed secretly to escape from Hengist's Tower, from the middle of that Saxon's lake where the false queen had
me jailed. Completely disinherited as I am today, I
can still find honor and the means to sue for what is
duly mine. I cry out for vengeance on that wretched
woman who has so long lived with you in mortal sin.

She deserves to suffer the just punishment she thought to inflict forever more upon me. I have desired to write these letters, but since writing cannot tell it all, I have entrusted my heart and tongue to this lady cousin. Believe what my ambassadress has to say, for she is well acquainted with all this business I have just related. I am having her escorted by a war hero who has an equal right to credence; he is Bertolais, the truest, loyalist of men in all these islands. I chose him despite his great age so as the better to bear witness that the mightiest of her human powers can *not* prevail against justice itself, and truth.

During this scene of the letters reading Queen Guinevere had remained silent, although in her heart indignation reigned. She gave no sign, however, of either emotion or wrath. She seemed to disdain any attempt to justify herself. She would not even look at her accuser. The king, on the other hand, was visibly disturbed. . . . Finally he turned to the queen: "Lady," he said, "come here. It is up to you to give her the lie. If her accusation is true, you have unworthily betrayed me and you would deserve death. Instead of the most faithful of ladies, you would be the most perfidious and the falsest."

"Sire," she told him coldly, "there will be no defense for me to present. It is up to the king to preserve my honor and his own."

This plot to murder Queen Guinevere and seize both the king and her property comes as no surprise to the reader. It is merely another attempt on her life, which is in this case aimed at both Queen Guinevere and King Arthur. The first attack was on her wedding night. The second occurred through the elimination of her father, King Leodagan, who suddenly was never heard of again. Merlin and King Arthur had done their best to destroy, dishonor publicly, destitute, and exile Seneschal Bertolais.

From some abbey, such as Deare in the north of Pictland perhaps outside Aberdeen, the next challenge to Guinevere suddenly emerges. The authors of the *Prose Lancelot* pick up the story again. Everybody loves a courtroom drama.

On an appointed day in February, the treacherous damsel from Camelot, richly clad in silks and furs, accosted King Arthur as he left early mass at church. This time she personally accused Queen Guinevere of treason. But the lordly Galehaut cautioned the king to require proof.

Then in calm, self-assured tones Queen Guinevere spoke: "God knows that treason has never lodged in my heart. I have no commerce with it, and I shall desire to be defended either in open court or by trial of arms."

"If judgment is to be given by courtiers, then the plaintiff must now forego a trial by armed champions," cautioned Bademagus, governor of the Grail Castle.

Bertolais then asked if his damsel could be allowed a delay before making such a difficult decision. King Arthur allowed her one day's grace.

The damsel then retired with all those of her party. They discreetly went to lodge in a house far outside Arthur's citadel; when they had ascertained that nobody from the king's household had followed them, Bertolais remonstrated with the damsel, saying that the Court's judgment might very possibly fall against her. He added that if that occurred, she could not escape the death sentence. On the other hand, if the case was to be remanded to armed combatants to try, she knew very well that King Arthur had united under his banner the finest flower of world champions. There was not among them one single warrior who would not believe that in defending his queen, he was defending the right. They would therefore have every advantage on their side because judiciary combat was indicated only in cases when the Court lacked both proof and witnesses. Her champions in such a last resort, Bertolais warned her, would in all good faith be defending a fraudulent plaintiff. But, as she knew, he added, they would even so be obliged, before combat commenced, to swear on the saints that the False Guinevere had justice on her side, and was not false, but true. Did she suppose that perjury stands when confronted with sincere oaths sworn by King Arthur's heroes?

The damsel was not unacquainted with law. She turned again to Bertolais for counsel.

He told her plainly what he advised her to do. There is a well-known, widely accepted principle among men: Never compromise your honor, he told her, when as a man you are in front of other men because men among themselves do not act as our Savior acts toward men, forgiving repentant sinners easily.

In order for her not to endanger her very life, he warned, and also lose her good name, she would be well advised to tread cautiously here. First of all, he argued, we will need more time to make our preparations, he said. We will just softly ask for a respite of a second day. Arthur will grant it; and, as soon as he has done that, we will have caught him!

This will be our plan, continued Bertolais. We will send one of your champions to announce to the king that what do you know, that there in the dark Forest of Caradigan dwells a fantastically huge boar, that for ages has preyed on the whole countryside thereabouts. King Arthur is mad for hunting prize game. He will ask to be guided to where this creature usually roams. The rest of your men will lie in ambush. When they see that the king has strayed off by himself, they will rise up, surround him, and have no trouble escorting his person over to Camelot. There you can enchant him at your leisure. You know how he enjoys his manor house beside the river. You will have all the time you need to cajole and persuade him you are his lawful spouse, until he falls into your arms.

The damsel liked Bertolais's proposal. She bade three of her men ride over to Arthur's Court to request in their lady's name a second delay. We are moved to grant it, said King Arthur. But this will be your last respite, he sent warning. Let her not expect another. Just as they were taking leave, another champion apparently not of their acquaintance asked for an audience. In other words, Bertolais and the lady set their plot in motion.

Their messenger prayed God would be with King Arthur. He came to inform the king of something he said he saw with his own eyes. In the Forest of Caradigan there lurked the most enormous boar anybody had ever heard tell of in the whole country. Nobody dared go near him. If Arthur did not attempt this hero's feat, which was to deliver this land from its ravages, he truly did not deserve the crown he wore.

At that time Lancelot himself happened to be seated next to the king. Arthur begged his counsel. "Do you hear what has been announced to me, Lancelot?" Arthur inquired.

Lancelot thought the man fortunate who could find the boar's lair and bring back his head! He said that none of Arthur's bachelors but would not consider himself lucky to hunt along this spoor.

"Let those," said the king, "come who have the heart to follow me. As for me, I'm not waiting for any one of them. Hey, there! You! Bring me my hunting clothes!" Attendants ran to serve Arthur. He mounted up. Lancelot, Galehaut, Gawain, Yvain, and several others followed suit. The damsel's man was instructed sharply to move out and lead the way.

After a while Bertolais's lackey crept close enough to the king to speak to him privately. The pig is pretty close to us here, he warned the king, but the noise all our horses are making will force him to run. He said that if the king really desired the honor of being the first to charge the beast, he had better leave his party behind.

The king thought it a good idea. He motioned to his men to take a side path so that only two beaters followed him into the densest thicket.

Even as he rode along, however, King Arthur was not absolutely duped. He began to wonder why he heard no sound at all from the underbrush, and why he saw neither beast nor boar. Then all of a sudden he found himself surrounded by foreign warriors, helms laced, their long-handled halberds strapped on, broadswords in hand—plenty of warning for Arthur not to try a useless resistance. Seeing himself surrounded, even so, King Arthur raised his own sword in a token show of might; but his horse fell struck to death beneath him. His two beaters were soon trussed up. He was himself disarmed. They tied his hands together, hoisted him up on a palfrey, and they all set off at a rapid gait.

The decoy who had lured the king into the hunt then rode toward the main party. When he had gone halfway or so, he sounded his hunting horn to bring together the king's men. "Listen to that horn," His Grace Gawain said. "That's the king's summons. Let's ride into the wind that way."

Thus, Arthur's escort sped so fast in the wrong direction that night had fallen before they were able to enter Caradigan's walls again, dripping wet, saddle sore, and worn out with worry. There stood Queen Guinevere anxiously awaiting them. At once she wanted to know why King Arthur was not with them. His Grace Gawain confessed to her that they had searched for him and been unable to find him.

Immediately Queen Guinevere suspected treachery. She burst into tears. In vain they tried to persuade her that she had no reason to fear for the king. "He wanted to be the only one," they said, "to kill the pig so he could tease the rest of us about it afterward. Tomorrow will be bad luck, indeed, if we are not able to find him easily."

The next day the British champions of King Arthur beat the bushes in the forest from one side to another, and up and down, without coming on King Arthur. They found his dead horse riddled with wounds made by lance points. They began to think that their king had met the same fate, or, if not, that he had been taken prisoner. Consternation swept over Caradigan as people learned of the rescue party's failure to find King Arthur.

No sorrow equaled Queen Guinevere's grief, which one can well understand. Even though she had for weeks been bowed down with the sorry trouble caused her by the wicked damsel's plot, she still held her head up proudly. Galehaut tried to comfort her. He swore they would find out soon by what misadventure the king had been stolen away. In any event, the lady personally had nothing to fear from that damsel's calumny. Bad fortune to that girl who had slandered the queen with such a foul pack of lies, Galehaut told her.

"I care nothing for that woman, Galehaut," the queen replied. "What I do fear is the meanness of men. Be so kind therefore as to warn your friend Lancelot not to try to see me in private as long as the king is absent from the court." Galehaut understood her prudence and the wisdom of her suggestion.

Defamation of her character was already being planned, the queen knew.

That very day, in fact, the queen left Caradigan for the safer refuge of Carlisle. She journeyed there under the guardianship of His Grace Gawain, His Grace Yvain, Seneschal Kay, and the men-at-arms from her own quarters.

Meanwhile, as soon as the damsel from Camelot heard that King Arthur had been captured, she reappeared at his Court in Caradigan demanding to be ushered into the king's audience chamber. The officer in charge, who was Bademagus, informed her that His Majesty was not at that moment in residence. He had been obliged to leave Caradigan. He had left Bademagus in charge there and deputized him to act in Arthur's stead.

"Not so," she retorted. "My case must be judged by the king's words only, spoken by his own mouth. I have come before him today, for my complaint names him the guilty party. It is he personally who must reinstate me in my full honor and royal rank."

Bademagus replied that officers of King Arthur were empowered to answer for the king during his absence from Court. They had plenipotentiary to speak and to hand down judgments in his name. Their noble birth and noble persons guaranteed the rightness of their judgments. It was a point of honor that she must respect.

The False Guinevere refused. She declared that only the king and he alone could hear her complaint and hand down justice to her. She waited right where she was before the Bed of Justice until all the other pleadings had been heard and the guilty parties sentenced. She sat there solemnly just as if she continued to hope against hope that Arthur would arrive before Court closed for the day. Then, bearing herself sadly, but as if outraged in her person, she departed for Camelot where all the time she had known she would find Arthur.

She had no sooner arrived home than she presented herself before the prison cell where the king was being sequestered. "King Arthur," she probably told him, "thanks to my honorable officers, you find yourself in my power." If he refused to recognize her as his legally wedded spouse, she told him, at the least he would be obliged to return to her here all those companions of the Round Table whom her father, King Leodagan, granted her as partial portion of her dowry.

King Arthur was totally hoodwinked. He made no reply at all to this business as he still, at first, failed to suppose that the damsel into whose custody he had unfortunately fallen could possibly be correct in her plea. But, as the days went by, the False Guinevere poured into his goblet more and more drops of a love potion that began to act on him. Every day she came to visit him, it is said. She came every day, they say, with sweeter and sweeter words and more caressing sighs, and she looked at him with eyes so tender and so passionate that little by little he felt himself soften. The king felt himself so drawn, probably by the force of her poisoned drops, that he finally became defenseless before her arts of love. What more could the medieval authors say?

He finally came to such a point, they decided, that he actually forgot about the legitimate rights of his legal wife, Queen Guinevere. So after a while not a night went by but he slumbered in the soft arms of the False Guinevere. He was only human and should, therefore, be pitied and forgiven, was the consensus.

Between February and Easter, however, Arthur began to come to his senses again, to become bored, and to complain of being kept so faraway from his own warriors. The damsel remonstrated with him. She said he should never think for a moment that she would give him up on her own free will. Once he returned into his own domains he could very easily mistrust her, who now had become his own true wife and queen. If she overcame him by force of arms also, he would please consider how she did it to lead him back into the consecrated bosom of Holy Mother Church. As for her, she said, she did in no way regret losing the crown he had set on her head. Even without his crown, she swore, she would prefer him to all the world's crowned heads.

For his part, King Arthur then swore, he loved her more than any person alive. Because he had been at Camelot beside her, he had totally put aside and out of his mind that other royal person who for so long a time had usurped her place beside him. Even so, he must admit, he added, that no great lady ever showed more knowledge, more goodness, and greater courtesy than did that other, first Guinevere of his, the one who was so long considered to be his legal wife. By her generosity and by her great birth she had certainly won the hearts of all, rich and poor alike. She was, everybody used to say of her, the very Emerald among ladies.

The False Guinevere sneered, knowing certain ladies use such outward shows because they have to hide what they really feel and are. Women always need to lie to impress people, she said. Arthur was inclined to agree, but just the same he could never cease to marvel when he recalled all the qualities that his first queen seemed to possess. To think that such excellence kept him also in sin for such a long time. His records would have to be changed to excuse his lapses, and his first queen was the recorder. That did present a problem. Such conversations caused the False Guinevere no end of unease. It was all very well that the king should show her the blindest of passions. She still trembled for fear that the aphrodisiac she employed would one day lose its potency. One day Arthur even asked her what more she wanted from him. She replied she wanted him to have her recognized by his nobility as legitimate daughter of King Leodagan and as his lawful spouse. He replied he was perfectly willing to do so. To avoid censure from both clergy and laity, he intended to reassemble the dignitaries of Camelot and bring them to recognize her all over again, as rightful heiress of Leodagan, and as her whom the King of the British wed before Holy Church. Following that, he would ask his barony down in Britain to confirm their testimony.

The False Guinevere applauded this resolve, and the king indicated Ascension as the day for the assembly at Carmelide when all convoked would recognize the Second Guinevere as the true queen of the British. At the same time King Arthur sent word to His Grace Gawain notifying him that he was fine in body and mind, and also notifying him to have members of British nobility present themselves in the fortress at Camelot on Thursday, Forty Days after Easter, i.e., the Day of Christ's Ascension.

The Lowlands, or contested lands that lay between the Roman Walls, had suffered not a little from King Arthur's imprisonment in his new wife's Pictish estate. His British barons escaped his vigilance to wage their unending, personal wars. Everywhere people suffered from their depradations. Those noblemen who under Arthur's eye had conducted themselves appropriately suddenly turned into the blackest villains, cutting the main roads, ravishing maidens, robbing widows of lands and revenues, whipping orphans, and stripping churches of valuable icons. Somebody had at least to attempt to govern them. Evil escalated on all sides.

Complaints from high and low poured into Carlisle, to Queen Guinevere constantly; for the very persons who were most guilty of the worst crimes suddenly came to their senses when they in turn were victimized. Then they recognized that some supreme authority needed reestablishment. The higher the lordship the more he expected to earn this distinction, if he caressed Fortune softly enough.

Thus, King Lancelot of Scotland, who was Arthur's "cousin," flattered himself that he would doubtless be elected king of the Lowlands. Of course, Gawain was an even closer relative of Arthur, because as Arthur's sister's eldest son he would normally inherit King Arthur's throne. By ancient law the king himself had no sons recognizable as heirs to his throne. But Gawain had already proven too beholden to Arthur, too happily his best man, altogether more interested in the high military command than in the patient administration of a kingdom. He would certainly refuse the succession.

At a general assembly of the nobility convoked to study the question, King Lancelot delivered the first address. He advocated first replacing Arthur who, for anything he knew, was already dead. He added that although it was a nice point of law, he believed that as Arthur's cousin he rightly claimed the kingship.

Prince Galehaut knew for sure that Gawain would never accept to be king while Arthur still lived, or could be thought to live. Arguing King Lancelot's naked ambition, Galehaut persuaded Gawain to offer a conditional reply. When Scotland's king approached Gawain with a proposal endorsed by the assembly, Gawain replied that he did not exactly refuse the kingship because that was the general will, but that he still hoped King Arthur, "his uncle," was not dead and that he would soon return.

At that time, he added, the barons who had elected Gawain would be released from their oaths of fidelity to him, and King Arthur would also pardon him for having assumed the rule during the king's long and mysterious absence.

The courtiers of the Lowlands easily perceived King Lancelot's disappointment and surprise when he witnessed His Grace consent to be elected only in order better to conserve the kingdom for the absent Arthur, were he ever to return alive. However, his enemies were dissenters who followed the majority. The assembly voted to recognize Gawain, the sister's eldest son, as the legal and rightful heir (by matriarchal or Pictish law) to the vacant or vacated throne. No sooner was Gawain inaugurated than unrest and troubles ceased. His Grace acted with force of arms, but as king in name only; the one who wielded the administrative, or real power, was Queen Guinevere.

One day messengers from Camelot finally arrived at Court asking for an audience with Gawain. They announced that King Arthur greeted him as his deputy, his nephew, and his friend. He enjoyed good health and the full liberty of the kingdom of Camelot, to which he summoned Gawain with pleasure to meet him, along with the noblemen of his southern or Lowland Kingdom, on the Thursday next of Our Lord's Ascension.

Before replying to the messengers, His Grace Gawain went to consult the queen. He told her they had good news concerning the king. He was in Camelot, to which he commanded them to journey to counsel with him.

Queen Guinevere was by then altogether too wise in the ways of men not to guess what His Grace had omitted. King Arthur was in Camelot, she agreed, which meant he was prisoner of or protector of her who had raised such a hideous, legal outcry. Gawain's silence as to what else the messengers had relayed to him allowed her no doubt as to what he was trying to conceal from her. She nonetheless put on a more cheerful face than she had shown lately and thus, let everyone note her joy that the king's good health and safety brought her.

For his part Gawain replied to Arthur's messengers that all should be as his uncle desired. He therefore informed the nobility of the Lowlands that their king, who was free and well, invited them to assemble at Camelot on the Thursday next, the Day of Christ's Ascension.

At once thereafter the wise queen summoned Prince Galehaut to counsel with her. She needed his advice very badly at that moment, she told him:

> More than ever, Galehaut, I am in need of your advice. It appears that the damsel at Carmelide has insinuated herself into His Majesty's confidence. That must be my just punishment for having undertaken a vow which was unknown to my husband. Ah, Galehaut! You know if Lancelot has deserved to be loved by the most moral, Christian, and most beautiful souls in the world. Even so, I shall never complain at my being misunderstood, and chastised for another, imaginary crime of the flesh. Let me finish my days in some black dungeon if such is what I shall have deserved. But I fear to die before I have formed firmly the honest desire to repent, for I should then be in danger of losing both soul and body.

Galehaut told her he could not doubt this expected judgment of the Court. One thousand warriors here, and including Arthur himself, will meet death before allowing anyone to threaten to take yours. He said he was leaving immediately for Camelot, and that he would be well escorted by men-at-arms. Were any one person or persons to dare condemn her, he and Lancelot would surely know how to annul their sentences and silence their very selves.

As the Thursday drew near, the queen prepared to leave the safety of the fortress at Carlisle under the protection of Gawain and the men of her household. Galehaut followed close after her with Lancelot and their armed vassals.

The false damsel at Camelot had already been declared legitimate heiress and queen by her nobles there. When he saw Galehaut and Lancelot again, King Arthur bade them welcome. He forbade the first queen, however, to lodge in his quarters; for that was now an honor reserved for the False Guinevere alone. The first queen, the real Guinevere therefore chose a lodging close by. She was continually surrounded, day and night, by nobles and barons from Carlisle, or Britain, who agreed among themselves that the king was blameworthy, that he did wrong to favor accusations against her.

On the Thursday morning Arthur addressed his newly arrived barons from Lowland Britain. The French medieval writers, not to be outdone by Geoffrey of Monmouth, wrote an oration for Arthur:

> Lords, I have commanded you to gather here because a king should decide nothing without counselling with his men. You know the complaint presented before us by the damsel and heiress from the kingdom of Carmelide. At first I considered her outcry to be spurious. Today I know that she has based it upon law, and that the deception therein stems from her whom formerly I considered my queen. Men of this country will testify before you that she is the daughter of King Leodagan of Carmelide: she whom I took as wedded wife was merely the daughter of a Seneschal. I am in need of your counsel concerning what I should do today to remedy my overlong misapprehension.

The king's words cast his nobles into such great dismay that no one person rose to contradict them. Gawain himself wept openly as if he had already witnessed the death sentence passed on his Queen Guinevere.

Then in the general consternation a single man rose to his feet. It was Prince Galehaut, the powerful son of the Giantess slain by Tristan. The medieval writers again rose to the occasion:

> "Sire, everyone here present recognizes you as every whit a king, which means to us that you in particular will never rush into an action you could re-evaluate later as totally wild folly on your part. I personally

consider that the queen has nothing at all to fear from this damsel."

"Galehaut," the king replied, "you cannot reliably ascertain the true facts behind this situation as have already ascertained the aristocrats of Camelot here. They belonged to King Leodagan. How can one doubt such eyewitness testifying?"

"Sire, at least one may now say it seems very peculiar that they should be presenting her so-called claim at this late date, and after all of them here have ignored it these many years. Have they not also right up until this present time considered our lady as their truly crowned queen?"

"I know for a fact," King Arthur replied, "that she is no such thing, and I have great regret on that account. I would much have preferred to have cherished my love for her whom I once considered my legal wife. I may without sin no longer so consider her. There is today no question of war or combat over this situation. The testimony of the noblemen of Carmelide suffices to teach us the truth in this matter."

All the bluebloods of Carmelide were then convened and ushered into the great hall. The accused queen was seated at one end of the hall; the accusing damsel sat at the other end. The king chaired the proceeding:

"All you judges, who now sit in judgment as my own subjects should do when summoned because I long since received your oaths of loyalty to me, are now about to become better acquainted with this plea for justice lodged with me. It touches upon these two ladies here present as defendant and plaintiff. The latter swears that she was properly and duly wed and so crowned queen, as befitted the only daughter of your lord king and lady queen, his spouse. The former, or defendant, is a lady I have considered up until this present time as my loyal spouse; she still persists in claiming that she is truly what the plaintiff now claims to be. You are here to learn and to decide the truth of all this. Swear therefore upon the saints I hold here before you that you will speak with neither love nor hatred in your hearts, and that you will recognize as queen she who veritably is such."

Then the aged Bertolais stepped forward, stretched out his hand toward the images of the saints that the king held and swore: God and the saints help him, but the damsel whose hand he holds *is Guinevere,* wife of King Arthur, anointed and ordained queen, king's daughter and queen's daughter of Camelot fortress. After him swore also the high-born nobles of that Court, and after them all the lesser barons and landed gentry from King Leodagan's domains. Among these notables there were some who even so swore for the true queen from Carlisle, but King Arthur heard, or failed to hear, these words as being of no account. He passed aside their trifling reservations, so deeply had the aphrodisiac acted on his system. His understanding had obviously been damaged.

The queen from Carlisle was adjudged guilty of all charges lodged against her.

This one day's work was the greatest spot on the reputation of King Arthur during his whole lifetime. Such was the consensus, or French medieval opinion.

On this occasion of a case that should have been thrown out of court, they thought, there followed a great and joyous celebration in Carmelide (Camelot), but deep and fearful mourning in Carlisle.

After he heard the verdict handed down by his judges, King Arthur inquired what should be done concerning her who had so long abused His Majesty. Guessing what was on the king's mind, Prince Galehaut of the Isles moved that this decision should be postponed until Whitsunday because any further decision needed several weeks for deliberation, given the utter gravity of the matter and the prestige of those concerned. He spoke in this way so that he could still be counted among the king's counselors, and, in fact, the king seemed still to acknowledge him as such. The king appeared to be grateful. He accepted the delay.

Meanwhile King Arthur entrusted to his nephew Gawain the warding of the queen from Carlisle. "Present her and yourself at Whitsuntide," he instructed Gawain. "My nephew, do not fail me in this if you wish to continue in my good graces."

"Sire," Gawain replied. "This is not the first time that the queen has been threatened with losing you."

He said it to remind the king how she had been, the very day of her wedding, almost at the point of being permanently abducted by relatives of the False Guinevere.

CHAPTER VII

The Testing of Guinevere

Guinevere is one of those supernatural beings who
are often assigned as wives to the greatest of
mortals.
—K. G. T. WEBSTER,
Guinevere: A Study of Her Abductions

IN ANY POLITICAL SITUATION, AS HERE WHEN A REALM OR TWO HANG IN
the balance, in-fighting erupts into open warfare every now and
then. Periods of relative calm only mask the evil faces of hatred,
envy, and greed. After the first plot to abduct Guinevere from her
father's fortress at Stirling on the eve of her wedding failed, the
young heiress gradually found herself, if she stopped to consider
what was occurring beneath the apparent calm of her months at
Arthur's Court, and as his crowned queen, deprived of all her
natural allies: half-sister, father, his seneschal, and then the king
her husband. Far sharper eyes than her own fortunately surveyed
her perilous situation from a distance. The Lady of the Lake
therefore dispatched Lancelot from the Isle of Man to Guinevere's side, to become her deputy, her true friend, and her secret
ally to the death. The two of them fortunately bound to their side
the powerful Prince Galehaut, Lord of the Isles. King Arthur had
gone north more than once to defeat both Picts and Scots if he

could not otherwise secure their submission. Meanwhile, Merlin required more and more time for his scholarship and missionary work. He ceased counseling Arthur.

Rather than hear the scenario of Guinevere's testing on charges of adultery with Lancelot according to any of her detractors, who inclined to agree with the charges, it would be refreshing to hear another side of her story from the college of French, or Angevin, writers who prepared the *Prose Lancelot.* They take his side and hers. In their royal view, because Lancelot was born of both royal and holy blood, he could not be wrong when he swore before God and his peers that Queen Guinevere was innocent and that he Lancelot stood ready to die to prove it. Why? Because noblesse oblige.

When Whitsuntide rolled around, they had it, all in Camelot saw Gawain true to his word, reappearing in the fortress of Camelot along with Queen Guinevere. From his apartments King Arthur processed into the hall escorted by various local nobility. The king urged his new attendants to observe the oaths they had solemnly sworn, which was to study what should be done with her who had by committing adultery so long maintained King Arthur in mortal sin. The visiting nobility from Arthur's Carlisle and points along Hadrian's Wall were of the opinion that King Arthur intended to hand down a light sentence for their queen; they could not have been more mistaken.

King Arthur no longer deserved the title of a just king, said the medieval writers. He sat there twiddling his thumbs while his new Guinevere screeched and threw herself at his feet, floods of tears streaming down her cheeks, screaming that she would kill herself if that "other woman" was not condemned to torture and death. Arthur actually yielded to her cries and no longer wished anything so much as he wished for peace and quiet, and the death sentence laid on his first queen, and for two reasons: imposture and adultery.

His Grace Gawain deliberated with the British barons from Carlisle to ascertain what or which action, if any, each of them proposed to take. As for himself, he had already decided, whatever happened, never to sit in any court where the queen could possibly be condemned to death. He would avoid dishonor by association.

The French authors searched for an alternate solution to the dilemma, which they treated as history and not as scandal inside Britain. Furthermore, they were less eager to accuse royal ladies of adultery and imposture, having in proximity as they wrote not only the immensely wealthy Eleanor of Aquitaine, not repudiated by the King of France much before 1152, but even more important, having before them the august mother of the future Saint Louis, Queen Blanche of Castille, twice regent of France, who had come up from Palencia into France to wed King Louis VIII.

The French authors took account of Prince Galehaut, who loved and protected Lancelot and who therefore extended himself to defend the queen. He cautioned prudence to Arthur's vassals in Camelot. Let us proceed gently with respect to His Majesty, Galehaut urged them. Because the king now seems determined to treat Her Majesty with the extreme severity allowed him by law, he said, let us all request a delay of forty days in which to weigh the evidence. Perhaps, once the king has returned to his own lands down in Carlisle, he will no longer remain so infatuated with her whom he has set in the queen's place. His motion was carried unanimously, and the request was formally submitted by Galehaut for the king's approval.

The king replied that he saw no reason whatsoever for him to delay sentencing. If Galehaut wished to disqualify himself, he could be replaced forthwith. This went for the others present as judges.

But they pleaded that because the Court's judgment had already declared the Lady Guinevere stripped of her titles of wife and queen, and of her estates, it was certain that the consequent judgment would pronounce on her the death sentence. Now, this was a sentence that the judges refused to sanction because those from Carlisle were unanimous in their decision that the Lady Queen not be in any way cruelly treated or injured in her person.

The king was angry. He decreed that others could carry out the proceedings and would do so that very evening. Thus, he dismissed the protesters from Carlisle and ordered the resident barons of Camelot to pronounce sentence forthwith.

The treacherous Bertolais spoke for them. They were willing, he said, to do this, but on one condition: that Arthur should preside as chief magistrate from the bench. If the barons from Britain disqualified themselves, then their sovereign must fill their places.

King Arthur understood that he could not refuse such a reasonable request. He, therefore, preceded their group into the Court chambers where the doom would be pronounced.

Prince Galehaut for his part also countered this move, however, by asking the British nobles from Carlisle what they planned to do if their queen was doomed, actually doomed, to death. His Grace Gawain repeated he would without hesitation leave his uncle's realm and never again set foot on it. When His Grace Yvain, son of King Urien (Rion), and Seneschal Kay swore the exact same vow, all the other British aristocrats followed suit.

Prince Galehaut praised God first when his turn to reply came. He said it was easy to see that the Lady Queen was beloved by the most patrician of warriors there and easy to know if they would ever have found her guilty of any such charge.

Galehaut then went looking for young Lord Lancelot, son of kings of the same name. Handsome, gently born, noble, and holy companion of mine, Galehaut thought of him. Lancelot must not be bent down with care. Before this day ends, Galehaut promised, Lancelot would see one of the slickest military coups anybody ever heard tell of. If the Court condemned the queen, he would by his own authority, promised Galehaut, declare a mistrial. He would call the king personally to answer for it and at once offer to fight the king on the field of honor or gladly to fight any champion Arthur cared to designate.

Lancelot forbade Galehaut to do any such thing. He was the only warrior designated to sustain her quarrels. If the king was displeased with him for this, then no great harm would fall on anyone else. Allow Lancelot to do what it behooved him to do, and only him, he pleaded.

Galehaut consented, because that was what he wished, but Lancelot was, like him, a member of the Round Table. Nobody could forget that. Therefore, when Lancelot heard the sentence pronounced, he was told to look toward Galehaut. He would give the high sign. At that, Lancelot was to walk toward the king and there before him boldly declare that he renounced all honors attendant on Arthur's House and also all honors attendant on services to the Round Table Order. Once he had freed himself, he would be blameless as he then refused to accept his sentence.

That is the way things stood when King Arthur rose and his barons at Carmelide followed him out of the hall where judgment had just been pronounced. He sat down, his barons clustered about him. The queen stood alone to one side. She showed no trace of emotion. Then Bertolais began to speak, for he clearly had been assigned that responsibility:

> Hear ye, lord barons of Britain, this sentence pronounced by command of King Arthur, against the woman who had been for too long a period of time his royal companion. In order to pay for such crime and make restitution therefore, the guilty party must forfeit her life. However, we should pay some regard to the honor she received for this long time, although she received it unwarranted, the honor, I say, of sharing the king's couch.
>
> It will have to suffice for her to be stripped of everything she brought with her the day of her wedding.
>
> Since she wore a crown upon her head, and falsely, her hair which received this crown shall be cut off. So shall the palms, or the inside of her hands, be sliced off since this flesh touched the crown each time she set it upon her head. The two cheeks at the two sides of her face shall also be amputated, upon which holy oils once were rubbed at her coronation.
>
> In that state she shall be exiled from the land of Britain, and she shall henceforth take especial care never again to re-appear before our Lord King Arthur.

The indignation of His Grace Gawain was great as he listened to Bertolais's words, and great was the anger of the other
British lords as they too listened to the unexpected sentence laid
on their Queen Guinevere. Each one of them, as the press of
emotion urged, declared loudly that never again would he sit on
any tribunal in any court where such a judgment had been ut-
tered. Prince Gawain was the first to say that if his Lord the King
had not taken part in this trial, those others who sat, consenting
accomplices in his Court that day, would be forever banished
from the society of decent men. His Grace Yvain concurred.
Seneschal Kay went even further, declaring himself ready immediately to fight every one of those men present on that judgment
bench, exception made for King Arthur, and that he considered
their sentence positively odious. In the midst of this tumult of
angry voices Galehaut raised a hand in signal to Lancelot.

At once Lancelot hurled himself through the assembled
crowd of barons, thrusting roughly with elbows and shoulders,
silently pushing them violently aside without a word of notice
or excuse. In the middle of the crowd he came on Seneschal Kay
who was trying to fray a passage toward the queen so he could
offer her his sword and service. Lancelot thrust him aside so
rudely, Kay spun around in a circle. When Kay whirled to face
him and ask what he was doing pushing him about, Lancelot
cried in a voice of thunder: "Back! Get back! Let a better man
undertake the care of our Queen Guinevere!"

Haughtily Lancelot stood then alone in the throng of stupe-
fied noblemen. Slowly Lord Lancelot raised his hand to his left
shoulder. Then deliberately he unhooked the gold penannular
brooch that held his superb mantle closed. In a shimmer of precious tissue the mantle dropped to the floor. Lancelot paid no
heed to where it fell or if anyone reached to raise it up. There he
stood divested of cloak, tall and slender in his close-fitting military tunic and battle dress. Thus stripped for combat he strode
resolutely up to the king's bench.

This confrontation between Lancelot and Arthur had been
a long time coming. Lancelot addressed Arthur directly, face-to-
face. He told him how he had been his warrior, how he had
accepted to become a member of the Round Table Order as

established by Merlin, how he had received the king's thanks on many an occasion. At this time he formally requested the king to call it quits.

Arthur asked him if he was serious. Lancelot replied that he was very serious indeed. Arthur replied that Lancelot should have no such dispensation. He also inquired how Lancelot could abjure his service and renounce such great honors as Arthur had laid on him.

Lancelot retorted gravely that he had already departed from Arthur's service as he heard the doom that had just been pronounced on Her Majesty. He fully intended at once to leave the king's household, to renounce his honors, and to resign from his ranks altogether, and forever more.

Arthur let him go. He could do nothing else. Lancelot, he said, had apparently no regard whatsoever for his companions, for the nobles assembled there. And so he gave him his hand on it, declaring him quit of all ties of good faith, good service, and links to himself.

Lancelot then sought permission to speak freely, for himself and for the noblemen of Carlisle. He insisted on knowing who had rendered this judgment on Queen Guinevere.

The king admitted doing so himself. Curtly he told Lancelot that no man could find it unnecessarily severe. Rather they would consider it far too lenient. He wished to know why Lancelot had asked.

He asked, Lancelot told Arthur, because he hereby declared whoever took part in that trial and in that sentencing perjured and liars. He added that he stood ready instantly to enforce that charge against Arthur as against the whole Court.

Still Arthur remonstrated with Lancelot, assuring him that he had not forgotten his services to the kingdom. He further urged his forgiveness, promising never to hate Lancelot. Truly, he had found Lancelot's conduct audacious, to say the least, particularly as he questioned Arthur's judgment. He ended by telling Lancelot the truth: that he would very soon meet a champion who would make him regret his words and his behavior.

Lancelot agreed that this was very likely but that he was ready to demonstrate the falsity of Arthur's sentence and ready to meet not one single champion of his but to go against the two best warriors he could find to accept the defense of his so-called just sentence. If he could not force two champions to admit they were perjured, he would hope that Arthur would string him up by the jaw.

Their confrontation was disturbed by Kay, who burned with outrage against Lancelot, first for having thrust him aside, and then for having been so insane as to offer to meet two champions at the same time. He must be drunk, was Kay's estimation.

Lancelot told Kay to stand aside and leave it to him, that Kay was too hot to be in command of his wits. He added that Kay should make no mistake about him, that he stood ready to defend the queen, not against two but against the three best warriors who sat and voted in that trial. They must beware of me, Lancelot told them, and do none of you from Britain think to stand before me today. He told Kay that he could join him if the king consented.

God forbids any three to challenge Lancelot, Arthur decided, although he added that one of his own men could probably handle three at once. His nobles at Camelot were incensed. They accepted combat and paid collateral security. Arthur still hesitated.

Finally Arthur warned all present to bear in mind that Lancelot was one of the most renowned and successful champions in the world. Arthur would not for anything see him die a shameful death.

Lancelot replied that the combat must take place. He repeated that the sentence was unmerited and, furthermore, that all those who did not fear to take part in it acted feloniously.

Then Lancelot knelt before the king and held out to him his own pledges. Despite his reluctance, the king accepted them as binding Lancelot to fight single-handed. The nobles of Camelot selected their three best men, who were the broadest shouldered. The oldest was barely forty years of age. Combat was scheduled for the following Sunday, the first Sunday after Whitsunday. Meanwhile the queen was to remain under house arrest while she awaited this judiciary combat to the death, which would decide her own life or death. Her own people feared the outcome. They could not help it (Ms. fr. 339, 751, 752).

Everybody soon learned how Lancelot had won the honor of defending the queen. His warning to Seneschal Kay was very clear. He would allow no person to share combat with him, much less, to replace him. For their part, the three mighty champions from Camelot openly boasted of being set to uphold the Court's verdict of death to that woman still claiming to be the queen. Lancelot ardently desired to rush them, all three at once, but Galehaut would absolutely not permit him to attempt such a feat. No, Galehaut told him. You are to meet them one at a time: one, two, three, in that sequence.

After having deposited their pledges with King Arthur, each champion went to be armed. Lancelot pulled on tight-fitting trews and buckled his halberd.

Then Gawain offered Excalibur to Lancelot. Excalibur was Arthur's sword that, at Merlin's direction, he had at age fifteen drawn from the anvil at the Chesters Fort on Hadrian's Wall. It was another Pan-Celtic "sword of light" (*calad*, "hard" plus *bolg*, "lightning") like the swords that Irish and Welsh heroes alike had taken in ages past from the pre-Christian god of the Underworld. The Irish *caladbolg* was so strong it could be used to cut off the tops of the hills. When Arthur drew it in his turn from an anvil, he understood that it had originally come from Vulcan or some other blacksmith who dwelt under a volcano and had wed the queen of heaven. To the most ancient Celts, the blacksmith god had created man. The *Prose Lancelot* associated Excalibur with King Rion of the Isles, which merely repeated this same Celtic tradition explained in 1136 by Geoffrey of Monmouth: that *Caled wlch* (Excalibur) came from *Ynys Afallach,* or Gaelic Avalon, i.e., the Gaelic-speaking Isle of Man. Thus when Arthur deputized Gawain as his commander-in-chief, he gave him Excalibur as a sign of his power (the Roman *imperium*). When Gawain in his turn accepted Lancelot as the warrior entrusted with communal honor, he lent him Excalibur. The sword, third after crown and scepter, constituted the ancient honors of Scotland.

When only his head and his hands remained bare, Lancelot mounted his palfrey and rode into the lists. Galehaut, Gawain, and others wheeled about and formed his escort. Before him rode young Lionel, who had been raised with Lancelot at the Grail Castle; he bore Lancelot's helmet and shield. A second squire followed, leading Lancelot's war-horse by his right hand and his Sword of Justice in his left hand. The lists had been drawn up between the king's house, the forest, the Forth River, and the salt meadow. The two queens had been seated at windows, the False Guinevere at the upper story, the real Guinevere on the ground floor, but surrounded by His Grace Yvain of Galles, Seneschal Kay, Giflet Fitz-Do of Carlisle, and the queen's brother, Bedevere.

Then file in the three champions of Camelot, also fully armed except for hands and heads. They were tall and handsome. Meanwhile, Lancelot had gone up to the queen at her window. She kissed him like a mother, in full view of all and commended him to the Virgin's son, Jesus Christ. Thus comforted, Lancelot covered his hands, laced up his helmet, and passed the laces of his shield around his neck. His richly caparisoned war-horse stood waiting. Lancelot mounted, took his sword from his second squire just as his three opponents had already done. Those onlookers who could not find a place to stand started climbing on the crenellated ramparts.

Lancelot rapidly grew impatient to hear the signal to commence. "Sir Gawain," he shouted, "what are you waiting for?" The horn sounded. His sword under his armpit and his shield over his chest, Lancelot kicked his horse forward with his spurs. The first of the three opponents awaited him. Their swords clashed and rang on their shields. The hasp of the opponent's broke. Lancelot's blade pierced chain mail and leather, pierced his heart, and came through his back. Lancelot rode past, rested his sword against a tree, dismounted, and tied his horse to some low branches. Then, shield over his head and his broadsword in hand, he returned on foot toward the felled champion whom he notified to stand up. There was no answer. He was dead. Lancelot unlaced his helmet, opened the visor, cut off his head, and wiped off Excalibur on the green grass of the meadow before sheathing it again.

His Grace had the horn blown for the second judicial trial.

The second champion arrived top speed in the lists, at a full cavalry charge. The two shocked at the top of their shields, and the opponent broke his sword. Lancelot broke his shield in half but without piercing his hauberk. Lancelot reached across and grasped his adversary about the torso, raised him up out of his saddle, and threw him over the croup of his own horse. Then driving his sword into the sod he rode back to the Camelot champion who had already picked himself up and had already covered his head with his broken shield.

"Don't worry," Lancelot called down to him. "I should be ashamed to fight you from horseback when you are afoot." He dismounted, tied his gigantic horse to a tree and strolled back, sword in hand, to his adversary. First Lancelot cut the strap holding the man's shield. Then he rained blows at him, hard at first, and then soft and searching. His opponent was soon bathed in blood. All of a sudden Lancelot hesitated, then backed away horrified; although his foe was already beaten, he still did not call off the fight and surrender. After casting about looking for a place to hide, he dragged himself over to the riverbank as if he could find a haven there. Then seemingly ashamed to die in such a cowardly way, he came back to where Lancelot stood waiting for him. Then he saw Lancelot raise Excalibur over his head.

"Ah, Lancelot," he cried. "Gentle warrior, from whom can a man expect mercy except from one so highly born?"

"You will receive it," Lancelot replied, "but only after you have recognized aloud that the judgment pronounced against our Lady the Queen is a false judgment, that all those who sat in judgment on her, and who handed down this verdict are ignoble and traitorous."

"Assuredly," he replied, "I cannot save my own life at the expense of these judges. They did their duty."

"Then say rather that henceforth they will be forever more disowned by every person of noble birth alive in the world today. As for you, who support such treason, you will have received her death penalty."

Lancelot again raised his sword. The other waited for him no more but fled across the field. When he finally ran out of breath, again he begged for mercy.

"Poor warrior," Lancelot told him, "why not let this good blade do its work? Is it not better to die rather than pronounce the craven's cry for mercy?"

"God be my witness," he sighed, "but you are right. I shall stand and await death from your hand. I could not have it from a nobler antagonist." So he remained standing, motionless, his head barely held by the hood of his coat, and the dangling shreds of his shield. Lancelot at one stroke made the sword fly from his hand. All the spectators looked on this sight with pity.

Carried away by the very depth of his desire for revenge, Lancelot slashed down at him with one furious stroke. Behind his foe he had glimpsed the queen's strained eyes trained on him. He cut through his antagonist's helmet and his visor with that one stroke. His sword Excalibur lodged deep in his skull, and the man's body slumped inanimate on the grass.

"Ah, my good, brave sword," Lancelot whispered to it. "He who wields you cannot miss his feats of prowess. He sheathed Excalibur, returned to his horse and showed again his old impatience to hear the sound of the horn, and see his third opponent head-to-head. As he waited nervously, he saw the judges from Camelot throw themselves at King Arthur's feet.

"Sire, we were wrong to let this combat commence before we had our champions swear they were defending a just cause. It will be better if we ask them this now, if they wish to take that oath. In fact, the one should swear now as to whether he believes the judgment just and the other as to whether he believes it stained with felony." It was true that Lancelot had not been obliged to swear that Queen Guinevere on his word was innocent of all charges. While the king prepared to satisfy his protesting noblemen, he heard Galehaut sound the third horn. Thus Galehaut avoided any possible perjury both for himself and for Lancelot.

The third combat commenced. Lancelot's antagonist was a celebrated champion (whose name has escaped us). He judged the war-horses to be of equal weight and skill. He, therefore, slit open the chest of Lancelot's horse, so as to force the challenger to fight on foot against a well-mounted, fresh defender. However, he figured wrong; for as his horse staggered Lancelot grasped his antagonist so firmly that both fell to the ground. Both wielded their swords on each other's helmets. Chain mail split and flew about. Crimson blood spurted hot over their clothing. Even so, Lancelot lodged his strokes more tellingly so that even those who were wagering on the Camelot warrior began to doubt he could win. Their fierce battle continued until 3:00 P.M. By that "fourth part of the day" the foreign champion had lost so much blood that he was having difficulty breathing. Then Lancelot pushed him harder and ever harder, chased him backward along the fence, and yet seemed in no hurry to give him the coup de grace. By that time, the Camelot man still raised his arm to strike but failed to deliver a blow.

Finally Lancelot struck him so hard he knocked him flat on the ground. Lancelot then pulled off his opponent's helmet. Then he looked up at Kay and angrily asked him if he wanted to be next. The felled champion still lay flat at Lancelot's feet. "Brave warrior," he begged, "have mercy."

"There is no mercy for the injury you have inflicted." The vanquished champion made a last effort to hang on to Lancelot's right arm, but he was again knocked flat by Lancelot's left arm. Then Lancelot put one knee on his chest and beat him over the head with his sword, and on his visor and over his helmet and on the hood of his tunic.

Barons and ladies who had counted so heavily on the fellow from Camelot begged the king to halt the combat. Arthur told them there was no way he could stop Lancelot or anyone else when the old Irish battle fury was on him.

"Sire," Galehaut suggested, "there is perhaps one way to calm his fury. Go beg the lady for whom he fights to ask him for his enemy's life. She will most certainly do whatever you ask of her."

"I am willing," Arthur replied, "for no price is too great to save the life of such a worthy opponent."

King Arthur then sought the queen who dutifully rose as he approached. "Lady," he began, "the sentence of the judges has become null and void. Your life has been given to you once more. However, this last warrior whom Lancelot has vanquished is going to die now if you do not request that he live. It would be such a shame, for he is a truly accomplished champion of great renown."

"Sire, if that pleases you, I will do what I can." The Lady Guinevere descended from her tower, walked across the green grass of the meadow, and threw herself at Lancelot's knees. "Dear, handsome friend," she said, "I beg you to show mercy to this warrior."

Seeing her in this humble position, Lancelot could hardly contain himself. "Lady, fear nothing for him. If you so desire, I will give him my sword rather than refuse him his life. Are you not she whom I am to hear first, she who armed me and cherished me, even when I was delirious with wounds?"

Turning to his prostrate antagonist, Lancelot told him, "You, Sir, I hold quit. I have no more quarrel with you." His men hurried to assist their defeated man and help him from the field.

If one of the queens that day rejoiced, the other felt differently. So did the barons from Camelot, every one who had sat in judgment on the queen from Britain, because every one of them was henceforth, as a result of their cruel and dishonorable verdict, declared so unsuitable as to be unworthy ever again to sit in a court of law.

The testing days of Lady Guinevere continued, however, even after Lancelot's victory; for she was not reinstated either as queen of the Lowland kingdom or as wedded wife to King Arthur. She did nevertheless make her way down into Britain, although not in the king's party—under Gawain's protection. His Grace showed her the same affection and deference as in her happier times. Before they reached Arthur's capital, they saw Galehaut approaching. "My Lady," he told her, "despite this sorry state of your separation and estrangement from the king, which shall last as long as God so wills it, you have continued so worthy and so gracious toward all of us that not a nobleman in all our state but will never leave your service. As for my part, I am honored, here in the presence of His Grace, to offer you the most beautiful of all my estates. It is a property very pleasant to behold, very fruitful in all revenues, very rich in soil and fruits, quite surrounded by fortresses. There, dear Lady, you will have no need to fear malicious intent still held against you by the new queen."

"I thank you very much, Galehaut," she replied, "but I may not receive such honor without permission from my lord the king. If it has pleased him to repudiate me, I am none the less obliged to act as he commands."

Next day as the king left chapel, he came on Queen Guinevere leaning on Galehaut's arm. She fell to her knees: "Sire, you wish me to depart, but I do not know where you wish me to go. May it be to a place at least where I may pray for my soul's salvation and fear my enemies no longer. Were one of them to dishonor me while I am under your guardianship, the shame would fall on you. All that is needed is one word from you and I shall be endowed with another estate, which is offered me more for yourself than for me. However, I shall refuse it unless you bid me otherwise."

"What estate is this and who offered it to you?"

"I, Sire," Galehaut replied sternly. "I am deeding to her the most beautiful and most pleasant of all my holdings. I am signing over to her The Sorelois. Once there, the lady will have nothing more to fear."

"Let me consider this proposal in council," the king replied. He called a meeting of his vassals from Britain to lay Galehaut's intention before them.

"Sire," Gawain told him privately, "you know, and we all know, that the lady was repudiated only because you so desired it. She had not deserved it. Probably we should, all of us, not have allowed it. At least, we counseled you unanimously to choose another treatment. When a sovereign lord will not trust his own men, he, and not they, must bear on his shoulders the consequent blame for the sorry results. My advice now is that at the least you guarantee the future safety of our lady. She would not find safe refuge anywhere in your kingdom. The woman who is going to replace her would not desist from further persecutions. However, you have ample choice. You may indicate as likely places for her retreat three safe domains: (1) the kingdom of King Urien of Galles, which at this time includes the southern isles (Sudreys) and the Isle of Man; (2) the kingdom of Lothian, which is ruled by my own father, King Loth, at Traprain Law; or (3) the ocean-bordered lands of The Sorelois (in Dalriada), which this powerful Prince Galehaut offers her as her own entailed property free and clear."

The king had no time to respond, for a vassal who was a close ally of the new queen requested an immediate audience. His Grace stepped out of the room as King Arthur asked this weeping lord, "What's the matter? What is the queen doing?"

"Sire, she has fallen into despair. She has learned that you wanted to retain your old concubine here on British soil. Please understand that if you are to do so, your queen will die of grief."

"Hurry up, then," the king urged, "go reassure her. I shall never do anything that could displease her." Returning again to Gawain's side, he told him: "Good Nephew, I realize that Guinevere cannot remain here any longer, or in any of my lands or secondary holdings. She would not be safe here, and I do not desire her death. Let her go into The Sorelois with Galehaut. I will have her safely escorted there by my own trusted guards." He then returned to the council, which unanimously endorsed his plan.

Then the king found Galehaut. "Fine, true Sir," he told him, "you are not my subject, but my companion-in-arms and my friend. I have not requested from you on behalf of Guinevere any gift of land, but because she could not reside here with any degree of safety, I entrust her to you and to your honorable intent. Keep her as you would a sister and promise me, on the love you bear me, not to undertake anything to her detriment or any endangerment of her honor." Having so said, the king took the queen by the hand and placed her beside Galehaut, her hand in his. Prince Galehaut swore to guard her as he would a sister. Arthur designated those of his men who would form her honor escort, and they followed her at once to the private quarters where she was residing.

"Sire," Gawain told the king, "you have now embarked on a new marriage. Believing that you were disentangling yourself from sin, you have soiled yourself even more, and in addition, you have lost the company of all those noblemen whom you needed most to keep close to your person and counsels. Both lords, Lancelot and Galehaut, have renounced the Round Table Order, which no ordained member has ever before done. Lancelot must be brought back and persuaded to become reinstated. You must at least attempt this."

"I agree," the king replied. "There is nothing, Nephew, that I am not ready to try except repudiating my new queen. Let us reason with him."

In Galehaut's quarters, Arthur and Gawain found the two, Galehaut and Lancelot, seated together. Both rose before the king. Arthur held out both hands to Lancelot and asked for his friendship. His Grace added his entreaties. "Good Lancelot," Arthur pleaded, "you have done more for me than I ever did for you. You were a member of my Round Table Order. I shall never again experience one moment's happiness if you do not accept to join us once more. Forget your reasons for resentment, dear Lord, and request the half of my kingdom. It will be yours. I offer you anything at all you desire, except my honor."

"Sire," Lancelot replied, "I feel no resentment toward you. Nor do I care for your lands, which I would not govern in any case. Nothing could make me remain here with you. At mass this morning I made an oath to leave this place." His words alerted the king that he had no hope of swaying Lancelot. He withdrew with bowed head, a heavy heart, and all that night never closed an eye. Then he remembered what Lancelot had told the queen, that he would never refuse her anything who had so kindly watched over him once during a long illness.

The next morning Galehaut and Lancelot paid their respects to the Court prior to departing for The Sorelois. Both king and the new queen stood to bid them adieu. The king went up to Guinevere's palfrey and addressed her: "Lady, I know that Lancelot loves you so much he would refuse you nothing you ask. Be so kind, if you ever hope to return to me, as to beg him to remain in the Round Table Order. You will easily win what we have been refused."

The queen listened quietly, showing neither surprise nor joy at the king's assurance of Lancelot's love for her. "Sire," she said, "Lancelot would have to love me immeasurably for him to accede to my prayers when he has already declined yours. But we should take great care, do you not agree, not to cause the slightest pain to those who love us. Were I to persuade him to rejoin your company, would I not be depriving myself of his? And yet he hås already served me better than have others from whom I should rightfully have expected more love and greater protection. I was ever your submissive and devoted wife, and yet you never hesitated to condemn me to torture and capital punishment. Only the supreme prowess of Lancelot preserved me from both. He remembered the only assistance I once was able to render him, when we were both embattled at the Saxon's Rock there on the Clyde River. That time I did no more for Lancelot than I would have done for the least of your defenders. And when Lancelot saw with his own eyes how quickly you forgot all the great feats of arms he had performed for you, when you allowed him to stand alone and combat three terrible challengers one after the other so he could, he hoped, deliver me from the lowest of all degradations, it simply is not possible now for me to believe that he should care about living at your Court among your elite guardsmen, when he could follow Prince Galehaut and her who owes him her honor and her life."

She fell silent then. The king blushed to have heard what she, and the world also, doubtless, thought of his recent conduct. Only Galehaut was near. Lancelot had already mounted and urged his palfrey out of earshot. Finally Arthur commended them to God's care but asked His Grace Gawain of Galloway to accompany their party to their safe destination. They did arrive safely in The Sorelois where, thanks to measures taken by Galehaut, the lady received the homage of his nobles. After having seen the queen receive these royal honors, Gawain returned south to Carlisle.

Following these gala ceremonies of her new investiture, the queen requested Galehaut, Lancelot, and her chief lady-in-waiting to attend Her Majesty. "Now you see a queen separated from the king who is her lord. Although I am the rightful queen of Britain, daughter of the king and queen of Camelot, I must expiate my sin for having shared my love with another, Lord Lancelot. But when a lady loves so noble and so holy a youth, how could she blush for this fault on her part? How could she not have been forgiven for her love of him? She could not be forgiven, some say, for Our Heavenly Father has no regard for our rules of polite society. The best way to stand in with Him is to stand out with your century. Therefore, I ask you, Lancelot, for a gift now, if you please: allow me to sequester myself even more closely than when I was running an even greater risk of being discovered. In the name of the love you feel for me, I would like to hear you agree now not to ask more from me than a kiss and a hug. Of those I have an abundance for you, and later, in a suitable time and place, I shall not refuse you the surplus of my deep affection. Do not suffer on account of my heart. It can never belong to anyone, even if I wanted it to. Dear, sweet love, know that I told His Majesty, when he asked me to persuade you to remain at his Court, that I loved Lancelot's company as well as I loved his."

"Lady," Lancelot answered her, "whatever pleases you could never displease me. Your will is my law. On you shall always depend my heart and all the joy that will ever come into my life."

Those were the conventions established by the queen for her new life, and Lancelot never once attempted to infringe on them (*Le Livre de Lancelot del Lac*).

Titles used in the preceding summarized translations come not only from the various *Prose Lancelot* manuscripts, but by authority of ancient texts such as the Welsh *Book of Llandaff,* which treats land charters and gives the life of Saint Dubricius (see *Merlin* by Norma Lorre Goodrich, New York, 1987, 1988). The book gives the following ancient titles: *Rex* (*Riogh* in Gaelic) for the English word *king, Comes* (count), *Optimates* (noblemen), *Tribuni* (military tribunes, who were at times the highest officers in the Roman state), and *Domestici* (household troops or guards) as well as dukes, earls, seneschals, stewards, judges, county judges, champions, sergeants, plaintiffs, defendants, counselors, councillors, and freeholders. As John Toland observed at the end of the seventeenth century in *The Critical History,* the title of "king" indicated to ancient Celts even before the advent of Christianity the supreme ruler, one king over all (*Rex unus est universis*). "The king bore all the envy," said Toland (p. 188), "and the Druids possesst all the sweets of authority." Such a remark makes one wonder who Galehaut was. A priest? It seems likely, for the more ancient Druid priests were also judges, and male or female.

Early Christian Fathers inside Britain were very upset by the murders of young wives by their husbands in Arthur's day. Saint Gildas had tried to save the beheaded young bride, but to no avail. Another such priest attempted to save the beheaded Saint Winifred in Wales, also unsuccessfully. Murder and mutilation were probably much more common than historians realized, occurring even when the young wife was not pregnant. Her pregnancy might have ousted her husband from her property is the assumption. A case similar to that of Guinevere came to the attention of an early historian of the barbarian invasions of Gaul.

Professor B. Zeller (1897), of the University of Paris, documented for his students the case of Visigothic Emperor Theodoric's daughter from Toulouse, who had been married to the son of the Vandal Emperor in North Africa, at Carthage. The Visigothic Emperor resided at his Court in Toulouse, now France. The Vandal prince suspected his bride of wishing to poison him. He therefore had her nose and both ears amputated. Then he sent her back to her father in Toulouse. Because of this injury, Theodoric joined Attila the Hun in the war against the Vandals where Attila thought he would be invincible because he had miraculously found, and was wielding, the very sword of Mars.

When threatened with disfigurement, Guinevere resembled her contemporaries enforcing what the Italian poet Ariosto also is said to have called "the harsh law of Scotland": l'aspra legge de Scozia.

CHAPTER VIII

The Abductions of Guinevere

There is nothing to indicate in the romance that
Lancelot has ever received from Guinevere a token
of her love. All that he possesses of hers is the
hair that he has taken from her comb.

—A. H. DIVERRES,
Arthurian Romance

As THEY COMPOSED THE *Prose Lancelot,* THE WRITERS WHO WERE COMMIS-
sioned to accomplish this long task certainly formulated a mental
construct that could contain places, times, personages, and
events. Twice in the preceding passages they allowed their own
world with their personal opinions and analyses to break
through into stern disapproval of King Arthur. The point is that
judicial combat itself was frowned on in their medieval France
and that it had at least once been forbidden by law. In fact, the
Count of Flanders had abolished it in his territories in 1116. But
famous authors continued to abhor it elsewhere and to castigate
those princes who still allowed dueling, much as the authors of
the *Prose Lancelot* castigated King Arthur for it. As late as 1455 at
Valenciennes, France, two "gentlemen," wrote the chronicler
Georges Chastellain, fought to the death in a judicial duel while
all the time the event was rendered more hideous to the spectators by the incessant death tolling of a huge bell. And Chastellain

was another world-renowned eyewitness, whose last pages on the abduction of Jeanne d'Arc were so revealing that somebody tore them out of his unique, eyewitness chronicle and destroyed them forever.

Chastellain's fifteenth-century England could very well be compared to sixth-century Arthurian Britain. The fifteenth century saw Great Britain reach such low points in human cruelty under King Henry V as were hardly reached anywhere: public torture of prominent persons, riots, cases of royal insanity, treachery by political leaders, executions of women, abductions, public scandals, low or no standards of morality in rulers and the clergy. The historian Henri Pirenne (1937) says that when the Arthurian kingdom collapsed after 542, the ancient world, then at the end of the sixth century, fell to its lowest possible point of dissoluteness and anarchy. The writers of the *Prose Lancelot* were very much aware of this collapse, and they reacted from their safer medieval centuries of relative peace and harmony.

The *Prose Lancelot,* whatever one may think of the Irish literary genre, or romance, stands as a huge, lengthy, composite testimony to the fall of the ancient world. Nobody studying this text can mistake it for anything else than a document concerning the ancient world in decay and dissolution. One reads it, as one always reads history, for insights into origins, of course; however, what one has here is glimpses of collapse. In Arthur's world as on into the sixth century we have seen that the ancient world was a world where property, i.e., vast landed estates, represented the economic system and government by territorial princes. Privilege accrued only to men of noble birth. There was nobody else. Royal birth, but holy blood also, distinguished one man most of all, ergo, Lancelot of the Lake. He alone was both royal and holy, said to be descended from Saint Joseph of Arimathea of biblical fame. Whispering voices beneath the texts have him descended from another, the holiest of all persons, however. The young Lancelot might well weep at such a heavy burden fallen on him.

In this ancient world of Queen Guinevere one finds no mention of cities, commerce, industry, ordinary people, trade, exchange, business, or human rights. Arbitrators deal for themselves and their class, which is the aristocracy. Real property dominates the queen's treatment, marriage, safety, and her very life. She is a salable commodity, if there ever was one. Below her must somewhere be masses of indentured, male and female slaves with short haircuts such as she barely avoided, and that thanks to Lancelot. No clergyman came forward to defend her in Carmelide, which is Arthur's Camelot. Both Merlin and the Lady of the Lake were apparently resident at the Grail Castle, faraway. Not until the ninth century, in any case, would the Church daringly oppose its authority and holy Christian Republic to the power of the princes: authority versus power. In Arthur's world it is land, birth, and sword that rule, that appoint themselves judges and magistrates—other qualifications were nonexistent— and that allow, and even sanction, *ordeals* and *judicial duels* in cases unsettled otherwise. These were, said William Paton Ker (1958), the darkest years of all dark ages.

The Germanic invasions had commenced in 406 and thrust across the center fringes of the Roman Empire, disrupting its terrestrial empire. Their law derived from land empire imperial. If Arthur was actually an emperor, as Welsh texts sometimes claimed, or even if he was to be envisaged merely as commander-in-chief, he was still a Roman-style ruler *and High-Priest also,* according to Julius Caesar's precedent. Then by Roman law Lancelot was identifiably the hero, or avenging arm of the law. The Roman Arthur wielded in any case regal power under the Roman judicial principle of society as its own prince, the two being interchangeably powerful and indistinguishable. Arthur stood unchallenged on home ground except perhaps by Lancelot and Galehaut, astride the apex of his world and property. He was the *Man* and only begetter and founding father.

King Arthur died, said the Welsh chroniclers, before Justinian, another Roman emperor who was also illiterate. The Welsh Annals claim Arthur died in 542; Justinian died in 565. Under Pope Gregory the Great (590–604), the Church finally became organized enough to challenge the princes; it would quote the Constantine Donation to argue effectively that Church and State represented henceforth two, equal, sovereign powers. But until then, it is uncontestably "law from imperial power."

There are other reasons besides inference and entertainment

for studying the *Prose Lancelot,* however, and for allowing it a measure of credence. It was composed while its authors still had available, and at hand, *The Northern Annals.* Thus, theoretically, authors commissioned by Angevins ruling in Britain, France, Aquitaine, Provence, or Spain to write the life and adventures of Lancelot, still had a reliable source in front of them. One notes, as a token example, that they name Lancelot's father, or grandfather, just as Geoffrey of Monmouth named Lancelot: King Anguselus of Scotland, or King Aiguisel of Scotland ("Anguselus" in Latin would give "Aiguisel" in Old French, which in turn would give us "Lancelot" in more modern French). *The Northern Annals* were lost in Scotland in the thirteenth century and have not yet been recovered. For this other reason, then, their text deserves scrutiny.

In one of her essays, the late Kathleen Hughes of Trinity College, Dublin, studied this very question. The list of names of the early Scottish and Pictish kings was last seen in Holyrood Castle in Edinburgh in 1660, she found. King Edward also removed many manuscripts from Scotland. The Scandinavians destroyed many more, doubtless. Gaelic manuscripts also disappeared in the twelfth and thirteenth centuries. Worse yet, the attitude in Scotland toward history, said Hughes (1980, 20) "we find hard to understand." "They did not want contemporary history, a year-by-year chronicle recording a few events," such as Georges Chastellain and Jean Froissart were to write for later French kings of France and England. Another great scholar, the Scot Robert L. G. Ritchie (1952), blamed the loss of *The Northern Annals* on medieval kings of Scotland, who passed out, or gave away, historical material during a reorganization of the Church in Scotland. The churchmen who thus acquired these priceless records may have been precisely the ones who seemingly either commissioned, *or who were,* Geoffrey of Monmouth, Chrétien de Troyes, and the compositors of the *Prose Lancelot,* among a host of other most-talented authors and historically interested colleagues.

Other very talented authors have puzzled at the loss of *The Northern Annals* of Scotland, but blamed it on the early clergy who were King Arthur's contemporaries. One such was the brilliant

Irish author John Toland (1670–1722) who studied abroad as well as at Edinburgh and Oxford, and who wrote voluminously. In his *Critical History of the Celtic Religion* he quotes (p. 93) a Dr. Kennedy's *Dissertation* as follows:

> Dr. Kennedy says, (p. 99) that Patric [Saint Patrick] burnt 300 volumes, stuft with the fables and super- stitions of Heathen Idolatry: unfit, adds he, to be transmitted to posterity.

That was nothing new, adds Toland, because he found such wanton destruction also in the Acts of the Apostles (19:19). "Mr. Toland was, at all times," says the Abstract to his book, "a rigid advocate for the primitive apostolic simplicity of the Christian religion" (p. 29); and he became a Presbyterian.

This was the Gaelic and/or Irish custom, wrote Toland (p. 185 ff.):

> There is one king . . . over them all; for they are as many as be of them, divided only by narrow channels [of the sea]. The king has nothing of his own, but shares of every thing every man has. He is by certain Laws obliged to observe equity: and lest avarice should make him deviate from the right way, he learns justice from Poverty; as having no manner of property, being maintained upon the public expence. He has not so much as a wife of his own, but by certain turns makes use of any woman towards whom he has an inclination; whence it happens, that he has neither the desire nor the hope of any children.

In more ancient days, before St. Ninian in the fifth century Christianized Galloway, where Arthur was born, Toland adds: "The kings bore all the envy, and the Druids possesst all the sweets of authority" (p. 188).

The foreign prince Galehaut seems in the case of Queen Guinevere's rejection and sentence to have obliged King Arthur to recognize international civility. The situation of Guinevere resembles twentieth-century terrorism in which the endangered victim cannot by physical force be snatched from the hands of her captors. Rather than capitulate unilaterally to the False Guinevere and to her terrorist seneschal, Galehaut negotiates with Arthur. His was the wise decision, for it all turned out well, except for the resident barons of Carmelide who bore the loss in wounds, in the deaths of two of their number, and, of course, in the huge expenses of Arthur's visit plus the visits of his courtiers from Carlisle.

We are left with several unanswered questions, chiefest of which is the identity of Galehaut. If we are to assume that the authors of the *Prose Lancelot* were the most capable and talented who could be found, and that they were, like all authors, held accountable for their work, what have they implied and said concerning Galehaut? First of all, they have given us a clue in his name: High Gael.

It is tempting to think that Galehaut was, in fact, a king of the *Gall gaidhel,* or stranger Gaels from Ireland whom the Romans were to call *Scotti* (Scots). As such, Galehaut would have been a king from the royal family of the *Dal-Réti,* whose kingdom (Dalriada) was being founded in the western half of Scotland, from Glasgow north, and which today is called the Highlands. King Fergus Mor (the Great) had led a settlement into western Scotland around the year 503, when Arthur would have been about twenty-eight years old. What makes a further association here with Galehaut, as one looks at the family tree of Dalriada, is one king's early death. When Galehaut heard his officers interpret his dreams and Merlin's *Prophecy,* he realized that he was to die an early death. Now, the first king of the Dal-Réti in Scotland also died early, in the year 510, in fact. His name was Domingart, a lordly name like Galehaut's. It was common in Ireland to assign a nickname to famous chieftains and kings. Only Domingart among these Irish-Scottish kings died before Arthur (d. 542). And the Galehaut of Arthurian fame died long before Arthur. He was, as far as Arthur was concerned, a foreign king. Saint Columba's biographer Adamnan believed that Domingart died in battle.

Three tribes from Ireland had migrated with Erc's son Fergus

Mor; they were ruled by three brothers: Loarn, Fergus, and Angus. They constituted the *Scoti Britanniae,* or Scots of Britain, and settled permanently after 510 in their province abroad, say the *Annals of Ulster.* Thus, as The Venerable Bede in his history of the Church was later to record, there were several ancient races in (what is now) Scotland, each with a separate language: Picts, Scots, Angles from Denmark, other Scandinavians, Germans, and the older North British, or Gallo-Romans to whom, according to the *Prose Lancelot,* Arthur belonged.

If cultural pressure from immigrant Scots predominated at Guinevere's trial, then the judicial combat was more probably held on the old Gaelic "White Day," or last day of summer. That would still fall on our Halloween, and not on Whitsunday in the spring.

If Galehaut was really the King Domingart who died in 510, and if Lancelot was descended from one of the immigrant Irish princes named Angus, then one understands their closeness and alliance. Furthermore, their league against Arthur and his British courtiers also becomes more likely and more understandable. The love of Galehaut for Lancelot, which has also been recently portrayed as homosexual, should probably be construed rather as religious awe: first because of Lancelot's double pedigree, both royal and holy; and second, because he was a king educated, or fostered, in Gaelic territory, which was the Isle of Man. There too, both he and Gawain were tested for candidacy by Archbishop Dubricius (alias Merlin), who decided to their sorrow that neither possessed the requisite qualifications to move up and become the next king of the Grail Castle. Lancelot was twice said to have been prostrated with grief at such refusals, at which reports he literally fell to the ground and sobbed. And, in addition, because Guinevere, too, was reported (Wolfram von Eschenbach's *Parzival*) to have been fostered on the Isle of Man, this also would help us understand their triple, close rapport and alliance.

Finally, when Galehaut offered her a safe and most charming residence in his coastal, western possessions, near the water and islands, we assume he meant either the Hebrides or the west coast between Glasgow and Oban, where the fortresses of Dalriada were located, or adjacent to the present Duchy of Argyle. This territory, which was already guarded by the heavy fort of Dunadd, would have been far too remote for Arthur to threaten in force, and in addition, it was very close to the refuges and holy islands of the Scots. Both Mull and Iona are quickly and easily reached by ship from Oban. But there are several thousand such island refuges off the coast of Argyle.

Galehaut's protests during the lengthy trial and proposed punishments of Queen Guinevere, and Lancelot's three judicial combats in her defense, have offered a window into law as practiced in the Dark Ages, actually in their final and declining days.

No glimpse at all survives in the texts concerning Guinevere's alleged abductions. Eight or so tellings abound in Arthurian literature, but all are either demonstrably fairy tales or so colored with fantasy as to be mere embroidery. Only one clue runs through each narrative, that Queen Guinevere was abducted from Scotland into Ireland. If each text does not precisely stipulate that the queen was forced to "go west," the clue "Ireland" constantly appears in one way or another, a clue to be unwound.

No notion of abduction as a heinous crime meriting the death penalty appears in the Arthurian accounts. Even through the Middle Ages, girls of high birth were commonly abducted by married nobles whose wives no longer became pregnant or who no longer accepted to become pregnant. The abductor usually imprisoned his captive maiden and kept her for his abuse until she gave birth to a son. Then he released her or expelled her from her prison. Such cases were well publicized in the fifteenth century when the persons involved, and the infant son, were celebrities. A Duke Louis of Orléans sired Count Dunois, who was Jeanne d'Arc's brilliant artillery officer, with such an abducted girl. The Duchess of Orléans raised the infant. She was the proud heiress Valentina Visconti of Milano. Her legitimate son was the great French and English poet Duke Charles of Orléans.

Also in the fifteenth century, Queen Guinevere's olden abduction was seen by Sir Thomas Malory, finally, as resulting from a military action on her part. Thus, as officer in an offensive action, Queen Guinevere was taken prisoner, he decided, on her recognizance and therefore legally held captive. In every telling her same captor was seen as some royal youth who desired to marry her anyway (to inherit her kingdom, and/or her Round Table).

That Guinevere, who had by marriage become a queen of the Celts, participated actively in campaigns, that she could have waged war by leading a war party, should not come as a surprise. Scholars of Celtic history report that their wives and women performed military service regularly, and that this practice continued until 700, when it was forbidden by the Roman Church. Certainly Roman historians like Julius Caesar reported the gallant defense of Gaul by armies of women and habitually by masses of them after the defeat and deaths of their husbands. In many battles the women all died in battle, and all intended to die in battle after having first slain their children. Not to mention the British warrior Queen Boudicca who alone has the honor of having defeated a Roman legion in pitched battle.

The *Prose Lancelot* contains its own version of Guinevere's abduction into a foreign land where unwillingly she "went west" (*Le Livre de Lancelot del Lac,* vol. IV, pt. II, p. 157ff.). Their story begins after the early death of Galehaut whom the queen mourns when the warrior Meleagant (Meleagan), who is son of Governor Bademagus of the Isle of Man, comes to Arthur's Court at Camelot to complain of Lancelot. The latter had accused Meleagant of having spitefully wounded him under cover of truce. King Arthur replied that doubtless Lancelot would give him satisfaction were he there, but that he had been absent for some time and his whereabouts was unknown. The queen showed presence of mind; she at once forbade anyone present to substitute for Lancelot.

Now that the stage is set for the most famous of Guinevere's abductions, we should change authors to allow perfect freedom to the most famous of French texts, the *Lancelot* of Chrétien de Troyes in Champagne. He picks up the story at this point in the action, but he tells it differently, or rather interprets it differently.

It is important to remember that the first of Arthurian authors, in point of time, was Geoffrey of Monmouth, who taught at Oxford and who composed beautiful Latin prose. He said nothing damaging concerning Queen Guinevere. But he has always been excoriated and, in fact, flayed alive by his English critics. Why? The answer seems to be that mightily as he tried to placate public opinion inside the England of his day (1136) by dropping an occasional reference to King Arthur having been inside England and born in Cornwall—the Cornwall in the south of England, and not the Cornwall in Scotland—he choked over it. Geoffrey's source, which has not yet been located, knew for a fact that King Arthur was inside Scotland where all his twelve battles were fought. Geoffrey was a true Celt. His heart creeps through his chest. He suffocates for King Arthur, King of the Celts. Geoffrey makes no damaging suggestions about King Arthur's queen except perhaps to say that her end is unclear, as was her relationship to Arthur's nephew Modred. Geoffrey is a nationalist, a Celt, and a defender of women, especially royal women who became queens of the Celts.

Soon after Geoffrey wrote *History of the Kings of Britain,* he was followed at Glastonbury in England by Caradoc of Llancarvan, who wrote a silly and anachronistic account of how Queen Guinevere was abducted to Glastonbury Abbey and there raped and held for a year. Because Glastonbury was not built until centuries after Guinevere's death, which is only one reason to spurn this text, its account should be discounted and swept under the carpet. It is at this very Glastonbury that damaging references to rape and scandal accumulate about Guinevere.

But now we must turn to Chrétien's most famous of abduction accounts, where literally Lancelot enters Queen Guinevere's bed at night and adultery is committed. The crime of adultery brings to the Celtic woman involved the death sentence. This most famous account is *Lancelot* written by Chrétien de Troyes. Here we must eventually come to a literal translation of his text, for it contains an error. That error of one word is capital. That one error condemns the queen as an adulteress.

Chrétien had already made a most peculiar error in this same text when he said that in order to reach the Grail Castle, Lancelot crossed the Sword Bridge, but that Gawain crossed the "Water

Bridge." What is a water bridge? A crannog? asked Roger Sherman Loomis. No. The phrase of Chrétien *pont evage,* does not mean "water bridge," as translators and even dictionaries have assumed. It is an error for *drawbridge: pont levage,* "lever bridge." While anyone can make an error, a translator like Chrétien ought not to make an error in a simple word like *lever.* One can safely assume, then, that Chrétien was not, in writing Old French, using his native language. The good translator likes to translate into his own native language; for even common language is very complicated at best.

A recent study by Eugene J. Weinraub (1975) of Bar-Ilan University, Ramat-Gan, Israel, bears out the original intuition in Goodrich's *King Arthur,* published in 1986, that Chrétien was not native speaking, but, like Geoffrey of Monmouth, a foreigner, inside France, in his case. Were Weinraub to discover that Chrétien was a member of the famous, rabbinical school at Troyes, one would believe it readily. As the Israeli professor says, Chrétien also started in his succeeding Old French text one of the world's hottest literary disputes concerning the Holy Grail.

The thought now is just as interesting: Chrétien probably also launched the titillating theory that Queen Guinevere committed adultery with Lancelot. And the corollary leaps to mind: Did he make another mistake in translation?

The reader is therefore burdened with a rapid summary translation of Chrétien, done just for the reader's convenience. We pick up the story where the *Prose Lancelot* left off:

The challenger Meleagant then went on to shame King Arthur because he had abandoned several of his men who had remained prisoners in the Gaelic land of Gorre (Man). The king had never launched a drive to liberate them, which was cowardly of him and therefore disgraceful. "Let the queen lead out a rescue party," Meleagant proposed.

"Sir," the king replied, "I pity our captives over there; and as soon as I can, I will mount a rescue operation. However, this has nothing to do with the queen. She did not in any way cause or allow them to be captured. Nor shall she set out to free them at the risk of her honor and her own freedom." Courtiers agreed with the king. It was ridiculous to think of sending the queen out into the woods. Therefore, although Meleagant left for home, he kept a sharp lookout for pursuit.

The trouble was that Seneschal Kay became very angry at not having been charged by the king to follow Meleagant and win renown by rescuing their captives in Gorre. He threatened to leave Arthur's service forever. The king loved his foster brother Kay so dearly that he asked Queen Guinevere to settle their misunderstanding. Tell him he may have whatever he wants from me, Arthur told the queen.

"Thanks very much," Kay replied. "Do you know what you have granted? You will have to allow me to lead out the queen in pursuit of Meleagant. I have no doubts about it. I shall liberate our prisoners in Gorre." The king claimed he was sorry he had granted this permission. As for Queen Guinevere, she shut herself in her chambers, thinking nothing was ever spared her: Lancelot had been rumored dead, Meleagant would probably capture her, Galehaut had died, Kay was entrusted with her life and honor. She wept, it was said at Court. Arthur found her expendable.

"Mount up," Kay told the queen. "Have no fear. I will bring you safely back." The queen mounted up. She did not answer. She knew better. They were soon out the gates and into open country. Meanwhile Gawain was so worried he set out by shortcut for the entrance to Gorre. He would await Meleagant there, just in case he had unhorsed Kay and seized the queen, which seemed all too likely.

Kay's party soon overtook Meleagant's in a thickly wooded area. "Let us move forward to open ground," Meleagant suggested. As they passed through a dense thicket, the queen saw an armed warrior hidden in the underbrush. She thought she recognized him as Lancelot, by his red shield with white bend, the same he had worn during their recent, victorious campaign at Dumbarton, Scotland. He bowed to her as she passed. "Oh," she thought, "it can't be Lancelot. I am too unfortunate for it really to be Lancelot!" Kay also saw the red shield, recognized Lancelot, and signaled him not to interfere with his command. Get back, he indicated to Lancelot.

No sooner had they arrived in the first clearing than Meleagant rode at Kay, pierced him through the shoulder, threw him to the ground, and took possession of the queen's reins. Kay lay in a dead faint flat on the ground. His horse bolted and headed for the stable.

Then Lancelot attacked and felled Meleagant first, and then faced the "horde" of his men, who managed to kill his horse. Then the "horde" set off at a fast pace, two of them holding the now half-conscious Kay in his saddle. Lancelot stood helplessly waving his sword at them as they rode away into the forest. The queen thought to herself, "It *was* Lancelot. Thank God I got to see him one last time."

When Gawain came on him, he let Lancelot have a spare horse. Again Lancelot caught up with Meleagant's party, but the coward cried to his men, "Don't try to fight him. You can't win. Aim for his horse." Again, Lancelot was left stranded on foot. His next conveyance was a cart driven by a (Pictish?) dwarf. The dwarf is not the least puzzling part of this passage. He was perhaps a Pictish prince, for even Gawain is sometimes referred to as a dwarf. One tends to think of the Picts as small people.

Lancelot still continued his pursuit of the queen's party, overcoming warriors when they forbade him free passage and always riding forward until he was stopped at the stonework around a fountain.

Having arrived there at the rim, Lancelot saw a comb on the ground. He stayed there rapt in such deep contemplation that he did not even stoop down to pick it up. His eyes closed as if dazzled. He did not know where he was. If the young damsel who had been riding with him had not dismounted and held him up, his knees would have jacked under him. As he came to his senses, he asked her what she wanted. "I wanted to hand you this comb that you seem to desire having."

"Many thanks, damsel. Give it to me." He took the comb reverently in his fingers and carefully unwound the hairs that were caught in it. He cautioned the damsel to guard the comb with care and placed the strands of hair against his bare flesh. The damsel's presence forced him to hide his joy. (She could not have known that the comb was Queen Guinevere's who so sadly had passed that way, leaving this token for [her acolyte] Lancelot to find. Her comb was similar to the golden comb she had years previously offered Lancelot as pledge of their [secret] troth.)

This passage also in the *Prose Lancelot,* as here much embroidered and interpreted by Chrétien de Troyes, stands as one of the most evocative word paintings in world literature. It recalls with its stasis, its symbolism of troth and golden comb, the tragic beauty of this Queen Guinevere as one of the world's most desolate and most haunting heroines.

Such an image, which is always presented in frozen time, of a sad, beautiful woman who once sat beside a fountain, or a lake, recurs with equal force in art, hauntingly in a painting called *The Enchanted Castle* by Claude Le Lorrain (1600–1682), which the artist painted in 1664 for Lorenzo Colonna. An exhibition centered about this work was mounted in 1982 at the National Gallery in London by Michael Wilson. In his guide to this exhibition (*Claude. The Enchanted Castle*), the art critic Wilson discusses such a scene: the "solitary brooding female," "the magical island," "the ideal beauty" contemplated in silence: Queen Guinevere, the biblical Ruth, Shakespeare's Miranda, Apuleius's Psyche, Ovid's Circe, Ariosto's Alcina and his Guinevere (Genevra), Tasso's Armida, and Botticelli's Venus. John Keats in 1818 speaks of such a woodland enchantment as Lancelot underwent:

> You know it well enough, where it doth seem
> A mossy place, a Merlin's Hall, a dream.
> You know the clear lake and the little isles,
> The Mountains blue and cold near neighbour
>   rills—
>
> And many other juts of aged stone
> Founded with many a mason devil's groan.
>   (*Claude,* p. 15)

Keats also envisioned such a scene as toward the west: "westward on a summer's night." In the distance was Guinevere's "golden galley," which would carry her into Gorre. He also thought of Lancelot's "enchanted spring" . . . "the foam / Of perilous seas," and "faery lands forlorn" (*Claude,* p. 16). Wilson made a final, telling point: "The picture's meaning changes according to the ideas and aspirations that the spectator brings to it," and that, it seems to the reader of the word picture in the *Prose Lancelot,* is the test of great art.

Lancelot's next hurdle was the Sword Bridge. Chrétien continues:

Queen Guinevere was being held prisoner in a castle before which a swift, deep river flowed. The river separated the land side from the small island on which the fortress towered over the Irish Sea. The place was called Gorhan, or Gorre (a Manx land of an ancient King Orry), we now understand. Chrétien says that as Lancelot approached, he saw Queen Guinevere leaning against one of the windows. Beside her stood the castle's governor named Bademagus (*magus,* "magician," Druid). Lancelot halted to stare down at the deep, black water of the River Neb, we add.

Lancelot prepared to cross the river, and in this case, Chrétien does the details very well for us: Lancelot took iron wire to hook up his flowing sleeves. He put on gauntlets. He coated his feet and trews with tar. He was armed as follows: helmet, trews, halberd, sword in his belt, and shield over his back. Thus protected, he embarked on the Sword Bridge, attempting to cross its steel blade, or to crawl across it. His hauberk was soon bloodied. The hero still kept his gaze fixed on Guinevere. She looked back from her castle tower. Chrétien says that Lancelot preferred a future reward to the pain of present suffering. He reached the far bank.

No sooner had Lancelot arrived at the tip of the sword blade, continues Chrétien, than he heard the loud roaring of two lions. Medieval illustrators loved the idea! They adored representing Lancelot in combat with lions. Never mind that the lion represents royalty and that Lancelot was either fighting dogs that looked like lions, or kings that were lions and lion hearted. These lions of Chrétien turned out to be magical beasts in any case, for as soon as Lancelot cut them to pieces they closed their own wounds and bounded at him again. Even Lancelot finally got the idea that he was being enchanted.

So back he went on the Sword Bridge, summoning the Lady

of the Lake by flashing his golden ring at her. This ring on his left hand must have meant their secret talisman, or it was his graduation ring from his august teacher. In any case, the treatment worked because the lions vanished from sight completely. At the same time Queen Guinevere either became fully conscious, or woke up, or was finally able to see clearly; for all of a sudden, says Chrétien, she recognized Lancelot.

This is the sort of treatment, in any event, that has made King Arthur and Company appear like fairies in some enchanted realm.

Guinevere and Bademagus then negotiate terms of peace, but all their efforts proved in vain. The son of Bademagus pursued his doom to the bitter end, refusing to dismiss Lancelot, insisting on meeting him again on the field of honor, and thereby committing suicide himself.

By his heroism that day and by his passage of the dread Sword Bridge Lancelot proved himself again the invincible champion of Queen Guinevere. He triumphed over another physical obstacle considered invulnerable, and he breached the castle's defenses where Arthur's warriors and his queen were being held in perpetual imprisonment, without bail.

After a first inconclusive duel with Meleagant, Lancelot was able to speak briefly to the queen and request a further, more private audience for that evening.

Impatiently Lancelot awaited, adds Chrétien in his *Lancelot,* the fall of darkness. He excused himself and went to bed early. At the agreed on hour he stole quietly from his chamber, scaled the garden wall, and crept to the queen's window. She was waiting for him there in darkness. He thrust his arms through the bars of her window, touched her hands, felt her body as best he could. He asked her if she wished him to reach her altogether. She replied she did not know how he could do that. It will be easy for him who desires it, he whispered to her. Then he told her that he was coming in her chamber, that no iron could stop him. Guinevere cautioned him not to make any noise for fear of awakening sleeping Seneschal Kay. The latter had survived the storming of Gorre, but he was sorely wounded.

Lancelot pulled the iron bars toward him so hard he made them bend and then pop out of their settings. He leaped lightly down into the dark chamber. The night inside was pitch black, for the queen had already blown out her night-light. Even so, Lancelot was disturbed to hear sighs and groans coming from nearby. It was Seneschal Kay, moaning in his sleep because his wounds had opened up again as they still did if he tossed and turned at night. When Lancelot slid onto the bed where the queen awaited him, he felt that his hands were wet. Chrétien says that both he and the queen thought that he was wet with perspiration. Not so. It was blood. He had cut his hands by pulling apart the iron bars of her prison window.

As Chrétien dwelled upon his most successful story, he added that the joy of the two lovers was very great that night, and that their embrace was very tender. One conclusion seems absolute: Chrétien understood nothing about true love as practiced in his century by the great Angevin princes and princesses of the Basque country, of Provence, or of their kingdoms inside what is now Spain and Portugal. Chrétien has Lancelot leave in the morning, and by the same window. Chrétien falsely claims that nobody ever dreamed of asking the queen how she had spent the night.

The author has Meleagant refuse to accept offers of peace urged on him by his father Bademagus. He even has Meleagant wander into the queen's chamber, awaken her from sleep, interrogate her about the blood on her bedding, and then reconnoiter Seneschal Kay's chamber and his bedding as well. He also had blood on his bedding, which is no big mystery.

Then follows a scene of jealousy during which Meleagant accuses Queen Guinevere of having also slept with Seneschal Kay. Meleagant even asks her why she will not sleep with him, when she seems gladly to sleep with the lowest fellow alive. After all, Kay is only King Arthur's foster brother. Actually speaking, the only relationship that Chrétien in these passages has got right is that of King, or Governor, Bademagus and his foolish, sex-starved, ambitious son Meleagant. The poor fellow has been pursuing royal personages for years now, and failing each time to advance in the world.

Meleagant then spouts defamation, which includes Queen Guinevere among the most treacherous of all human beings, which is to say, women. After such attacks and such vilification of Queen Guinevere, he turns to his main antagonist, the hero Lancelot. He supposes loudly that Lancelot will never again dare to meet him in single combat, and that he will not dare either to perjure himself by declaring the queen innocent of charges of adultery. For his part Lancelot wonders if Meleagant's wounds incurred at their last battle, which was stopped by the pleas of Bademagus, have even had time to heal. Lancelot cannot believe his ears, that Meleagant should be standing before him pleading for another drubbing.

Before the two meet in their final battle, it is made clear that Lancelot will kill Meleagant for having publicly impugned the honor of their queen. Meleagant did not become flustered until he sat watching Lancelot ride casually into the lists and cross the field toward him.

As usual in the single combats of olden days the two champions taunt each other to bring their blood to the boil. For his part, Lancelot intended that Meleagant and the witnesses also should know that Meleagant had once before defied the order for a truce and under cover of that cease combat had treacherously wounded his opponent. Lancelot also reminded the persons present that Meleagant had, after that first combat that had been halted, had Lancelot captured and imprisoned in a tower of his own. Lancelot added that he would have died of starvation there, had he not been rescued by a royal damsel. Even so, his health had been so damaged that he required a long time to recover.

Lancelot further charged Meleagant with wishing to capture the queen when she had no defender and of planning to have her burned at the stake.

More than any other aspect of his own world, Chrétien de Troyes loved martial combat. He must have seen many jousts inside northeastern France to give such a full and passionate description of the duel to the death between Lancelot and Meleagant. He tells graphically how the two entered the lists, how they spurred at each other without wasting a second, how Meleagant's sword was split or cracked at the first onrush. He delights in Lancelot's unerring aim that cut Meleagant's shield, drove through his forearm, which he then pinned to the cowardly Meleagant's tunic.

Chrétien understands from firsthand experience seemingly how Meleagant would have fallen over backward and then have slipped under his horse's belly. Chrétien loved the sight of sparks from metal against metal, the sight of blood spurting. He also pictured the sound of blows falling, the clanking of chains bursting open the hauberks, the shine of blood and the red of wounds. He knew Meleagant would have vomited blood from his gaping mouth. He knew Lancelot would press him back and back, come closer and closer, swing harder and harder. At what should have been the final moment, Meleagant dodged the blow, but in so doing tripped himself in his own harness and sprawled on the bare ground.

Lancelot took advantage, as he had planned to do. He jumped on the prostrate Meleagant.

The governor rushed out to plead for his son's life. Lancelot ignored him. He looked to the queen. Thus Queen Guinevere was allowed to show her sense of clemency, which would have become her mightily. There was a moment of silence on the field. Meleagant lay on the earth. Lancelot had his sword raised. He stood awaiting instructions.

She raised her arms, her thumbs down. Thus, she commanded Lancelot to show him no grace.

Meleagant crawled backward in horror. Lancelot went toward him. With one blow he blew his head across the fence and onto the grass.

As he was sheathing his sword, Lancelot saw Kay coming up to congratulate him. Kay helped Lancelot unhook his shield. "Sire," Kay told him, "the whole world salutes you and proclaims you the flower of valor!"

These thrilling pages in Chrétien's telling are celebrated justly in France as perhaps the best and most dramatic pages in all Old

French verse. Chrétien has always been hailed as a genius. Nobody can deny it.

However, there is at least one mistake in the preceding passages, which has changed history from then to now, and again it occurs in the commonest of words: *bed*. Probably only a native speaker of English, as of French, could use at random, and correctly, the commonest words of the language. It has happened before in an Arthurian text: *bed* for Bed of Justice, or Court. At the appropriate time, we shall see that Lancelot did not go into or onto the queen's "bed." Therefore we shall have to think again about the blood that was shed that night.

Chrétien's trouble was threefold, at least: (1) he jumped to a hasty conclusion about a queen's morality; (2) he was charmed and amused at his very salable story, or version; and (3) he really could not care less whether Lancelot and Guinevere were adulterers. Chrétien was being well paid by Eleanor of Aquitaine's son-in-law there in Champagne.

Let us allow the *Prose Lancelot* to tie up another loose end, however.

Meanwhile King Arthur and his kingdom lay low under interdiction by the Church, during which sanctions the king learned that the False Guinevere had suffered a stroke and was now paralyzed in her lower limbs: *"Et en cele nuit prist nostre sire de la fausse genieure . . . quele perdi tout le pooir de ses pies & de sez mains et de tout son cors fors des iex & de la langue"* (*Le Livre de Lancelot del Lac*, vol. IV, pt. II, p. 73). It was during the night that Arthur heard she had lost all sensation in her feet and hands and in all her body except her eyes and her tongue. *"En autretel auint a bertholai"*; And the same befell Bertolais. Their bodies began to decay. The stench was so awful people could hardly go near them even for a minute. King Arthur was very distressed. He sent for doctors far and wide, but no doctor he could employ was able to reverse this condition of theirs.

When King Arthur asked the False Guinevere what he could do for her, or what she wanted him to do, she begged him to allow her to return to her own native land and birthplace (Ms. fr. 1430). "How are you feeling today?" he inquired.

"Badly," she replied. "The wise men know nothing at all

about my illness. I wish they would let me go home to my birthplace. Once out at sea I would not be contagious or a danger to anyone. And I would only leave the ship to enter my native fortress."

"Lady, such an ocean voyage would only aggravate your condition. And, furthermore, you might die during the crossing. . . . Lady, you are embarked already on the adventure of death. You should look not to losing both soul and body."

"Sir," she told her confessor. "God is taking revenge on me for having abused Queen Guinevere."

"You must confess this publicly," he told her.

"That way will I save my soul?"

"I think so."

"Then I will do it."

Poor Bertolais also made a public confession of his guilt. Everybody felt very sorry for him. Queen Guinevere was thus exonerated of all the original charges that had been laid against her and was declared King Arthur's lawful spouse and queen of his kingdom. Everyone marveled at the malice and treachery of the False Guinevere.

After she has duly officiated at an altar to administer a sacrament to the postulant Lancelot, Queen Guinevere suffers an eclipse. Even the prolific medieval writers of Old French lose track of her. All of them fall strangely silent. Did she die?

Elsewhere, however, somebody picks up her track. The German translator of King Richard the Lion Hearted's *Lanzelet* (Lancelot) text from Carlisle thought she and not they had fallen asleep inside the wooden stockade called "Peel Castle," or palisaded fortress. If so, then she was the prototype of the "Sleeping Beauty" fairy tale. Then Guinevere, the tale stipulates, was mythologically reawakened by clattering King Arthur, Gawain, and Lancelot storming her "Peel" stockade on the Isle of Man.

Or, regrettably, Queen Guinevere failed to awaken because she had already died of venom in an adder pit, which honorable fate realistically became a Dark Age chieftainess like herself. Because of her birth, position, and renown she deserved a quick death, and not the slow torture reserved for other captive heroes and northern chieftains. If on the other hand she died groveling

and writhing, such anguish might explain Alfred, Lord Tennyson's (n.d.) depiction of her near death in southern England. But
such accounts fail to stand up in the face of folk tradition and
Queen Guinevere's memorial, which stands today in Scotland.

Before we turn to that very living folk tradition, and to those
famous witnesses of our own days, and to her memorial inside
Scotland today, we have one more medieval writer to deal with,
and to credit.

One last, late German protonovelist, Heinrich von dem Türlin, who wrote in the thirteenth century, understood Queen
Guinevere's fate differently from Chrétien, who saw her in fairyland. For their part, the French had let her go to focus on Lancelot
and Arthur in their final years. The authors of the *Prose Lancelot,*
thus, abandoned the queen in favor of male, or epic material. At
the same time, Heinrich inside Germany tried his hand equally
at an alternate solution. What in stark reality were this Guinevere's final days? What was her fate? Where on the upside-down
Wheel of Fortune had she lodged? Who slung her around by the
braids?

Heinrich had the benefit of his many predecessors, of course,
so much so that he grasped their old plot perfectly well: Guinevere challenged at Carlisle, her departure into the wild forest, her
glimpsing of her secret champion, the warrior's dreadful com-
bat(s) in the wooded glades, and the queen's pitiable protests.
But he also heard of a punisher who whipped her and tore her
hair.

Heinrich went even further than that, however, depicting a
determined manhandling of the queen that almost ended in her
rape. That rape did not occur. The queen managed to repel the
attack Heinrich wrote in chapters 9 and 10 of *Diu Crône (The
Crown).* *

There were reasons for the manhandling of the queen, Heinrich reminded his readers, and a valid reason for the attempted
rape as well. Before her wedding to King Arthur, the maiden
Guinevere had been affiancéd to somebody else. Therefore her

*Please see the marvelous new translation into English by J. W. Thomas: *The Crown*
(University of Nebraska Press, 1989).

first suitor attempted to assert his rights, to which he was legally entitled. This reclamation of his lost property caused him to attempt passionately and manfully to rape Queen Guinevere, Heinrich thought. Heinrich seems also to have been following a much more archaic explanation, however, and one that he could not fathom. The text stipulates that Guinevere's madly inflamed but spurned lover, years after her wedding to King Arthur, wanted *to uncover her naked hip;* he wanted to see her naked hip. From that detail, which he did not understand, Heinrich interpreted rape, saying that from this concession the spurned suitor intended to move to rape, which is to say, to intercourse. But here the German author sidestepped the morphological pattern and so doing misinterpreted the cue entirely.

Heinrich's original source had certainly spelled it out for the informed: The warrior wanted to identify the queen by seeing her "crown" birthmark or tattoo. No rape was intended, and, as we in the twentieth century are informed, rape is not a crime of passionate love in any case. Rape is an act of hatred and violence. The rapist intends to humiliate and injure the victim. Traditionally in the theater and in fiction, however, rape has casually been depicted as an excusable crime, due to the placement of the male sexual organs. Even in French law the male is usually excused and the female blamed. The argument goes that she is able to control her sexual drives, but that the male is physiologically incapable of so doing. He may thus even be excused for rape leading to first-degree murder.

Heinrich must be praised, however, for having remembered Guinevere's spurned suitor, who became her abductor. Earlier texts had identified him as King Urien of Moray or of Gorre (Isle of Man) or of the Out-Isles, and also in Chrétien's case, as the foolhardy Meleagant whom Lancelot eventually killed. We are to understand that Guinevere had been betrothed to another prince before Arthur and Merlin forced her father, Leodagan, to give the heiress to them. Most texts admit such a complication, which upholds the logic of the story in most older accounts. Heinrich was also correct in identifying Gawain as one of Guinevere's rescuers at the Peel Castle. Heinrich's identification of Guinevere's punisher as her own brother is a new note, which does not sit well with the reader. Nor does it satisfy the equation.

Heinrich rises finally to true, manly grandeur in his final solution to this brief, preliminary adventure in the forest. After the failure of the attempted rape, Guinevere has to witness a terrible combat between her spurned suitor and her brother. They fought, not once, but daily, and to the death, if possible. They mounted up, rode, and hacked at each other until each fell unconscious to the ground. There on the forest floor Guinevere wept and urged them daily to halt. She also rushed to attend to each as best she could. Having neither bandages nor towels, she dipped her sleeve into water and bathed their faces and brows. After they had one day in battle-frenzy killed their own horses by cutting off their heads, she still tended them. She even saw them rise to their feet again and continue the slaughter. They staggered over and around her, in fury. This went on for days in a wild wood where the three of them had neither food nor shelter.

The two combatants were eventually exhausted. Having gone for days and nights without food or proper medical care, neither one could so much as pick up his weapon. Neither could lift a hand to strike. Silence reigned in the forest. Both sprawled on the ground at the queen's mercy.

At this point Queen Guinevere showed her true mettle. She managed to get each one to stand and then to climb up on her horse, which was probably her palfrey, a small, white, Galloway pony. Heinrich himself specifies that it was a white horse that had remained alive. In this way, and by painful and slow stages, Guinevere led the two of them back to the citadel gates of Carlisle. All the way the queen walked beside the white horse.

Before making this sorry entrance into Carlisle, which she had left triumphantly with a war party, the queen halted to clean the warriors again, as best she could, and to wipe down her own little horse with fresh leaves and mosses. Then, taking the point again, she guided her party into King Arthur's chief western fortress, where her wounded champions could be attended to by the best doctors available. It took them a full year to recover. It is not certain that Gawain, after his injuries connected with this expedition, ever fully recovered his health.

People in Carlisle, formerly Camelot, did not blame the queen. In fact they found her conduct not only exemplary, but outstandingly brave and resourceful. They found her altogether praiseworthy, so much so, in fact, that they thought she should have been elected, then and there, to the Round Table Order of chivalry.

It should come as no surprise, therefore, that the conclusion to Queen Guinevere's story must come from her own people, which is to say, from local, native historians.

CHAPTER IX

The Priestess Guanhumara

> There is not *one* person, indeed, not *one* living
> being, that has *not* returned from death.
> —LÁMA ANAGARIKA GOVINDA,
> *The Tibetan Book of the Dead*

IF BEFORE GOING FORWARD WE TAKE ANOTHER BACKWARD GLANCE AT
Queen Guinevere's journey to the Grail Castle on the Isle of
Man, we understand that she had gone to the Otherworld. There
in the Otherworld, as the ancient Irish had explained, she performed ritually a priestess duty for Lancelot. From the famous
static scene at the fountain where she left behind her the comb
and the mirror, which usually figure together, Guinevere was
entering another space and time. What she made in theological
terminology was a descent into hell, called katabasis.

This descent was made by Guinevere, and King Arthur had
let her go, we now understand, because he was to follow her
there, and for the purpose of initiating Lancelot. Acolytes progressed there from one stage to another. This was Lancelot's
second initiation at this same place. Both times he had been
directed there, or lured there, for the deliverance of Queen
Guinevere.

Thus we now sense fearfully that knowledge of the Holy Grail was a long process undergone by a special few, all of whom were noble, heroical, worthy, and courageous. We also now know that there were at least two stages of initiation, but we suspect that there were many more than that, or higher degrees of initiation. As far as Lancelot progressed, he remained under the tutelage of Queen Guinevere.

That Queen Guinevere was the "psychopomp," the person who escorted souls to the Otherworld, makes her resemble the most ancient of priestesses, like the Cumaean Sibyl at Rome. We shall not see or hear from the living Queen Guinevere again.

So now, unfortunately, we have lost Guinevere. No chroniclers will do more than allude to her fate. From now on we have not much more to go on—as we proceed to untangle the webs they have spun—than analogy, comparison, deduction, and conclusions. As of now, the major source of all history, which is the written word, has in her case run almost dry.

As we have suspected, Guinevere was not only a priestess but probably the High-Priestess of the Picts: virgin, minister, initiator, sibyl, and figurehead. Her magic helped Arthur win his wars and stabilize his kingdom. Her purity and prestige bowled over Lancelot, who would have died for her. Her ability to descend into hell and return alive upon the surface of the earth again proclaims her a priestess. And she officiated on the Isle of Man, in the land where the Gauls for centuries had recruited their priestesses: Ireland.

From Matthew 16:18–19 to Revelation 1:18, and the intertestamental books written in the Holy Land from the death of Christ to the destruction of Solomon's temple in Jerusalem (A.D. 70), we know that the well or abyss, over which Lancelot jumped in his first Dolorous Gard adventure, dropped him into the realm of death and hell.

After he had entered the Copper Mountain, which the German authors of Arthurian manuscripts pleasantly termed the Mountain of Salvation, he saw the priestess, or Copper Mistress, herself. Through the *portae inferi,* or gates of hell, he glimpsed her regal figure clothed in malachite.

Guinevere was also the angel personified who, like Saint

Peter, held double keys, one to the bottomless pit and one to heaven. Jesus said to Peter, "Upon this rock I will build my church; and the gates of hell shall not prevail against it" (Matthew 16:18). The one key binds and the other looses. These keys are traditionally held by an angel or by Saint Peter in Rome. That angel here was Guinevere. Her Pictish sculptors, when they came to remember her, carved her so: an angel in a short gown.

A scattered series of tests show the events of a priestess' life, in this case that of Guanhumara. The name was given to Guinevere in the first of Arthurian texts, as we have recovered them today: Geoffrey of Monmouth's *History of the Kings of Britain.* It seems to be her priestess name.

Each test comes down the ages by means of a story recounting Guanhumara's adventures. Some stories read like descents into hell, which we know were made by other holy figures. The story or myth of the White Stag on the other hand refers us back, whether we realize it or not at first, to Saint Peter and the founding of his Christian Church at Rome.

Simply to read each story is not always enough to comprehend its true significance. In the case of the White Stag adventure we know its real meaning because the test or hunt for the White Stag was not successfully performed by Arthur and Guanhumara/Guinevere alone in the Dark Ages and not inside Britain only. King David of Scotland (b. 1084) also followed the White Stag to Salisbury, now a suburb of Edinburgh city, where he founded Holyrood Abbey. Centuries before his time, but a mere hundred years after Arthur and Guanhumara, Duke Ansegise followed the White Stag to Fécamp (France) where in 658 he founded Holy Trinity Abbey. Several abduction stories also relate testing and holy adventures of Guinevere as the priestess Guanhumara. From her stories we also learn of King Arthur's holiness, for it was perhaps he or they who, before King David of Scotland, first founded Holyrood in Pictish Edinburgh.

The late abduction or journey to the Isle of Man in the Irish Sea seems to have constituted Queen Guinevere's longest test. The authors of the *Prose Lancelot* were doubtless as surprised as modern readers to discover in the end that King Arthur, too, had arrived and that he presided there in the kingdom of death.

During the days when the *Prose Lancelot* was being written, its authors did not need to include any explanatory material to orient their readers, for this was the Celtic subject par excellence: *"C'est dans toute sa pureté le génie celtique qui n'aime que ses rêves,"* said Emile Mâle (1950, 317). In this descent into hell of Queen Guinevere we have, in other words, "in all its purity Celtic genius, which loves only its dreams." The Church fought a bitter war in defense of its doctrine of hell and Purgatory, which in medieval times Waldensians and Albigensians (Catharist heretics) bitterly died opposing, as did certain famous reformers and lesser Protestants.

What we have read in this section of the *Prose Lancelot* is a very old story telling how a holy person, who is Guinevere, descends into hell to release prisoners from their tortures. They have long dwelt in Purgatory, which we are to visualize as a concomitant state between life and death, this intermediate state designed for the expiatory punishment of venial sins. The sinner's purpose must satisfy divine justice; he must undergo temporal castigation still due God for remitted, mortal sin. Biblical doctrine recognized divine judgment, forgiveness of sins, the mercy of God, and temporal punishment due to sins.

Purgatory was recognized, and is recognizable from such texts, because it has a specific geography; it lies beyond a swamp or meadow, across a body of deep water spanned by a bridge usually covered with metal spikes, under an overhanging cliff or rock precipice, beside a chasm, which deafens because of a thunderous din of booming water (like the blowhole on the island of Oahu). Thus the medieval Purgatory took the long and fearful route from more ancient descents into hell undertaken by Odysseus, Theseus, Orpheus, Aeneas, Herakles, Thespesios, the Canaanite god Baal, and Christ as well as the greatest of divine women such as the Sumerian goddess Inanna, the Mesopotamian goddess Ishtar, the Eastern Orthodox Christian Virgin Mary, the Delphic Oracle Psyche, the Roman or Cumaean Sibyl, and now this Queen Guinevere. Celtic peoples were so enthralled by their own visions of Purgatory that they maintained for centuries the so-called Purgatory of Saint Patrick in Lough Derg, Ireland, despite absolutely clear orders from several popes that it be shut down. This particular Purgatory had nothing to do with the historical Saint Patrick, of course. It was a wet, dangerous place underground where devout people had themselves shut inside stone slabs for fifteen days, and apparently there were casualties. Henry of Saltrey, a monk on the Isle of Man, wrote a Latin treatise about it, which the medieval, Arthurian poet Marie de France translated into Old French.

As for Queen Guinevere, her adventure commenced like a military action, which is how Chrétien de Troyes developed it, and Sir Thomas Malory but three hundred years later. And they were right to do so because Guinevere was a battle queen, concerning whom there is considerable evidence besides the *Prose Lancelot.* However, one can see now from the *Prose Lancelot* text that there is a lacuna. Guinevere proceeds as if she were leading a military action, Lancelot tracking Meleagant's party and catching up with them, then Lancelot and Gawain in hot pursuit, but Guinevere and Kay being carried fast away. However, the sea crossing to the Isle of Man is missing.

Suddenly the authors give us the dire warning where Lancelot halts beside a fountain. There he also sees the fatal mirror—a familiar symbol of death, recognized as such throughout the world, and identified by C. G. Jung as originating and stored in the "collective unconscious" of the human race. The very sight of the mirror triggers an automatic reaction in Lancelot. He falls into a dream state. The text halts abruptly. It too falls into stasis. Time is suspended.

The art critic Wilson at the London National Gallery understood this descent into hell. Painters also depicted it. One looks at such a painting with open eyes, but sees in the mind ancient heroines, Guinevere's peers, who were goddesses before her in the most ancient religions on earth: Ishtar crowned, Isis with her horns of the moon, chaste Diana at her temple at Ephesus, Psyche descending the lava tube into the Netherworld, the holy women who were the Delphic Oracles without number over centuries, all before recorded time. Their oracle at Delphi, like Guinevere's Isle, still sprawls in sun-bleached ruins on the slopes of Mt. Parnassus, under brooding cliffs, beside a stream issuing from a cleft in the cliff, above the sea and Pleistos River. The cave of the Cumaean Sibyl on the north hook of the Bay of Naples is another such holy site. By analogy, if by no other way, then Guinevere also was a great, but later and perhaps Christian, priestess. The churches on Man stand on more ancient, oracular sites. It is ground so holy it takes the breath away.

After the capture of Queen Guinevere and the exciting pursuit of her abductors by Lancelot, authors dropped their readers into static time and pure, if haunted illusion. Reality they suddenly replaced with dreamy subreality, surrealism. Lancelot fell or dropped, at the mere sight of a mirror, into delusion and dream. When did this stasis end? When did Lancelot regain full consciousness again?

The answer from the *Prose Lancelot* will soon become clear: a year later! In other words, the section of text between the mirror episode and the duel to the death between Lancelot and Meleagant comprises the descent into hell. Concerning the latter, the *Prose Lancelot* gives us the barest account, and doubtless because the doctrine of Purgatory was in their day in flux and hotly contested by puritanical Albigensians and Waldensians, who had been branded heretic and who were finally condemned to death en masse.

The idea of Purgatory (which meant a place of cleansing and purification, such as an ancient oracle at Delphi in Greece, or Cuma in Italy), was that a person could, before death, undergo agony that would reduce sufferings after death. But houses also are "purified," as during spring house-cleaning, *domus purgantur*, just as persons, fortress walls, and fields were ritually purified in concrete ceremonies. Thus one may assume that what transpired with Lancelot and Guinevere, between the mirror episode and the duel where Meleagant died, was likewise a ceremony of purification. Lancelot was the testing candidate; Guinevere, the officiant.

According to Church doctrine of Arthur's day, then, mortal sin incurs the loss of the soul in hell. Venial sins are those committed by the just in their daily lives. Guilt is forgiven in the case of sin, but punishment is not necessarily forgiven. The punishment for sin must be paid by the sinner, and paid either in this life on earth, or in the next life hereafter.

What makes this Christian doctrine so remarkably applica-

ble to the Guinevere-Lancelot experience in Purgatory is its duration. Guinevere herself remarks on the lapse of one year between her capture and Lancelot's arrival at the hell locale: "I have
not seen Lancelot for a year now." Second, we realize the an-
guished duration of their traumatic experience with its sense of
long, suspended animation. Christian doctrine also clarified that,
holding that the soul in Purgatory floated in such suspended
time. In Purgatory there is no partitioned, hourly, or earthly time,
as we know it, all the while the soul hanging suspended, suffering acutely. Last and most tellingly, there is no speculation available to the sufferer. There is sight, to be sure, and apprehension—
but no ability to think, to reason, to theorize, or to speculate.
Thereby it was truly Purgatory.

Obviously these views of Church teaching were to be con-
siderably modified by various councils (Lyons in 1274, Florence
in 1439, Trent in 1545–1547), which would certainly have made
medieval authors tread cautiously in whatever they felt it safe to
rewrite via the *Prose Lancelot*. The sad circumstance of the sinner's
pain troubled everyone, and especially St. Bonaventure, who felt
that this pain must have resulted particularly from the sinner's
sense of loss, such as from God's partial aversion to him.

This thought also fits well with our *Lancelot* text as with the
correlation of Guinevere and the ancient Emerald. The hero
looked to her as toward a beatific vision, equating her perhaps
not only with the green emerald or beryl, as revered in South and
Central America, but with the blue emerald, which is the modern
sapphire. Indigo blue, as in the ancient MacKay tartan of Scotland, as in blue jeans, was the sacred color of the Celts.

The corollary would equate Queen Guinevere with the notion or fact of a guardian angel even though angelology also
remains today a theologically troublesome area. The thought of
a female angel is probably still more unacceptable, but female
angels with outspread wings guarded pilgrims to the goddess
Diana's temple in Ephesus, and for centuries, as they also protected them at the Delphic Oracle. Lancelot considered Guinevere his dread guardian, certainly, and also certainly an angel.

There was no question of sexual intercourse between Guinevere and Lancelot, and she had at the time of her exile into Prince

Galehaut's territory so stipulated. Lancelot looked up to her for help and approbation while he undertook the painful crossing of the Sword Bridge, precisely as he had looked up to her the first time he saw her face, which was in Arthur's Court at Carlisle.

Therefore it follows that Guinevere was not merely a crowned queen, but higher than that: a virginal priestess. In the centuries since her death she has now, it is hoped, been purged and purgatoried, branded, and excoriated enough as childless, barren, sexless, and sterile.

Many descents into hell end with the sinner's release immediately after he has been allowed the briefest glimpse of Paradise. If Dante in the *Vita Nuova* could with propriety figure this beatific vision as the luminously lovely, glowing face of Beatrice, then perhaps the authors of the *Prose Lancelot* may be allowed some latitude with Queen Guinevere. True, they never said in so many words that Guinevere was Lancelot's idea of Heaven, but they certainly implied it. They probably drew considerable consolation and courage from the knowledge that they had most of the world's greatest authors behind them, all the ones who were considered major in the Middle Ages or whose works were known, if only by hearsay: Herodotus, Homer, Lucian, Plutarch, Lucan, especially Vergil, and Ovid. From Plutarch's descent into hell of Thespesios in the first century to the Christian *St. Paul's* descent in the fourth, there were seven other, very famous Christian visions before Ireland produced the awesome, most influential *Tundale* descent, which remains the most imitated, and then the tragical *St. Patrick's*.

The ancient view throughout the centuries consistently held that the soul must be freed from the guilt of venial sin, and from man's inborn inclination toward sin. The sinner himself needed guidance, as Lancelot needed the priestess Guinevere, for he could count on no free decision of his own in the matter. He could only passively accept to confront raging lions, to cut himself on the Sword Bridge, and to weep at the fountain. When he bent the bars—if this was not an illusion—to reach Guinevere, he acted through no will of his own. He was intent on a blood communion.

The Gaelic forests of Scotland were haunted by ancient

ghosts of ancestors, says Sir Walter Scott in his appendix to "The
Lady of the Lake," such as a goblin dressed in antique armor "and
having one hand covered with blood." This "Red-Hand" haunts
Glenmore just as the "tall, emaciated, gigantic female's figure"
appears there today out of the mist. She is called "Noontide
Hag." Such ancient memories trouble Highlanders to whom "any
unusual appearance, produced by mist, or the strange lights that
are sometimes thrown upon particular objects, never fails to
present an apparition to the imagination of the solitary and mel-
ancholy mountaineer." Scotland is a weird world, it is true, and
subject to strange phenomena. The forests are dark green, the
rocks are dark gray, the lochs are colorless and leaden. But in
daytime the sky shoots vast streamers of orange over all, and at
night the northern lights play up and down the zenith in columns
of blue and red flames. And the starkness and loneliness turn the
mind toward the hereafter and the underworld. The "dark forest" by itself is a common symbol for the beyond. And today the
Lady of the Lake lifts Excalibur from Loch Katrine.

The geography of the Underworld was already ancient,
doubtless, when Homer described Odysseus's descent beside the
white rock or gate or entrance into hell. Even in ancient Egypt
the *ka*, or *döppelganger*, figured there in such death and/or initiation ceremonies. In the Lancelot text, Arthur's double is the
suffering, moaning Kay. Guinevere's double has just died. Lancelot himself once had a twin, for which reason the hero was
thrown into the "Lake" to drown; he was rescued by its "Lady."
The second-born twin was in ancient times always considered
the child of a demon, not the child of the husband. A mother of
multiple births was therefore condemned to be slain immediately; for her second or twin's birth found her guilty of having
had intercourse with the Devil. Kay here proved, if not evil, at
the least boastful and useless. The False Guinevere had certainly
proven herself evil, and so her atrocious suffering was what she
expected. We note again in passing how sad it is still that neither
Guinevere has a mother. The mother must either have died at
childbirth or been executed shortly thereafter. In Arthur's case
the *ka* is explained away as a foster brother. It was said by
Merlin, who witnessed it and, in fact, arranged this cover story,

that Arthur was only "nursed by Kay's mother." Was his own mother executed at his birth? Almost everyone found her missing from Arthur's life.

The *Prose Lancelot* omits much of the usual metal transformations and evil blacksmiths usually haunting hell, but Bademagus probably represents the dark ruler Vulcan or Pluto. The many-headed, monstrous dog Cerberus, to whom Psyche gave a sop of bread dipped in honey to stop him from biting her, was here multiplied not into heads but into the priestess' "rabid" lions. The River Styx flows dark and Stygian enough. The priestess Ariadne's talisman, a protective thread, becomes the Lady of the Lake's talisman, a golden ring. All descenders are spitted or impaled, as was Lancelot. All are cut like him. In ancient Germany the hero also saw the death goddess, for that deity or priestess was female like the Greek and Roman Persephone/Proserpina. Her name in German was Hel, and she gave her name to the place. The appearance there in hell of the priestess Guinevere, therefore, comes as no surprise. Neither does her "palace" appear there anachronistically; it also is a feature of that far western, dark, Irish land of purgation and death. Lancelot's punishment was surely that in that dark light (*atra lux*) of the Roman poet Vergil, he could see the paradisiacal face of Guinevere, but that to his sorrow he lost the beatific vision.

Christ's Harrowing of Hell is celebrated liturgically at Matins on Holy Saturday, as at Easter Vigil. The Irish *St. Patrick's Purgatory* is so explained:

Saint Patrick went to preach in Ireland. God made miracles for him because he was worthy. (v. 189) He drew people there out of their mad [pagan] religion (v. 201). He frightened them about hell and showed them the great joys that came from believing in Christianity.

Along about Easter an old man came to confession. The Saint found an interpreter and heard him. When asked if he had ever killed anyone, the old man said, "Five." The Saint explained the crime.

People wouldn't believe him because they couldn't see. The Saint prayed, kept vigils, fasted, etc. Jesus re-appeared to him, giving him a Gospel and a staff.

Then God took St. Patrick to a desert, a wasteland [*uns lius guastez*] (v. 301). In a desert,—a wasteland which was uninhabited,—[he saw] a completely round pit, and it was wide and altogether deep inside. And understand that she was black, and outsized hideous! Next he told him that herein was the entrance found of the Purgatory. After confession he could climb down in and stay there one day and one whole night long (v. 317).

The Saint realized that anyone of these pagan people experiencing this vigil would upon exiting be cleansed of the error of his ways. He then built an abbey (v. 337) for canons and other people of the good life.

The pit truly is in the cemetery toward the east. He made doors to the round wall which encircles it [her]. The reason was so that nobody could enter it except by his permission, nor otherwise descend down into it. He entrusted the key to the prior and forbade him neither at night nor by day: to let enter nobody, unless by his permission, and also by permission of all those in the abbey.

Men came down into this pit, suffered horribly there, glimpsed there the hard pains of hell, and the joy of delivery therefrom. It was called "St. Patrick's Purgatory." The name of the place was Rigles (v. 377).

Patrick died and went beside Christ.

Afterwards there was a very old prior, so old he had only one tooth left (v. 383). He had a "habitacle" built for himself near the dormitory so his feebleness and old age would inconvenience nobody. He used to say "Here have I pains and sorrows. Joys and delight shall I have elsewhere" (v. 406). He lived until he died, on cold water, bread, and salt.

Lots of people in St. Patrick's time went down into the Purgatory and died. The canons wrote it all down. Those who wanted to test themselves, confessed to the bishop, who gave them a sermon afterwards: "Sirs, for God's sake, do not enter it down there (v. 441) . . . that dark pit (v. 450). . . ."

When the bishop couldn't stop them, he sent them to the prior, who kept them for fifteen days in penance in the church.

And thus he would show them the pains (v. 476) which down inside that place they would find, and that nevermore they would return if they were not to have an unshakable belief in God, and veritably hope.

When he was unable to stop them, he let them go down; and he locked the door. Next day those who came up had a service said for them and the ones who didn't come up, knew for certain that they were lost (v. 502).

These lines from *St. Patrick's Purgatory* were written by another Cistercian monk, Henry of Saltrey, around 1153 and translated into Old French by the Arthurian writer Marie de France. They are contemporary with Geoffrey of Monmouth's rediscovery of King Arthur and Queen Guinevere, and the publication of his *History of the Kings of Britain* in 1136. Henry was, like Geoffrey, a Cistercian or White Monk in England during the reign of King Stephen (1135–1154) to whom Geoffrey first dedicated his royal history. The canons who organized and maintained this Purgatory Henry of Saltrey wrote about were canons regular of St. Augustine, who settled there in the twelfth century. In their day, the pit had become a cave on an island in Lough Derg (Red Lake), County Donegal, Ireland.

At the rate reported of fifteen thousand pilgrims per year, then at least nine million people journeyed there in Ireland to experience Purgatory. Pope Alexander VI ordered the Purgatory closed in 1497, and so did the Irish government from Dublin in 1632. In the year 1790 it was still open and in use.

Marie de France said in her opening verses that she translated Henry of Saltrey's Latin text because "when souls leave the
body, they are received by good angels, but bad souls are by bad
angels taken into torment." In her Arthurian poems Marie de
France often expresses, despite her authorial control, an anti-
Arthur bias. She is frankly pro-Gaelic and pro-clerical rather
than warlike.

Several texts mentioned thus far in this attempt to understand what transpired between Queen Guinevere and Lord
Lancelot are closely interconnected in several other ways: by
subject matter, by the central hero, by the authors who may have
known each other, by materials that were probably shared, by
localities so precisely described as to have been seen personally,
by the same religious orders and religious instruction and beliefs,
by the use of the same biblical texts and the same liturgies, and
by the same places of residence of their characters. Three such
authors we know were Cistercians in Britain.* Chrétien de
Troyes also had either resided in Scotland or, if not, had certainly
traveled long and wide inside southern Scotland. Jocelyn of Furness was a Cistercian who wrote the *Life* of King Arthur's
nephew St. Mungo (*Kentigern*, "Chief Lord") of Glasgow, Scotland, but Henry of Saltrey was also a Cistercian who probably
resided for years on the Isle of Man itself, as did Marie de France,
who from textual evidence inside her writings and by her pro-
Gaelic stance, seems to have also resided there. There was for
centuries a celebrated nunnery—several times reendowed by
Irish princesses—at Douglas, the capital of the Isle of Man. It is
impossible to think of Marie de France otherwise than as a nun
or abbess like the Arthurian Lady of the Lake. Finally, Queen
Guinevere ended her abduction and superintended Lancelot on
the Isle of Man. Geoffrey of Monmouth was the greatest Cistercian of the three men.

King Arthur himself was not only finally but supremely
present on the Isle of Man, which was also an original ancestral
home of the more ancient Pictish tribes, when Queen Guinevere

*Geoffrey of Monmouth, Henry of Saltrey, Jocelyn of Furness, and probably Marie de
France. There were 530 Cistercian abbeys functioning in the twelfth century.

and Lancelot enacted the final ceremony of the latter's Purgatory experience there. This means that the king presided after having reconquered the Isle of Man, which had reportedly lapsed after having been Christianized—some say by St. Patrick himself—in the year 444. The later Patrick of the Irish Purgatory was an unscrupulous abbot, who was disciplined, sent to Glastonbury in England, and interred there in a grave still called St. Patrick's, or King Arthur's. In any case, the islet off the west coast of Man, which faces Ireland from this center of the Irish Sea, is still called St. Patrick's Isle, and the ruins of his original church are still there—roofless, which is a great pity and a sad sight.

Tending to their charge, which was to compile the adventures of Lancelot, the authors of the *Prose Lancelot* made no attempt to narrate King Arthur's reconquest of Man, his plan to remove the Holy Grail from Dumbarton Rock on the Clyde River (downstream of the modern Glasgow) to Man, his Grail experience, much less the heroic and brutal victory there of Perceval wielding his poleax in Arthur's name. Only the Perceval manuscripts tell of this reconquest of the Isle of Man.

The place of Lancelot's Purgatory, or initiation experience, was most certainly one of the early Christian churches on the Isle of Man, either St. John's Church at the Tynwald Hill on the road from Douglas to Peel and St. Patrick's Isle or on St. Patrick's Isle itself. The latter seems likelier because the geography fits better: beetling cliffs on Man overlook the islet, the River Neb flows into the Irish Sea at St. Patrick's Isle, and Man itself is symbolized by the triskelion, three legs within a wheel, or the tripod figuring one of the world's oldest oracular centers.

Christian churches stand, in Europe at least, on the sites of more ancient, pagan temples, as in the Isle of Man. The ruins of St. Patrick's Church are only one of many churches in decay, parts of which still stand in lovely, orange, crumbled stones on St. Patrick's Isle. The cemetery also, with graves under graves going back to King Arthur's day, has recently been excavated. The St. Patrick's Purgatory at Lough Derg stood in a cemetery like the one on St. Patrick's Isle, beside the largest church (also now roofless).

Incidentally, Arthurian texts mention another such cemetery inside another such round wall as at Lough Derg, but that still exists on the Bannockburn Battlefield near Stirling Castle (Cameliard/Camelot), Scotland. The church is called St. Ninian's, because he first Christianized the Rhinns of Galloway, before King Arthur's day. Here also Lancelot once descended underground and was overwhelmed at the sight of a sarcophagus containing the body of a celebrated saint. The sarcophagus was surrounded by flames from many candles. Perceval saw this same tomb as well. It was Perceval's young father, who would live only a short while longer before dying in battle, who took his son there to show him the sarcophagus and have him hear a recital of his own royal and holy genealogy. Perceval was obviously another ancient Scot, either Pict or Gael.

Many such narratives swing the reader back and forth between Scotland and Ireland. The latter was in Arthur's day when, even unconquered, Man and Ireland supplied Britain with Bards, priests, priestesses, and theologians of renown and overwhelming erudition, like Pelagius, Patrick, Bridget, and Merlin. The ancient Gauls also claimed that their priestesses were imported from Ireland. And even the Greeks entertained a learned celebrity from Gaul as chronicled by the Irish scholar John Toland, but so did the Roman orator Cicero, who was himself a renowned theologian and still very admired as such.

One turns therefore to ancient books of Ireland itself and Scotland to see whether Guinevere is a solitary example of a northern priestess, or whether Irish records know others like her. W. F. Skene, who is considered perhaps Scotland's most distinguished, recent historian of ancient Ireland and Scotland, edited a collection of ancient stories, which the Irish say outnumber all those from Europe put together. The particular stories Skene edited and introduced from 1868 to 1887 had been collected by James Macgregor (1862) of Fortingall, a Dean of Lismore, which is a place in both Ireland and Scotland, and named in his memory: *The Dean of Lismore's Book.* These ancient stories present many priestesses as quasi-historical personages. They originated, says the learned Skene, from the two races of Ireland and Scotland: Scots and Cruithne. Cruithne is the Irish word for the Irish Picts who inhabited northeastern Ireland (Antrim and Down) just as the other, more mysterious Picts inhabited eastern Scotland north of Stirling. The Dean of Lismore's stories originate then from Ireland, from the Picts or Cruithne, and from the Scots—who after 503, says Skene, had migrated into northwestern Scotland and particularly into Argyle—and from the Picts around Perth, or northeastern Scotland. The many priestesses in *The Dean of Lismore's Book* throw light on Guinevere in Purgatory and Lancelot as her initiate in a long line of great initiates: Aristotle, Plato, Cicero, Pythagoras, priestesses, and oracles.

The Scottish-Irish poet Ossian remains a major source of ancient history among the Gael or Scots of Scotland. These Ossianic poems, which were collected by the Dean of Lismore, give us today a clear idea of terminology and of ancient geography A.D. 432, just prior to Arthur's birth (c. A.D. 475). What he says also applies not only to Merlin, Lancelot, and Perceval but also to Guinevere as priestess. Ossian speaks of the following:

Alba (Alban): Scotland north of the Forth-Clyde line.
Breatan (Dunn Breatan): Dumbarton on the Clyde River, downstream from Glasgow.
Lochlan: Northern Germany—then Celtic, said Skene, whence originally came the Cruithne (Picts) and the Tuatha De Danann into Ireland.
Lochlanach: Invaders from Scandinavia.
Feinne: Finn's bands of warriors, who contacted invaders of both Ireland and Scotland, i.e., the Cruithne and the Tuatha De Danann.
Fenians: personages inside his poems, as collected by the Dean of Lismore.
Finn MacCumhal: the Irish and Scottish warrior.

The historian Skene points out how ancient priestesses defended their homelands before Guinevere and Arthur replaced them and did likewise. The rulers often bore names containing the syllable *gal* as in Galehaut.

The Ossianic poems portray priestesses and judges who were royal women like Guinevere. In fact, it seems to be common knowledge in Ireland that the priestess who acted as supreme judge had the last two syllables of her name like that of Guinevere: *Guanu* plus *Mara.* In Ireland the priestess performed rites in Purgatory, and she was also severely tested. One of the tests routinely undergone by Irish priestesses was for virginity. She must remain virginal.

Guinevere was even once said to have been tested for virginity by being required publicly, at a session of Arthur's Court, to disrobe and slip on a white garment. That notion also occurs in *The Dean of Lismore's Book* where six wives are similarly tested. The robe would not fit either Diarmad's wife, or Conan's, or Oscar's, or Finn's, or Angus's daughter, but only MacRea's wife who was Deirg's daughter and the future mother of the poet Ossian himself. Therefore, of the six chieftains' wives—Maighinis, Gormlay, Naoif, and the others—only Ossian's mother survived the ordeal, as did Guinevere, of course, who remained forever virginal. The dean's book contains three more beautiful elegies by Queen Gormlay of Ireland; but Guinevere is said only to have kept King Arthur's Annals, none of which in the original has survived. Nor has any of the sculpted or incised tomb lids she commissioned survived although many such were made, as art historians report, on the Isle of Man; and the *Prose Lancelot* attributes them to the Lady of the Lake. That Lady was not Guinevere, of course, but Lancelot's teacher and perhaps Guinevere's as well.

Some say that Queen Guinevere also was tested for virginity by means of a mantle that, had she been guilty, would have burned her to death. In front of certified witnesses in King Arthur's Court, the queen courageously proved her innocence. She calmly put on the terrible mantle. She was not scorched in any way. This test proved her virginity. The queen was a priestess.

Queen Morgan le Fay, who was Arthur's youngest half-sister, disliked him intensely and continually and openly defied him. She also openly plotted his disgrace and death. The "Queen of Orkney," who was another half-sister, publicly upbraided him for mistreatment of her youngest son whom she had richly endowed and sent to Court. The king claimed he never saw the boy's attendant riches. Under attack, however, he changed his story, coming to agree that he did see the prince's dwarf loaded with riches and treasure but did not know they actually belonged to his sister's young son.

Among her many attempts to assassinate King Arthur, Queen Morgan once sent him a "burning mantle." The king's life on that occasion was saved by an emissary from the High-Priestess, Lady of the Lake. She warned King Arthur in time, that he should not put on the garment until he had asked the donor herself to test it on her own person. When the donor hesitated to comply, she was ordered by the king to put the mantle forthwith on her person. So doing, she was so utterly consumed by flames that she died before them all. Sir Thomas Malory tells that story marvelously (vol. I, book IV, chap. XVI).

Lancelot once replaced his cousin Bors and fought another judiciary duel, this time to save Queen Guinevere from being tied to an iron stake and burned to death, Sir Thomas Malory (vol. II, bk. XVIII, chaps. I–VIII) also recalled in the fifteenth century.

The queen had prepared a feast for twenty-four members of the Round Table Order. To please Gawain, who particularly delighted in fruit, she had ordered many delicious apples. Sir Pinel poisoned the apples, which caused one guest to die at the table. But Gawain himself did not eat a poisoned fruit.

The queen was doubly condemned to death: as murderess and intended murderess of Gawain.

In Lancelot's absence Bors agreed, although reluctantly, to champion the queen at her ordeal. He was excused, however, when Lancelot appeared at the last moment and saved her from the bonfire.

Even when faced again and again with imminent death, the queen had stalwartly continued to proclaim her innocence. Although Lancelot saved her from this burning, even he was still not sure of her innocence.

It required finally an intervention by the august Lady of the Lake, by means of her emissary, to disclose the name of the real murderer and exculpate the queen. Sir Thomas Malory, who remembered all this, probably only repeated what many before him also thought: that Lady found out the truth "through her sorcery and enchantments," and not because she, too, was a High-Priestess, clad in white, mounted on a snow-white palfrey, incapable of dishonesty.

To recognize Queen Guinevere as High-Priestess will undoubtedly open doors to persons seeking knowledge. Another such door, for example, suddenly swings ajar in the sacred Welsh tale of Gereint. Guinevere's champion Gereint from the Welsh *Mabinogion* (1974) collection of stories is the same hero named Erec, or Guerec, in the courtly French *Erec et Enide* romance by Chrétien de Troyes. Neither telling can be considered much more than a frivolous, romantic adventure until Guinevere's true profession reveals it as a real conflict between her priesthood and King Arthur, as her royal personage against his imperial power, as conflict between her champion and his, and as their earthly opposed to their unearthly kingdoms. With a start we realize that their two realms are contiguous and the crossings, free but dangerous.

The Welsh Gereint tale revolves about King Arthur's hunt for the White Stag. But the tale is postulated on what has before seemed superfluous and extrinsic: Arthur and Guinevere worshiped in separate churches. Did they, indeed?

Although Queen Guinevere asked to accompany the King's Hunt, she was not awakened early enough, or she overslept. In short, King Arthur left her behind. He also took with him all the horses, except for two. However, Guinevere and one maiden set off unescorted, in pursuit. Fortunately for the queen, she was immediately joined by Prince Gereint, who, as everyone then knew, had been born at a time when the gates of Heaven itself happened to stand ajar. This day he was royally clad in a purple cloak; at its four corners were four golden apples, fruits of the Tree of Knowledge (Genesis 3:3), fruits also of the prophesied new Adam, who was Christ (Song of Solomon 2:3). From this point onward, the Welsh tale rises into prominence in our eyes, to a rank at the least worthy of being esteemed a true repository of ancient wisdom.

Queen Guinevere and Prince Gereint meet on their arrival at the gloomy forest of this world a somber deity, a dark warrior accompanied by a white lady astride a snow-white horse. She is richly appareled in Oriental brocade as if she also were a priestess from the Lady of the Lake's domains. Queen Guinevere's maiden and then the unfortunate, or fortunate, Gereint are scourged on their faces until blood streams down their cheeks. Their punisher is a (Pictish) dwarf. The queen sternly orders Gereint to follow him. Thus he has proven able to venture into the Otherworld where he will furthermore defeat the dark warrior.

The defeated, black-mounted warrior was none other than Edern (Edeyrn), son of (ap) Nudd, brother of Gwyn ap Nudd. The latter warder of Hades was finally slain by Lancelot because he had abducted Queen Guinevere to his sacred realm across the sea. Chrétien had called him Meleagant. Edern managed, after his defeat by Gereint, to stagger into Arthur's Court, barely alive. Whether he recovered enough to accompany Arthur to Rome, or whether they had both returned from Rome before the king undertook his hunt of the White Stag seems to have been forgotten.

The Welsh tale stipulates that Arthur, aided by his hunting dog Cafall, slew the White Stag, cut off its head, and returned home triumphantly. He gallantly, or because he was so obligated, handed over this important trophy to Queen Guinevere. She, in turn, awarded it to Prince Gereint's sweetheart Enid (Enide), who was the white-clad maiden.

This tale, which exists in Welsh and in Old French, opens wide the one most mysterious portal, which is that Celtic myth peculiar to King Arthur's ancient world. The Hunt for the White Stag, that adventure that King Arthur achieved personally, stood athwart the perilous route to the Castle of the Holy Grail.

Masked by hands far more initiate than our own, ancient authors knew perfectly well what we today only discover by analogy and the practices of comparative literature. How gratifying to understand finally here that a body of esoteric knowledge revealed in Arthur's day only to select and royal initiates, and even then only to those who had advanced thus far on the perilous path to hidden knowledge, can perhaps be to some degree unraveled.

Thus, Queen Guinevere's priestly profession may eventually help us fathom the Quest of the Holy Grail.

Ancient authors now have indicated four stages along the esoteric path to knowledge. The hero, in this case King Arthur in person, after having exhausted all available sources, must apply to beings older than man, in this order: (1) the Ouzel, or European Blackbird, who was Merlin himself; (2) the White Stag, or *Blanc Cerf*; (3) the Eagle, and (4) the Salmon of Knowledge.

King Arthur may have beheaded the White Stag because, after having plundered his lore, he in that way slew the pagan horned god Cernunnus. Subsequently, it would seem, he then placed a cross between his antlered head and planted it above the Castle of the Horn where the Grail reposed.

Toward the close of King Arthur's life he decided again to have Queen Guinevere once for all burned at the stake for adultery with Lancelot. Sir Thomas Malory (vol. II, bk. XX, chap. VII) explains it as follows:

> And the law was such in those days that whatsomever they were, of what estate or degree, if they were found guilty of treason, there should be none other remedy but death; and either the men or the taking with the deed should be the causer of their hasty judgment.

Although Gawain, Lancelot, Gaheris, and Gareth counseled King Arthur, begged him not to condemn her, but to continue steady, holding his fellowship of warriors together, he would not ignore the old charge or rescind his last sentence.

Queen Guinevere, therefore, again was led outside the city walls of Carlisle, where she was publicly "despoiled" of all her clothing down "into her smock." Then, shamefully displayed, she was shriven by a priest while "lords and ladies wept and wrung their hands" in pity (Malory, chap. VIII).

When Lancelot's deputy saw the queen so stripped and then

shriven, he notified his royal master. Lancelot was waiting. He rode onto the field.

In the ensuing melee more than twenty-one members of the Round Table were slain, even those who were merely present as witnesses hostile to Arthur and unarmed. In those two days King Arthur lost a total of forty companions-in-arms, most of them dead from split skulls, Malory calculated.

As soon as he had rid the field of combatants, Lancelot called for a "kirtle and gown to be cast upon" the naked queen. He then conveyed her safely away to his Joyous Gard(e) Castle, which King Arthur then besieged. "Queen Guinevere," Lancelot once more told the king, "is a true lady unto your person" (chapter XI) and that's that.

"Alas," said King Arthur after Lancelot had one day unhorsed even him, "that ever this war began."

But when the royal Lancelot mounted and rode out of Carlisle for the last time, there was "sobbing and weeping for pure" sorrow at his departure from Arthur's realm.

But many still to this day believe that it was not Lancelot, but Queen Guinevere herself who brought down the king's realm because she committed adultery with Lancelot. Nothing avails. The thought that Guinevere was innocent, as both she and Lancelot solemnly swore before God and public, many times over, has never been accepted.

Nor has it ever occurred to anyone that Queen Guinevere was a High-Priestess and as virginal as the Lady of the Lake, or as Saint Bridget of Ireland, or as Saint Geneviève of Paris.

The Arthurian corpus over and over again takes sad adieu of a sorry, guilty, and, therefore, despicable Queen Guinevere—a woman no more evil and impure than contemptible, oversexed women everywhere, it claims. The biased view of womankind prevails, and the practice, which is called "Project and Deny."

Whether or not she was guilty of adultery, the life of Queen Guinevere was filled with trials and testings, descents into hell, and initiations. The old charge of adultery with Lancelot has over the ages remained the most repeated. It still clings to her although an Irish scholar, and one of the best in the world, long ago disculpated her of all charges of this nature. All he did was to bring up the question of mistranslation in the *Lancelot* of Chrétien de Troyes.

The famous Irish scholar to whom we are endebted was John Toland (1670–1722). He had not wasted his years of study at Edinburgh, Glasgow, Oxford, Leiden, and other high seats of learning. Beware, said Toland, of mistranslations. They are such terrible pitfalls as to attract spiders' webs of disaster all along their wake—for centuries, if not forever.

One must beware of certain Gaelic words linguistically prone to misinterpretation. One of them is the word for *bed.* When ancient Irish writers speak of a *bed,* said Toland, they very often mean an *altar.*

With what sorry result? When you think they are talking about somebody going to bed, or Lancelot getting into the queen's bed, they are speaking about a religious rite that is being performed. He did not go to her bed. He went toward her altar. She was the priestess, and he was the acolyte.

Even the English word *bed* has several meanings among which is in masonry the place or foundation on which blocks are embedded. Altars were so constructed, by fixing stones or bricks in layers. That construction occurs strikingly as one of Gawain's more hideous ordeals, called the Perilous "Brick" or *Atre Perilleux* (from the Greek *ostrakon*). In this dangerous purgatorial ceremony Gawain also walked or rode into a cemetery in darkest night. He came to a tomb. Lancelot also proceeded in darkest night to a barred gate, we are to believe, where he cut his hand, so urgently did he desire sexual relations with Guinevere. What a low idea of human aspiration have we in this impoverished telling! What a hero dripping with perspiration!

But Toland also warned us of what others in our own century, notably Jung, have been saying in book after book. Is research into origins always fruitless? And, in any case, who is to halt the desire we all have to know? Before this descent into hell was Irish and before it was Scandinavian, and before it was Greek Orthodox Christian, what was it? What was its actual origin? Can we know? And how can we know that we know?

Indeed, a most ancient wisdom, which comes strangely from Tibetan Buddhism, explains very clearly what the *Prose Lancelot* left so inexplicable, and explicated so unsatisfactorily.

Guinevere is the guru, the White One, Lancelot's teacher as he descends the planes of his being to the *Sidpo Bardo,* or lowest level of incarnation, where in anguish he thirsts for a return to the womb and is about to experience rebirth into another reincarnation. He has failed, and so he must return for another cycle of life with all its anguish and sorrow, and endure on earth to become another human being. He has experienced the Sword Bridge among other torments such as the rabid lions, which were so many karmic illusions. In his dream state of progressive degeneration he fears self-sacrifice and cuts the palms off his own hands, which was his beloved teacher's sentence at Arthur's Court. He suffers horrible visions of ultimate degradation: adultery, self-immolation, murder, the drinking of blood from skulls, and rebirth. In this guarded state of which the great initiates could never openly speak, on pain of death, he implores the Divine Mother's protection during his fourth dimension. He sees visions of humans mating just prior to his own rebirth. Lancelot was to be born again, into a better life, it is hoped.

The White Priestess decides his destiny: human bondage again. Her words were whispered and, as always, so were the teachings from Tibet, now printed as the *Bardo-Thödol,* once known only by hearsay across continents and through the ages: to the Delphic Oracle in Greece, from her to the Greek Sage Pythagoras, thence to the Cumaean Sibyls in Naples, then to the Druid priestesses like Velleda in Gaul, to and from the ubiquitous Celts as they crisscrossed the known world. Oral transmission has sufficed until now.

Strangely, the Albigensians heard it in southern France from their own brand of White Priestess, or Puritan, who is Purgatory related: Man is a stranger in an unknown land. Man lives here in exile from God who was his home. He came, trailing clouds of glory, from elsewhere. Elsewhere is his real homeland. Their Gnostic priestesses taught it: *Nous sommes d'ailleurs;* We come from somewhere else.

As crowned queen of the Celts, Guinevere was authorized to wear robes of seven colors on her person. Seven was the greatest number allowed to anyone. When solemn priestess, she wore a white veil of sheerest linen, and a long white robe. She wore white, or no color at all, as priestess Guaṇhumara. If even her title as priestess was Sanskrit or Tibetan, then it may originally have been something like *Dhyara Mara,* White Illusion. Like her more ancient and classical predecessors, Guinevere had many, many names.

CHAPTER X

The Mistress of the Copper Mountain

"When to Pohjola thou comest,
All the slope with stakes is bristling,
All with heads of men surmounted,
And one stake alone is vacant,
And to fill the stake remaining,
Will they cut thy head from off thee."
  —*Mother's warning to the hero not to
  venture into the realm of the Mistress of
  the Copper Mountain,* Kalevala, *Runo
  XXVI, tr. by W. F. Kirby*

AFTER THE MAJOR SCHOLARS WHO HAVE WRITTEN EXTENSIVELY ON DARK Age Britain and who have focused on Arthurian affairs and personages have been weighed, all are found wanting when judged against Heinrich Zimmer. Even the best theory, that the Picts were Scandinavians, is not precise enough for one to narrow it down to certain traits. Zimmer's twenty-one sources thoroughly cover the question of Picts in Scotland where he agreed, supported, and expanded the findings of Sir John Rhŷs as presented to the Society of Antiquaries of Scotland, May 9, 1892. Rhŷs had given sixteen inscriptions in Pictish to the society, beginning, "1. ehtarrmnonn, 2. Drostenipe Uoret et Forcus, 3. Maqqo Tal-luorrn-ehht Vrobbaccennevv, 6. Iddaiqnnn Vorrenn ipua Iosir." Thereafter Rhŷs (1891) sounded the death knell of the Celtic theory:

> Here we have a certain number of inscriptions which appear to be more or less Pictish, so let the advocates of the Celtic theories come forward and explain these inscriptions as Celtic . . . take the carefully written and punctuated Ogam [writing]—xTtocuhetts: ahehhttmnnn: heevvevv: Nehhtonn, and let them explain it as Welsh, and I shall have to confess that I have never rightly understood a single word of my native tongue. If they cannot explain it so, let them explain it as any kind of Aryan [Indo-European]. Till then I shall treat it as unintelligible to me as a Celt, and as being, so far as I can judge, non Aryan.

Thus, Zimmer allows another than himself, who was also a masterful scholar and proficient linguist, to speak for him: the Picts were non-Aryan.

Zimmer's major and well-demonstrated conclusion, that the Picts were not Aryans, that their native language was not any variation of Indo-European, also makes the most sense as far as Queen Guinevere is concerned. She has always sounded like a foreign princess, even though she was born on the east coast of what is now Scotland. She came from Camelot, which is Stirling, still Scotland's most important naval harbor and a mustering center. For this reason, she was King Arthur's chosen bride with a dowry referred to even centuries after her death by its most remarkable building, the Round Table, a building so striking, so unique, so mysterious that it comes down the ages as the very symbol of her husband, King Arthur. For this reason, not only because her real estate was so essential but because she was a foreigner, Queen Guinevere has always walked veiled in mystery. Because she was so strange, because she spoke with an accent, because she did not belong, because she had been deprived of mother and father, she always attracted powerful and kindly disposed champions like Lancelot, Galehaut, and Gawain.

Because Queen Guinevere was Pictish—which meant not even Scandinavian and not even Teutonic, not Indo-European at all—she has survived in all our hearts as the most glamorous, which means the most magical, of foreign women. The French authors, who have always trained an eye on gorgeous, high-stepping ladies, were sure she was on the order of Botticelli's Venus—tall, slender, blond, and pink like the Lady of the Lake, her only competitor in the beauty department. The revered Lady too was praised as blond, tall, languid, white clad, blue eyed. English Victorian painters, on the contrary, saw Guinevere as tall, but slightly stooped, saturnine, dark skinned, curly haired, and black eyed. When King Henry II's cousin Abbot Sully at Glastonbury exhumed her there, or said he did, he found her golden haired. That was altogether wiser of him. This abbot of Glastonbury, Henry of Sully, traded on his royal birth to promote his abbey by exhuming Guinevere's body and Arthur's, he said, at Glastonbury. He continued to fabricate Arthur sites after he lost his bid for the abbacy of Salisbury, England, and had to move across the Channel to France. It was he who gulled Gerald de Barry into identifying the corpses exhumed in 1191 as Arthur and Guinevere. Gerald also was refused promotion and preferment.

Another controversy that swirls today just as vehemently as ever concerns Guinevere's Pictish social customs, granting women unheard-of freedoms, that even the Romans had assailed. By Roman law a daughter or a wife fell under the absolute jurisdiction of her father and then her husband. He was her absolute ruler who legally wielded all power to dispose of her person any way at all he chose. He could kill her himself or have her killed by someone else at any time or place, by any means, and for any reason, without question or repercussion. He could send her into gainful employment as a prostitute, as he pleased. He could cut her hair and sell her as a slave on the auction block. In Rome a daughter and/or a wife was obliged to worship her father's ancestors as he directed, for he was her only priest. When she married, in a ceremony of mock capture and rape, she

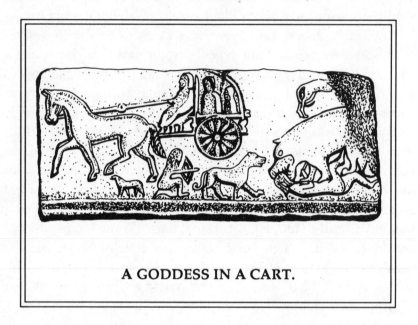

A GODDESS IN A CART.

was obliged henceforth to worship only her husband's gods, and then he became her only priest. Even the official city priestesses, or vestal virgins, were commonly and routinely buried alive for any trifling offense, such as wearing a pretty dress or a piece of jewelry that aroused jealousy; and the vestals were daughters of Rome's highest aristocrats. And so the Romans protested Pictish customs. They found Pictish women free agents at all times. Today we read their protests and wonder all the more about the mysterious, foreign Picts whose language nobody can read and whose ladies were free and sometimes very wealthy.

The controversy that still swirls inside Britain has to do with these same distressing Pictish customs, which, willy-nilly, are recognizably matriarchal. Queen Guinevere brought King Arthur the Round Table. If she ceased to own it, then the False Guinevere owned it. If Queen Guinevere died, the property reverted entire to her half-sister. In neither case did it descend to Arthur. There lies our prime example of matriarchal law. But a large and imposing line of British scholars continue to deny that Scotland ever lived under matriarchal law or matriarchal custom. Therefore it was only the Picts who lived under such matriarchal law and such custom and not the Celts. Guinevere, but not Arthur. King Loth, Lancelot, and Gawain, but not Arthur. Custom segregates the Picts.

Heinrich Zimmer even unearthed evidence that Pictish law vanished because it was officially and legally outlawed. When the bishop of St. Andrews named Turgot wrote his biography of Queen Margaret of Scotland, he found archives that before the year 1100 ordered some matriarchal laws rescinded. As of that date certain matriarchal customs were forbidden by the queen: (1) a son was forbidden to wed his stepmother after her husband's death and (2) a brother was forbidden henceforth in Scotland to wed his brother's widow.

Both changes in the law damaged women and were aimed at depriving women and their children of support. Stepmothers and widows were destituted by these changes, effected by Queen Margaret's supposedly kind hand (and her reputation held her most holy). Their minor children were apt to become wards of the state. One might suppose that Queen Margaret was praised by her counselors and petted as most saintly because she let herself so easily become their dupe.

Thus we come to Zimmer's prime methodological approach. Language, he decided, is a sorry crutch. We do not know the Pictish language, nor what words by way of language Guinevere spoke. We have no words from King Arthur anyway, but only Geoffrey of Monmouth's translation of his words into Latin. And anyway, nobody in Britain respects or believes Geoffrey, much less his words—only Americans and non-British believe him. Not language, because so few Pictish letterings have survived, but law, Zimmer decided, would be a better approach. The Picts have been known for ages. They were reported living in northeastern Ireland and in eastern Scotland north of Stirling from 55 B.C. to A.D. 844–899 when they were overruled by Kenneth Mac-Alpin in the united kingdom (Scots and Picts) of Alba. But Pictish laws were once unique in Scotland:

1. The mother decided her child's tribal member-
   ship and right of inheritance.
2. The sister's son succeeded to the throne, i.e.,
   Modred. Thus when Modred is accused of rape,
   or of having abducted Guinevere during Arthur's absence overseas, that charge is false. He
   was the rightful heir and her protector. Historians of Scotland have admitted it.
3. The daughter takes her mother's name or her
   maiden name. Thus there were understandably
   two Guineveres, both born to the same mother.
4. No king's son inherited the Pictish throne.
   Thirty kings named Brude governed the Picts.
   No one was a son of Brude. Pictish succession
   can only be explained by mother right. The Venerable Bede had concurred that right was *magis de
   feminea . . . quam de masculina,* "more from the feminine . . . than from the masculine." W. F. Skene
   had also agreed.
5. Parishes were coterminous with tribal lands;
   thus Arthuret in Scotland (north of Hadrian's
   Wall) was, and is, a church on lands of Arthur's
   mother's people.

Zimmer accuses historians as having always written as if all their
material from Dark Age Scotland were Celtic; they were wrong
to think so.

6. The ancient historian Julius Solinus Polyhistor
   (c. 34) reported the king had no real wife. He
   borrowed wives one at a time. He had "neither
   desire nor hope of issue." The only king's son
   who could reign was the king's son by his sister.
   Ergo, Arthur was accused of incest by other Celts
   who mistook his choice of Modred as an admission of guilt. Thus Modred was intended to be

king because he was the son of Arthur's eldest half-sister, and she belonged to the Pictish or "female royal race."

The Venerable Bede had said that the Picts were a very ancient people, that they came to Britain from overseas, that they were Scythians from the North, and that they spoke a foreign language. Their Christian ministers had to preach to them in this foreign language even in Bede's day, in a language that was not English (Anglian), not P-Celtic (Welsh), and not Q-Celtic (Irish) either.

His study of Pictish laws, which surface so easily from Arthurian stories not otherwise even comprehensible except as inhuman anomalies, led Zimmer to the following, final conclusions. The Picts were either Finnish-Esthonian or Iberian or some third race. They were definitely not Celts, who were known from either 3500 B.C. or from 5000 B.C., as patriarchal. Several possibilities arise as corollaries, continued Zimmer: matriarchy probably precedes patriarchy in a society, unless matriarchy and patriarchy rise together in a society. If so, however, they rise in opposition the one to the other, and it seems clear enough that matriarchy dies out before it ever develops into patriarchy.

The "fierce" blue eyes, the red hair, and the heavy frames that Tacitus assigned to the Caledonians, as Agricola saw them and fought against them in northern Scotland, rules out the Iberians as their ancestors, because the Iberians "had that swarthy complexion which does not go along with red hair," added Zimmer's editor G. H. Others reply that some Gauls may have been very tall people with lighter hair, although those Gauls reported by Tacitus as very tall (*Chatti*) appear to have been Celts. On the other hand, the fathers of Pictish kings could be non-Pictish. Zimmer concludes:

> There was only succession-in-the-female-line as modified by Christianity, by Christian views of the world, and by the Christianized Aryan-Celtic culture of the Irish and of the Cymri [Welsh].

We should not attempt now to repeat past unsuccessful effort. Let us not compare modern Finnish words with ancient Pictish, urged Zimmer. That will not convince anybody. No more should anyone attempt to compare modern Basque speech with ancient Pictish fragments, which are all we have. The key will have to be matriarchy and Pictish law.

Did the ancient Finns, for example, follow a legal system recognized and still recognizable, provable, as matriarchal? What about ancient Iberians? Any trace of matriarchy there? If not, then the Picts belonged to a third, now unknown stock. Why? Because we know that Pictish society was matriarchal; in fact, matriarchal traces existed in Scotland well into historical time.

The huge body of Arthurian literature crosses the line between prehistory and recorded history, witnesses the collapse of the Roman Empire and the period of migrations from which will emerge new governors and a so-called five-hundred-year medieval period of peace in Western Europe. Queen Guinevere herself rises before oblivion and obloquy to represent the coming federation of her Roman ancestors, her Celtic or British husband, and her own overseas Pictish peoples defeated at Stirling-Camelot on the Firth of Forth. For centuries the Picts had stopped Rome at their northernmost outposts. By Guinevere's time she and her peoples were being persuaded to enter the larger society of Christian civilization. The southern Picts along the Nith River in Galloway had already built Candida Casa and worshiped Christ there before Guinevere's birth; Saint Ninian may already have had a nucleus of worshipers at Bannockburn, an easy walk from her birthplace.

Three educated women loom very large in Arthurian literature, for they and their kind are doomed: Queen Guinevere, Morgan le Fay, and the Lady of the Lake. All three ladies had probably learned to read and write with Merlin at the Grail Castle. All three are so related to him and his educational center, by one or more of the medieval writers commissioned by some French lord or lady to write Arthurian history. These three women stand out in their pages as educated, dominant, strong, and priestlike. All three deal with priestess tasks that come down the ages from most ancient temples of the Hittites and their satellite kingdoms in Asia Minor, from Crete, from Mycenaean Greece, classical Greece, Libya, North Africa, Gaul, Ireland, Scandinavia, Germany, and Scotland. Thus a veiled Guinevere remains preponderantly in the ancient world of priestesses rather than in the medieval world of priests. In this way, she looms very tall, a stark anomaly. She and the Lady of the Lake, both under Merlin's wing, dominate their world.

There is no doubt but that Guinevere was a renowned priestess, able in the Virgin Mary's recent Oriental pattern, as told in Apocrypha, to descend into hell, to receive her acolyte Lancelot in hell, to perform a religious ceremony invoking blood sacrifice and communion. Every great priestess from time immemorial had solemnly done no less.

By definition, then, when Guinevere performs a religious service, its account reads as mythological, because myth springs from such a mysterious ritual. Because Guinevere dropped her cares and the world, and its mundane war, at the fountain where Lancelot came on her symbol—the comb—she became, and her story too, a myth.

These three greatest priestesses of Arthurian literature stand alone, so tall they overwhelm the mere lords and ladies of Arthur's Court. The new French literature of Christian France, even a mere hundred years later, has no such priestesses. At Fécamp, France, a hundred years after Guinevere's death, they had only the bones of such priestesses, as relics. Irish tales have a few priestesses who flash momentarily in and out. Ossianic literature from Scotland has poetesses and young heroines heartbreakingly sad, pitiful mostly in early death and unfulfilled love—but no ancient priestesses as great as Guinevere and the Lady of the Lake. Nor does Scandinavian or German literature have more than glimpses and verses from their Druidical priestesses. Is it possible that priestesses occurred and lived primarily among the Picts? Is Guinevere a lone modern example of a queen-priestess in the manner of Hittites, Egyptians, proto-Greeks, and Roman Sibyls? How could she skip a thousand years and thousands of miles? And yet there she is. Her ceremony at the Grail Castle most resembled *The Tibetan Book of the Dead* (1960). The answer must lie in her Asiatic, distant origins. The Picts may well be the missing link that needs to be reexplored.

In his essay "Matriarchy among the Picts," Heinrich Zimmer left a conclusion, and walked away: Either the Picts were from Finland, or they had come from some other place. Why Finland?

Finland preeminently boasted a matriarchal society that has continued visibly until today, which books, testimony, government subsidies today (in 1990), and doctoral dissertations from Finland, Germany, and Scotland continue to study with great amazement. Because Finland alone boasts an ancient matriarchy, then did the Picts come overseas from Finland?

Even in Arthur's lifetime the king of the Orkneys boasted such a king-mother—a Finnish queen and priestess named Gunnhild against whom charges of magic making were brought. And the earlier Ynglings also boasted a Finnish queen named Drifa (*Ynglingasaga*). So why not Arthur, a conqueror bent on consolidation of races and their amalgamation by force and by marriage?

Today Zimmer can be answered affirmatively. He can also be bolstered by literature, another new body of evidence that he may have intended to mention. That body is the very ancient, Finnish national epic, the *Kalevala*.

The only large, lengthy body of ancient literature from northern Europe that suggests the persons, the scope, the tone, and the barbaric customs of Arthurian literature comes from Finland. In addition, and here is the key resemblance, the *Kalevala* contains not one or two, but many priestesses and their temples, both very reminiscent of the Arthurian. Both bodies of literature were similarly recovered from folk memory, tradition, legend, and mythology. Geoffrey of Monmouth has no source as yet discovered. The *Kalevala*, even less, has been restored only from word of mouth. The poem was recovered by one doctor (M.D.) from ordinary speakers in Finland and in Russia, just as Irish fairy tales were recovered by an American schoolteacher during his summer vacations.

Last of all, the *Kalevala* is infinitely beautiful. An Italian literary critic termed it epical-lyrical. It is so ancient that it has even lost its place-names, its heroes' twelve battles à la Arthur, its memories of real wars, and its genealogies. It has not lost its matriarchy—nor have the Finnish peoples, who are of Asian and not of Indo-European or Aryan origin.

The sad story of the first Finnish maiden priestess named Aino comes early in the *Kalevala* (Runo IV) and cannot but make one think of the poor maiden Guinevere rolled in her bedding and carried down to the water's edge on her wedding night. Aino went toward her woman's temple, which was a necropolis because it stood in a field *surrounded by alder trees (champs élysées)*. There she was raped by a hero whom she called "an old man." In despair she immediately after the attack divested herself of all her sacred objects: cross, gold ring, necklace, and scarlet ribbons

**COMB, MIRROR, PICTISH LADY,
HER DOG AND MAIDENS.**

of a priestess. From her waist she even dropped her holy, copper belt of a priestess, before returning home crying loudly. She told her mother how she had lost the gold from her forehead, the silver from her hair, the blue fillets from her temples, and the scarlet ribbons from her braids. "Go to the mountain," her mother advised her, "and take new treasures woven by Moon priestesses for you." Her mother also told her to dress in a white linen robe and that then she could be married. The story goes on very much like Marie de France's Arthurian poem *Yonec,* which ends with the raped maiden running to the refuge of the Grail Castle mountain of salvation.

The young Finnish priestess chose to live thereafter, like the Arthurian priestess, under the waters of the lake. First she dressed in finery from the mountain hoard. Then she journeyed to the shore of the lake to which she offered her finery. After having returned her treasures to the earth whence they came, she sat like the mermaid in the Copenhagen harbor on a rock sadly until it sank beneath her and she drowned. She drowned like the dove, which is the bird of death, says the *Kalevala,* thus explaining anew Guinevere's four doves that were borne before her at her coronation. By that token Guinevere was also one of the Furies and a priestess of the dead.

Who remembered this young Finnish priestess of the lake? The four forest creatures sacred to priestesses: bear, wolf, fox, and hare. This last creature, which is usually depicted as the white or Easter rabbit, was especially revered by priestesses in ancient Europe as in Central America by the Maya. Aino's mother turned to stone and wept rivers just like Niobe of Asia Minor whose sculptured image is still visible on the mountain behind Ismir, Turkey. Who remembered Guinevere?

After Aino's rejection of her rapist, the old magician goes to the far distant, cloudy, misty, northern land of Pohjola to seek its maiden as his bride (Runo VIII ff.). The hero *Väinä*möinen whose name gives his origin, *Fin*land, there woos another reluctant daughter of this Hyperborean realm that, since it is not Lapland, could have designated any other cloud-covered, northern realm, such as Orkney, Iceland, or Man. This maiden argues that she lives like a strawberry in her parents' home, but that as his wife she would be a "chained household dog" or a "slave" of all tasks. She tests him by a labor during which he wounds himself with an iron tool and has to delegate the completion of his labor to the blacksmith. That hero-of-all-accomplishments, Arthur's Lancelot, finally forges the talisman that the maiden and her aged mother of Pohjola must have. This talisman will heal them, feed them, and protect them during natural calamities. It is the Holy Grail.

The maiden's story thus repeats the most famous of Arthurian plots. As a maiden Queen Guinevere rejected Arthur for Lancelot, requiring the latter to transport her Pictish talisman, which was the Holy Grail, from its older site, Dumbarton, after it had been seized by "Saxons." Arthurian texts specify that the Grail was conveyed to Avalon for safer keeping after Arthur, Lancelot, Gawain, and Perceval recaptured Avalon, rechristianized it, and constructed a "castle" in which to house this utterly precious object.

The maiden's mother in the *Kalevala,* she who is represented in the Arthur texts by the Lady of the Lake (Irish Sea), receives from the blacksmith (Lancelot) the talisman. It is a "Sampo" described as a corn mill, a salt mill, and a coin mill. It provided the Finns with food, trade goods, and treasure. The maiden's mother, who was an aged crone, bore the talisman to her Copper Mountain, or in Arthurian terms to the Grail Castle called in German texts "the Mountain of Salvation":

> Now rejoiced the Crone of Pohja,
> And conveyed the bulky Sampo
> To the rocky hills of Pohja
> And within the Mount of Copper,
> And behind nine locks secured it.
> There it struck its roots around it
> Fathoms nine in depth that measured,
> One in Mother Earth deep-rooted,
> In the strand the next was planted,
> In the nearest mount the third one.

Even so, the maiden, daughter of the mistress of the Copper Mountain, refused to marry. The hoodwinked craftsman took three days to paddle home across the lake.

Not only do we have Queen Guinevere, Lancelot, and the Lady of the Lake in our scenario, but on this island (Isle of Man) in the Irish Sea or "lake," we also have stored the precious talisman of a people, to say nothing as yet of its Copper Mountain. Furthermore, Aino's aged suitor reappears on the Isle of Man as the rich Fisher King who dwelt beside the river that Lancelot's Sword Bridge crossed; and the aged suitor Väinämöinen also was wounded, as was the Fisher King. Each man also descended into the Underworld where he was ordained priest. Arthurian texts agree their Fisher King was lord-priest of the Grail Castle; and he must die first. Lancelot's Sword Bridge figures prominently in the *Kalevala* as a sword bridge of ax blades.

Certain Celtic scholars noted over the years that the original, prehistoric inhabitants of the Isle of Man were Pictish tribes. Their native giant hammered until he had learned the songs of creation. Arthur too hammered, but on his foes.

The *Kalevala* abounds in abductions of maidens or marriages consummated by force on maidens kidnapped by their suitors. The story of Lemminkainen, who is like King Arthur a Heracles-type hero, tells how entrenched among Finnish virgins was their function as priestess. Another maiden's name was Kyllikki (Runo XII), and she wept all the way to his home where the hero's sledge was carrying her. Their marriage ended by his divorcing her, for she could not forego her ritual dancing in the village with fellow maidens. Such dances around a Maypole were also charged against Joan of Arc in that they proved her, said her English judges, a pagan priestess. Today a statue of Joan stands in Winchester Cathedral.

When suitors journey again to the far north where the choicest maiden lives with her parents in Underworld Pohjola, they learn of a ceremony performed by the Mistress of the Copper Mountain (Runo XVIII). The crone forecasts their arrival and her daughter's future by placing "rowan-faggots" on a log in the fire.

If the log with blood is flowing,
Then the strangers come for battle,
If the log exudes clear water,
Then is peace abiding with us.

When honey oozed from the crone's log, it indicated suitors. The "Mountain Ash, or Rowan Tree, was a sacred tree in Finland as in Scotland," writes the editor (Runo II, n. 29). The herring heroes fish for, adds the editor, "are better known in Scotland and Ireland." Their *sea* means "lake," as in Arthurian texts. Their heroes are dark haired, but their heroines are always blond. The many narrators who recited the *Kalevala* to Dr. Elias Lönrot between approximately 1834 and 1849, some 22,000 verses, knew its adventures had occurred in Finland (Suomi, Carelia, and Lapland), in Russia, somewhere else in the far north, in the Underworld, and on the Island of Women. They remembered many myths common throughout the world—the fountain, the Golden Bough, and the Phoenix, for instance. They honored above all gods the Water-Mother Ilmatar because she had created the universe and the earth. While the narrators did not mention the Isle of Man, they did speak of an Ingerland or Ingermanland. Their journeys westward may have been even easier in prehistoric days. Some geologists believe that during the glacial period an arctic sea called the Yoldia Sea covered southern Finland and Sweden, thus connecting the Atlantic Ocean to the Baltic Sea and White Sea. These geologists note that land in that area is still rising.

The *Kalevala* appears much older, much more primitive than Arthurian literature, however, chiefly because such great respect is offered mothers, the mothers of heroes and maidens alike, but especially to the Mistress Louhi of the Copper Mountain, and to Ilmatar who created earth and the seas. No consideration at all is shown brides or young wives. Marriage by capture obtains in this primitive society as the usual courting maneuver. But when the blacksmith's wife was torn apart by wild animals into which her dairy cows had been metamorphosed, nobody cried. When she sat down on her milking stool, beasts attacked her:

> And the wolf sprang fiercely at her,
> And the bear came fiercely after.
> At her mouth the wolf was tearing,
> And the bear tore at her tendons,
> Halfway through her calves they bit her,
> And they broke across her shinbones (Runo
>   XXXIII).

The summary of the death of Ilmarinen's wife concludes the rune laconically.

> Thus it was the young wife perished,
> Thus the fairest housewife perished.
> Whom the smith so long had yearned for,
> And for six long years was sought for,
> As the joy of Ilmarinen,
> Pride of him, the smith so famous.

Even so, the scene is unforgettably poignant because there were no tears, and the manner of death was so unusual and terrifying. Today, when a similar scene is seen portrayed, sculptured on a Pictish gravestone in Scotland, the connection with the *Kalevala* springs instantly to mind.

Guinevere's function was that of a priestess called Guanhumara, where the first part of her name appears even to be a corruption originally of Diana, so that she is being called Diana plus mara, or mother goddess. As such, her role also would have been to assist in childbirth. The *Kalevala* tells how the pregnant girl was helped into the bathhouse. Then Diana was invoked:

> Noble one, *as gold all lustrous,*
> Thou the oldest of all women,
> Thou the first of all the mothers,
> *Knee-deep in the lake descend thou.*
>
> .   .   .
>
> Free the damsel from her burden,
> And the woman from her sufferings,

> Free her from this grievous torment,
> And release her from her sufferings (Runo XLV).

If these verses mean what they say, then the goddess Diana was represented by an image sheathed either in gold, or in some gold-colored metal such as copper. She is also the Lady of the Lake who rose with Excalibur in her right hand. In any case, young priestesses were copper-belted. When one such tried to repel Ilmarinen's advances, she was turned into a sea mew, or tossed back into the lake, condemned thereafter to struggle, as the priestess in human form had done, and scream and moan. When maidens were wanted by young adventurers, the fellows even embarked on a three-month voyage to some distant island refuge. One hero was very well received in some distant isle like Skye or Man off the coast of Scotland:

> Thus a thousand brides be found there,
> Rested by a hundred widows;
> Two in half-a-score remained not,
> Three in a completed hundred,
> Whom he left untouched as maidens,
> Or as widows unmolested (Runo XXIX).

Another hero arose from the sea as a Pictish dwarf completely sheathed in copper:

> Decked his head a helm of copper,
> On his feet were boots of copper,
> On his hands were copper gauntlets,
> Gloves adorned with copper tracings;
> Round his waist his belt was copper (Runo II).

The tiny man also declared himself a "mighty water-hero," and before the gaze he grew and grew until his head reached the clouds. He it was who had come, like Gawain, to cut from the Druid oak the Golden Bough:

> He who took the branch from off it,
> Took prosperity unceasing,

What was broken from the summit,
Gave unending skill in magic.

Gawain and Arthur's other heroes also sought Golden Boughs and also traversed the seas, sailing alone and in company with younger adventurers. Unlike the *Kalevala,* the Arthurian geography of sea voyages seems limited to crossing the Firth of Forth, lighting beacons along the coasts, journeying to and from the Continent, going from Galloway to the Isle of Man, thence to North Wales.

The Arthurians also knew fortresses decorated with severed heads, for Merlin's Carlisle, so adorned, resembles the *Kalevala*'s Sariola. Both Scotland and Finland have "island refuges" enough for hordes of amorous heroes to descend on by driving their vessels "upon the headlands." The Point of Ayr on the Isle of Man is just such a convenient, sandy headland. Finding brides abroad was altogether much safer for Finnish heroes: for, if a man raped a native maiden from his own family or clan, he was obliged, relates the *Kalevala* (Runo XXXVI), to go into exile for nine years, volunteer for battle if he survived this exile, and if he survived battle, then commit suicide.

When the great hero Lemminkainen was not invited to a wedding in Pohjola, he arrived, like a mythical Merlin, to the feast unbidden, caused a great scandal, and fought a conjuring duel with the master. The magical spells by each shaman demonstrate the importance of animals to the cultural life of the community. This love of animals—which amounts to a belief in their superhuman powers of comprehension and survival in a cold, harsh world—recurs lovingly on the Pictish sculptures of Scotland. Such a trait, or its absence, characterizes a body of literature. Frankish epics, on the contrary, show neither admiration nor appreciation for nature, no love of animals, and a cruel disregard for horses. Thus its verses are easily recognized as typical. The *Kalevala* is worlds apart.

First Lemminkainen conjured up a mighty ox with golden horns. This same creature, the horned ox, said Bayley (1952, vol. 1) in his study of Arthurian symbols, represents the revered Grail Castle itself. The master responded by calling up a wolf to devour the ox: pagan victory over Christianity. Lemminkainen then sang for a white hare, which is the preferred and darling creature of all priestesses worldwide. Then the master conjured up a dog (Pictish hero of the Dog Clan) to devour her, a scene that at least one Scot saw sculptured on Queen Guinevere's tombstone: fierce dogs devouring her (the hare was the priestess Guanhumara). Then other significantly totemic animals were called up: squirrel, marten, fox, hen, and hawk to eat her. The contest ended with the master of Pohjola losing his head.

> In the ground stood stakes a hundred,
> In the yard there stood a thousand,
> On the stakes were heads a hundred,
> Only one stake still was headless.
> Then the lively Lemminkainen,
> Took the head of the poor fellow;
> From the ground the skull he lifted,
> And upon the stake he set it (Runo XXVII).

Guinevere's father Leodagan, or Ogre generally, received a very detailed if repulsive origin in Finland. The Ogre came from the devil's coal fires, his heartstrings and mouth from the horned cow, his brains from a foaming torrent, his intelligence from a cataract, his head from a rotten bean, his eyes from flax seeds, his Toad's ears from birch leaves, his tongue from a spear, his beard from barley, his gums from the Death Maiden Kalma. The Ogre sometimes assumed the guise of a black snake (priest); but Ogre, anyway, is our spelling of Orcus, the Roman god of the Underworld. It is another name for Hades, or Pluto.

Everybody else attended this famous wedding feast in Pohjola, and especially the familiar animals who mostly enjoyed Väinämöinen's music: squirrels, ermines, deer, lynx, wolves from the swamp, and the beloved bear (Arthur) awakened on the heath "from his lair among the pine trees." The forest mistress watched over them as she too listened to the conjuring contest. The birds also assembled: eagles, hawks, ducks, swans, and finches. The Daughters of Creation sat on an arch of air, on clouds, or were the rainbow, weaving golden threads and silver with their combs and shuttles.

Runo XLI goes on to explain Guinevere's comb, or rather, the comb and mirror that symbolize her not merely in Arthurian texts but also in the sculptured stones of Pictland, now eastern Scotland. All the time the sea mermaids,

> Cousins of the reeds on lakeshore,
> At the time their hair were brushing,
> And their locks were deftly combing,
> With a comb composed of silver,
> And with golden brush they brushed it.
> When they heard the strains unwonted,
> And they heard the skilful playing,
> In the waves they dropped the brushes,
> Dropped the comb among the lake-waves,
> And their hair unsmoothed was hanging,
> Nor they smoothed it in the middle.

The same was probably done by Guinevere. When she arrived at the water, which in her recorded instance was a "fountain," she dropped her comb. Thus we understand that from that very moment she became a High-Priestess. All at once she ceased leading a war party and undertook her primary function. She dropped her hitherto useless comb. Like the mermaids from prehistoric Finland, the Pictish Queen Guinevere then tossed her head. She wore her hair thereafter in tangled locks. All priestesses from forever wore their hair in snake locks like those of the blue African goddess, Medusa of the Atlantic Ocean. The Water-Mother Ilmatar, oldest daughter of Creation, also sat on her rock and wept over water, and all the other priestesses wept too, for the beauty of the tormented bride and her deathly bridal music. They also wept because of the theory of history that dominates the *Kalevala:* The present is a time of evil. It is one of the commonest of the common *topoi* of literature: all good old days lie in the past, say most or all ancient epics.

The *Kalevala* is such an epic because its runes are nationalistic in thought and character, lyrical in praise of the motherland. It was assembled over the middle decades of the last century from native singers called *laulaja* or *runoja*. As shaman of his people, Väinämöinen often appears, as Merlin does, controlling wind, weather, and storm and wearing the hawk on his wrist and a fire stick in his right hand. The Finnish poem falls naturally into two parts, which are the conquest of the maiden of Pohjola (Guinevere) and the search from Finland of the lost Sampo (or from Britain, of the Holy Grail). As the octosyllabic alliterative verses end, Väinämöinen has stolen the Sampo from Pohjola. The crone Louhi and her eagle chase him over the seas. Although they overtake him, they break the Sampo. Only one piece is left to be carried back to Finland, for which reason cold, bad times, less food, worse weather, deadlier winters follow, and illnesses are about to decimate a people.

The Finns have been known to history about as long as the Picts have been known, the former early in the second century A.D. named by Tacitus and identified as *Sitones*. The name *Fenni* was also used by classical historians to describe this ancient people residing then along the Gulf of Bothnia, whose allied tribesmen kept arriving in Finland down into the seventh century. They spoke, and still speak, a Finno-Ugric language belonging to the Ural-Altaic family, because these early tribes migrated from Siberia and the Volga River area. Ethnically they are believed related to the Mongolian race. French scholars, like the encyclopedist Beauvois, list them as *Kvens, Tavasts, Carelians,* and *Iugritkot (Ijors)* around the Gulf of Finland. Tacitus took the *Sitones* for Teutons. From ancient times, the Finns faced Russia, however, and not Germany. They mined gold, silver, iron, and copper in Finland and traded primarily with Russia, which they traversed last in their centuries of migrations from Mongolia. If they were also the Picts, then one could expect them to have kept some knowledge of eastern Buddhism.

The ancient Finns were governed by a woman such as the ruler of Pohjola whose maiden was a prime object sought by Kalevalan heroes, just as her most precious Sampo was also the cause of a second long conflict. They were governed by a woman: *Hiiden emoentae,* "a country of Amazons." The word *emoentae* is fairly close to the Hittite *emetchi,* which is Asian for our word

Amazons. It means matriarchal, or "descended through women."

The Anglo-Saxons referred to Finland as *Moegdalund,* "Land of Maidens." The Scandinavians called it *Kvenland,* "Land of Maidens." Today the Norwegians still call the Finns *Kvens* and Finland, *Kvenland.*

According to a religious practice commonly attributed to the Finns of Maidenland, the priestess officiated at an altar. To placate the gods and make her service acceptable in their sight, she required her worshiper to draw blood from some part of his body and offer it on her altar (bed).

When Chrétien de Troyes (c. 1172) writing his *Lancelot,* came across the word *bed* in the material brought him from Scotland by the son-in-law of Eleanor of Aquitaine, he could make nothing of *bed* and *blood* except a story of Queen Guinevere's adultery with Lancelot of the Lake. And so, helplessly, Guinevere was tarred with the disgraceful brush she has forever endured.

But Guinevere was really the malachite Mistress of the Copper Mountain. In other words, she wore what the Provençal poets of southern France also recognized as "the green gown of the Saints"—*"la robe verte des Saints."*

CHAPTER XI

Pictish Sculptures in Scotland

These stones are the national monuments of the Picts, and an astonishing manifestation of their genius. In beholding them and in recognising the details of their apparel and accoutrements we are as near to the Picts as one can be, or is ever likely to be.

—STEWART CRUDEN,
*The Early Christian
and Pictish Monuments of Scotland*

AT THIS POINT IN HER LIFE QUEEN GUINEVERE HAS DROPPED OUT OF THE major narrations of her perils and testings. Acceptable written sources are now lacking, which drives the inquirer in another direction and to other knowledge. The procedure that comes at once to mind is a series of questions: What happened to Queen Guinevere at the fatal battle of Camlan where King Arthur and Modred both died? Had not Lancelot and Gawain died before the battle commenced? Arthur had set out for Scotland, say the Scots, to which he was conveying Lancelot's body for burial. Gawain, it has always been thought, was interred on some sea-coast near Arthur's harbor, or landing place. The next questions follow logically: Are the English accounts, that Guinevere died in an English nunnery, correct? And were the stories endorsed by both Henry de Sully and Gerald of Wales correct? Or are the French officials at Holy Trinity Abbey in Fécamp, then Normandie, correct that Henry de Sully, if he was abbot at both Glastonbury and later at Fécamp, was sadly a propagandist intent on attracting money to his abbeys and promoting tourism, rather than searching for the truth?

The last chapter on King Arthur from the *Vulgate Cycle of Arthurian Romances* (1916) concludes as *The Death of King Arthur* (vols. VI and VII), a death at, or following, the terrible rout of Camlan. That battle used to be situated in Cornwall, England, or at a *camlan* (crooked glen) in Wales; but since the recent discoveries of O. G. S. Crawford in Glasgow in the 1930s, it has also been sought by historians and archaeologists at the Camboglanna fort on Hadrian's Wall, a site easily approached from Carlisle or Brampton, England. *The Death of King Arthur* narration, which follows the *Prose Lancelot,* commences by situating Queen Guinevere, for her own protection, in a nunnery (p. 193 ff.).

King Arthur was obliged to fight his nephew Modred, who was his sister's youngest son by King Loth. Evil gossipers had always preferred to believe Modred was in reality Arthur's own son by his sister, and thus inherently evil because the product of incest. Whether or not Modred is Arthur's son, he will be stamped out anyway by Arthur in person. Modred has been besieging Guinevere in London, we are then asked to believe, which this rather poor concluding text so translates, mistaking, or choosing purposely, *Londinium* (London, England) for *Lodonesia* (Lothian, Scotland). Modred had improbably called up his liege lords from Ireland and Scotland to his aid in London, however, rather than summon them, much more credibly, to Hadrian's Wall on the northern border of ancient Roman Britain. So we have needed a new scenario for Arthur's last stand at Camlan.

It is unlikely that Queen Guinevere trembled at the thought of battle between Arthur and Modred because whoever won would kill her: Modred because he was her enemy; Arthur, because he believed she slept with Modred as well as with Lancelot. How wearisome this last text!

This account continues with the dubious scenario that Gawain had already been slain and was interred near Scotland. Therefore, Guinevere fled to a nunnery in southern England, which had been built and endowed, we are asked to believe, by her Pictish family ancestors. Arthur meanwhile prepared for battle at the Roman fortress of Dover Castle, which is equally impossible because during Arthur's lifetime Dover was firmly held by Anglo-Saxons. Thus, in this poor text all is masterful nonsense and confusion.

There is no notion of ancient geography, and equally no believable scenario: Here, Arthur and Modred wound each other mortally at Salisbury, England, where no such battle ever occurred. If Lancelot also dies in southern England, would he be interred up in northwestern Scotland beside Galehaut and the Scots kings? Was Bedevere not even there to represent his sister Guinevere and throw Excalibur into the Lake, or sea, or loch, or English Channel? This botched account is sometimes ascribed to Walter Map, a courtier of King Henry II. In other words, these Arthurian Annals were also botched—purposely, to bring Arthur down to Glastonbury.

Sir Thomas Malory, another English writer, although a genius, wrote in English a masterful but only slightly less muddled death of Arthur three hundred years later: *Le Morte d'Arthur.* Following Walter Map's lead, Malory also located Arthur and Modred (Sir Mordred) in England, on the Straits of Dover. There he has Gawain die so that his ghost may appear, like the ghost of Hector in Vergil's *Aeneid,* to warn Arthur of impending catastrophe. "Sir" Bedevere is incorrectly present for encounters and battles at Glastonbury, London, Canterbury, and Barham Down.

After Arthur's death, Queen Guinevere (Guenever) again entered her nunnery in southern England, of which (the dead) Modred was king. By now we have heard just about every error, except that Lancelot starved himself to death and was buried at Joyous Gard located improbably at Alnwick or Bamborough instead of on the west coast of Britain. However disconcertingly Malory's geography falls on the eye, his wonderful prose systems nonetheless herald an English language thereafter to be ranked among the greatest literary languages of the world, even equal to the earlier volumes of the French *Prose Lancelot.*

A third famous (or infamous) English account of Arthur's dying tugs the heartstrings even more poignantly. The poet is Alfred, Lord Tennyson, Victorian Poet Laureate. In "Guinevere" (c. 1842) from the *Idylls of the King,* written again some three hundred years after Sir Thomas Malory, Tennyson follows him and Walter Map, shutting Guinevere in her nunnery at Almesbury, England, where Arthur condescends to forgive her sins and bid her adieu:

> She sat
> Stiff-stricken, listening; but when armed feet
> Thro' the long gallery from the outer doors
> Rang coming, prone from off her seat she fell,
> And grovell'd with her face against the floor.

"Do you lie here on the floor?" Arthur asked her. "Well is it that no child is born of thee," he tells her.

> I did not come to curse thee, Guinevere,
> I, whose vast pity almost makes me die
> To see thee, laying there thy golden head
>
> •   •   •
>
> And beauty such as never woman wore,
> Until it came a kingdom's curse with thee—

He would ever have been virgin but for her, he also reminds Guinevere; and because it is his doom, he loves her still. Thus Tennyson wrings it out dry like a twentieth-century soap opera.

In England, Guinevere was always portrayed thus, as all hateful flesh and groveling womankind. She was interred in Glastonbury, also, they said, where King Henry II claimed he had her exhumed and further claimed falsely that her corpse's golden hair, shut inside the sarcophagus for six hundred years, crumbled into dust when it met the outer nighttime air. The claims of

Gerald de Barry, the Abbot Henry de Sully, and King Henry II have long been found spurious and politically motivated: Declaring Arthur dead rendered his Scots and other Celts no longer a threat to an English sovereign.

Our first set of questions can now be answered: (1) we still do not know what happened to Queen Guinevere at the time of the fatal battle of Camlan where both King Arthur and Modred died; (2) the English accounts that Guinevere died in a nunnery inside England are false, and particularly so because southern England was then being overrun by pagan Saxons; and (3) propagandists inside England during the reign of King Henry II fabricated false testimony concerning the end of both Arthur and Guinevere. Therefore, the sparse texts we have are all largely incorrect. That made no difference to the writers involved or to the false witnesses. Whom could it concern? None but a Scot. We must now come back to square one and our first questions, for the plot thickens and interest mounts. Who was the Scot? And who else was aroused?

After we hear his voice, and read his words, we shall have to follow the others, pilgrims all on the road to Guinevere's grave. The historian of Scotland will have led us to our answers, and we shall finally know what happened to Queen Guinevere after her own people from Pictland recovered her person. And we also shall be able to visit her grave. The thought is comforting.

For even murder will out, they say, and somebody from somewhere was bound to raise a voice in protest. It was a scholar, a lone Scot personally safe at the University of Paris, one Hector Boece, in the sixteenth century, who challenged the Englishmen: Walter Map, his King Henry II, their Abbot Henry de Sully at Glastonbury's Benedictine Abbey, Sir Thomas Malory in the 1500s, and the unborn Alfred, Lord Tennyson in Queen Victoria's nineteenth century. Nobody should be surprised at what happened to the lone Scot's dissenting, academic voice. Hector Boece, like Geoffrey of Monmouth in Walter Map's day, was branded the worst of liars.

Anyone who challenged the established view of King Arthur's history rapidly became a nonperson. Hector Boece has suffered his ignominy along with Geoffrey of Monmouth's contention that King Arthur fought at Dumbarton, Scotland, and vacationed four miles away, on Loch Lomond, afterward.

While studying at the august University of Paris itself, Hector Boece wrote in 1527 the two-volume *History and Chronicles of Scotland.* It was retranslated, while Tennyson was gearing up to depict his "groveling Guinevere," in Edinburgh by John Bellenden in 1821. The work was well known in Britain as well as on the Continent by 1544.

Boece tells how princes in Arthur's day were educated, like King Rion (Urien), *on the Isle of Man,* how Merlin personally dreamed up the dragon banner for Uther and Arthur, how King Loth ruled the Picts (*Pichtis*), how Pelagius was their contemporary theologian, how orthodox or French Christianity was in a touch-and-go posture then, how King Loth married Arthur's sister or Aunt Anna so that, according to the laws of "Albion," Loth's sons *Modred* and *Walwan* (Gawain) would succeed to a throne. King Loth was Arthur's ally and confederate, claimed Boece, "in this manner: That Arthure suld rejose the crown of Britane during his life, and eftir his deith the sounis of Loth sall succeid." While Gawain continued to serve under Arthur, Modred was betrothed to his ("Gawolane's daughter") because Modred was the greatest of the northern princes of Britain. Modred was "Gawolane's . . . gudfader," in Scotland, under King Conrannus.

King Arthur died, claimed Boece, in the sixteenth year of his empire and during the reign of the Emperor Justinian (483–565). King Rion (Urien) succeeded Conrannus on the throne of Scotland:

> This historie sall have faith with thaim that ar auctouris [authors] thairof; for we know fermelie, that Arthure deceissit in the time of Justinian, Emprioure, quhen the Gothis, Bergundians, Vandalis, and all othir nationis, invadit the Romane empire . . . [then were horrible wars between Goths and Franks, but no mention by historians of Arthur]. Nochtheless, sen we ar set to minnis [diminish] no mannis honour nor fame, we find that Arthure wes, in glore of mar-

cial dedis, na les vailyeant than ony othir princis of Britane, and likit his realme equaly in polecy and riches (p. 83).

Boece ends this chapter by explaining that Arthur chose his successor Constantine by free election.

In chapter XII Boece proceeds to relate Arthur's ending by saying the bad times commenced at the death of King Loth. Modred was immediately kinged (in Pictland), after which he sent word to Arthur to that effect. Arthur replied that King Loth's death dissolved all his old ties (to the Picts). At that news King Rion (Urien) "of the Scots" opted to join King Modred's forces. The final battle of Camlan was joined at the river "with mair cruelte than evir was hard in ony world afore" (p. 86). Which river? The battle was fought in a place "ful of mos and marces" (the moss and marshes of the Forth River at Bannock-burn, Scotland). This place below Stirling Castle was forever a battlefield, everyone knows. The Scots and Picts on that swampy land lost twenty thousand lives. The Britons and Bretons under Arthur lost thirty thousand lives, including King Modred's brother "Walwane" (Gawain). On the morrow King Arthur's camp was laid waste and taken. Boece continues: Queen Guanora (Guinevere) of Britain and her ladies with her, was taken hostage by the victorious Picts; Queen Guanora was carried by the Picts to "Dunbarre" (Dunbar) Castle (not on the headland east of Edinburgh, but on Barry Hill); her sepulcher is today in the town of Meigle, Boece added, which is in Scotland, "ten miles from Dunde" (Dundee). Boece gives Church records as a principal source, naming Turgot, Bishop of St. Andrews, Scotland.

This astonishing news from Scotland via the University of Paris, sent a shrill contradictory message still heard by all persons interested in knowing the truth about the battle of Camlan in 542, about King Arthur, and even about Guinevere herself. That she, but not Arthur, should have a tomb and a monument in Scotland could not fail to send eager researchers there. The ancient Welsh *Triads* insist Arthur had no grave, probably meaning that his bones, or relics, were distributed among the allies. But that there should be any grave, much less a sepulcher for the queen, struck a common chord among all born genealogists. As Sir Walter Scott explained,

> The Highlanders are as zealous of their rights of sepulture as may be expected from a people whose whole laws and government, if clanship can be called so, turned upon the single principle of family descent.

What was true of gravestones and monuments for the Highland Picts was no less true for their allied Scots from Ireland, both peoples swearing by square stones, coronation stones, and fatal stones: "The Scots in place must reign / Where they this stone shall find." The greatest *cromlech* in Ireland, wrote John Toland, was once a circle of twelve obelisks on a hill in Brefin "all covered with gold and silver," "the lesser figures on the twelve stones about it being only of brass." One stone in Brefin was called "Golden Stone," or *Clochoir*. They "became the prey [of] Christian Priests."

No sooner were Hector Boece's words written, declaring there was both grave and gravestone for Queen Guinevere, that it was being preserved and standing still in the old Pictish town of Meigle, Scotland, than the trek of the specialists to Meigle began. Boece finished his studies in Paris meanwhile and took a position at the University of Aberdeen near where St. Columba had founded Deer, and the *Book of Deer* was written only a few decades after Guinevere's death. Historians say that by 1544 everybody interested in King Arthur knew about Guinevere's gravestone and where it was. Boece's contemporary the king's antiquarian John Leyland (c. 1506–1552) was all agog for antiquities, as was William Camden (1551–1623), the queen's antiquarian. The Camden Society at those dates actually started publishing historical documents from ancient Britain but unfortunately, no *Northern Annals*.

William Shakespeare himself went to Scotland, and if so, to Glamis Castle, and if there, to Meigle, in 1589, it has been said by an early biographer named Knight. It was Charles Knight who published *William Shakspere. A Biography* (London, 1843; New

York, 1971) in which he asked in chapter VIII: "Did Shakspere Visit Scotland?" Knight traced his question back to 1599 when it was asked by William Guthrie, historian of Scotland. Guthrie was seconded at once by Archbishop Spottiswood, renowned historian of the Church of Scotland. Shakespearean players, it seems, under King James VI, certainly visited Scotland in December 1599; "Shakspere" was probably among them, agreed the Archbishop. The playwright's presence inside Scotland, where he verified his Macbeth material, was studied next by Rev. James Scott, who found earlier Shakespearean players there, in fact, as of June 3, 1589. In London (1818) to study the Annals of Aberdeen, William Kennedy also came to assert that the Shakespeare dramatist certainly visited that ancient, northern capital of the Picts, probably in 1601.

Charles Knight expanded his proof that Shakspere himself was really in Aberdeen in 1601. Otherwise, how could the playwright have included in *Macbeth* so much current information about political events of 1601, "topographical knowledge" of the Pictish country around Perth and Meigle, and detailed accounts of the numerous witchcraft trials in ancient Pictland?

John Anderson, another Scot, also endorsed Knight's proof, adding that he had found in 1828 in Macbeth's castle in Inverness papers demonstrating the "extreme accuracy" of things Scottish in the *Macbeth* play attributed to Shakspere, or to Shakespeare. Not only did the playwright speak correctly of Elgin, Forres, Nairn, Glamis, and Perth, "the minuteness" of this topography, he continued (1971, 426), sounded like "individual, local knowledge." Both *Macbeth* and *Othello*, he found, are full of "Scotticisms." Whoever he was, the playwright knew Pictland.

Why should this most famous dramatist of all time not have accompanied his troupe to Scotland and there added to what the English chronicler Holinshed had written about the Pictish Lord Macbeth, his Lady Macbeth, and the murdered King Duncan of Scotland? The trip on foot, added John Anderson, could not have taken more than ten or twelve days, "Richmond to Edinburgh."

In 1945, however, this question of the dramatist in Scotland took a much more serious turn. Then the proof broadened to include *Hamlet* most particularly. In 1945—and, in fact, from boyhood to his grave—the greatest of modern Renaissance scholars, Professor Abel Lefranc at the Collège de France for thirty-six years, dropped a bomb. Abel Jules Maurice Lefranc (1863–1952) identified the platform said to have been at Elsinore Castle in Denmark, as the real platform in Edinburgh Castle in Scotland. And among many other pieces of equally intriguing evidence, Lefranc identified Hamlet as King James VI.

Thus, it has made a difference whether the researcher sought an illiterate "Shakspere" as *Macbeth*'s dramatist, or some other person such as the noble William Stanley, whose coat-of-arms was *"Shake Speare,"* and who was the patron of the troupe of actors, said Lefranc.

Shakespeare wrote *Macbeth* in about 1606. And Macbeth's wife, say the Scots, was Pictish queen Gruoch, who centuries earlier had endowed the Monastery of Deer for St. Columba. And *Macbeth* is a Pictish tribal name: *MacBede,* "Son of the Dog Clan." Shakespeare's Macbeth killed King Duncan in 1040 and died in about 1058. He was Thane of Glamis Castle. Glamis is a mere couple of miles from Guinevere's monument in Meigle, somewhat too Gothic, and too far from the living, Scott quipped, and too near the dead. But the plot continues to thicken because Guinevere's monument is said to have been funded by an even earlier Lord Macbeth, Thane of Glamis. It was Macbeth's Pictish queen, however, whose claim to the throne of Scotland was stronger than her husband's. And among very ancient royal personages names always alliterate: the Burgundian Gundobad, Gifeca, Gislhere, Guíki, Gernot; and the Pictish or Finnish Gunnhild, Graoch, Gruoch, Guinevere, Guanhumara, Guanora, Ganora, etc. (Olrik, p. 44).

By 1560 the word from Boece had gone out and spread abroad so fast that a Henry Sinclair identified as "Dean of Glasgow" or as "Archdeacon in Glasgow" journeyed to Meigle, a Pictish town within the Bishopric of Dunkeld. He went to Meigle to see the "Thane of Glamis Stone" that had been so well set at some ancient time that it was still standing upright in the midst of a dense forest. The stone was beautifully sculptured. On it

GUINEVERE MONUMENT.
Side I.

GUINEVERE MONUMENT.
Side II.

Sinclair made out real pictures, such as "a goddess in a cart" (Chrétien's text is called *Lancelot, or the Knight of the Cart*), two horses drawing her, horsemen sculpted under her figure, footmen accompanying her as outriders, dogs flanking them, hawks (merlins), and serpents (snakes represent priests or priestesses). It was called the "Thane of Glamis Stone" because a Macbeth, Thane of Glamis Castle nearby, had commissioned it in memory of the "goddess."

Local tradition repeated that the goddess had in life been one of the "two terrible Ladies" of Meigle, the second of whom was Shakespeare's Lady Macbeth. Before that second lady forced Macbeth to kill their King Duncan, she cried words that would as well have become Guinevere in hell:

> Come, thick night,
> And pall thee in the dunnest smoke of hell,
> That my keen knife see not the wound it makes,
> Nor heaven peep through the blanket of the dark,
> To cry, 'Hold, hold!'
>
> (*Macbeth*, I, v, 48)

Shakespeare took this plot from Raphael Holinshed's *Chronicle* of 1577 where the terrible Lady Macbeth of Meigle was also terribly portrayed. The words of the three weird sisters Macbeth had met on a blasted heath encouraged him to murder King Duncan and seize the throne of Scotland, Holinshed wrote, "but speciallie his wife lay sore upon him to attempt the thing, as she that was verie ambitious, burning in unquenchable desire to beare the name of a queene." Holinshed's source was our same Hector Boece.

The *Macbeth* edited by William J. Rolfe (1885) shows the famous actress Mrs. Siddons dressed in magnificence as the tragic Lady Macbeth and shows also King Malcolm's sculptured gravestone at Glamis Castle, which is (or was, because its upper corners had been excised) very similar to the stone Henry Sinclair saw at Meigle in 1560.

A hundred years later the report of a magnificent, sculptured stone at the small country town of Meigle was collected by a James Kirkwood, as follows:

Queen Vyonar [Gwenhwyvar] wife to Arthur King
of the Britans about the year 500 falling into Disgrace on Suspicion of Adultery was condemn'd to be
torn by Dogs; but escaping she fled into Scotland
dying on a Hill of Stormond (where she had liv'd
some time) she was buryed at Meigle in Perthshire.
About three miles from the Hill, where she is buried
there is a Stone higher than a man with her *picture and
dogs tearing* in one side, and on the other men pursuing
her. There's an other Grave stone where her servants
were—her Servants were buried.

Macfarlane's Geographical Collections repeats anonymous seven-
teenth-century reports also alleging sculptured stones in Scotland, of remarkable aspect:

the Stones at Meigle cut with several Figures and
Hieroglyphicks said to be the Burial-place of Queen
Vandora, who had her Dwelling three miles North
upon a Hill called Barray. The Ruines yet remain,
and shew it to have been a huge Building of stone.

One of the most famous persons to visit Meigle in the eighteenth century was the poet Thomas Gray (1716–1771), in 1765;
he was made professor of modern history and languages at Cambridge University in 1768. In the second volume of his correspondence, he wrote in September 1765 (1935, vol. II, 891–892):

We set out then the 11th of Sept: & continuing along
the Strath [valley] to the West pass'd through Me-
gill, where is the tomb of *Queen Wanders, that was riven
to dethe by staned-horses for nae gude, that she did.* so the
Women there told me, I'm sure. thro' Cowper of
Angus; over the River Ila, then over a wide & dismal
heath fit for an assembly of Witches.

Gray's editors provide notes to say the famous graveyard poet
traveled south to the large town of Cupar Angus, that Meigle is

a small market town in Perthshire, about five miles from Glamis
Castle:

> The largest of the remarkable group of sculptured
> stones at Meigle, 8 ft. high, is reputed to commemo-
> rate the death of Guenevere [*sic*], King Arthur's un-
> faithful Queen, whose name in the north took the
> form of Wander, Guanora, or Vanora. It is said that
> she was imprisoned on Barry Hill in Alyth parish,
> distant three miles from Meigle. . . . Hector Boece
> gives a full account of the Meigle tradition. Bellen-
> den, translating him, says that all women abhor the
> stone, "and specially the sepulture of Guanora, as the
> title written thairupon shawis—all wemen that
> stampis on this sepulture shall be ay barrant but
> [without] ony fruit of their womb, sicklike as
> Guanora was." (Reported to Gray's editors by Sir
> Herbert Maxwell.)

The famous traveler Thomas Pennant passed through Meigle before 1776. He took the trouble to inquire of people there
what Guinevere's original burial had been:

> It is reported that her grave was surrounded by three
> Stones, in form of a triangle, mortised into one an-
> other. Some of them have holes and grooves for that
> purpose, but are now disjointed and removed to dif-
> ferent places.

Pennant was so much disappointed there that he decided
finally there was "no genuine tradition" of Guanora at Meigle.
Macbeth did not die near the tumulus in the Meigle churchyard,
as sometimes claimed locally. He fell in battle many miles away.
There were no Pictish monuments at Arthurstone, which was
merely an estate so named by its owner, a Mr. Murray charged
to preserve the Meigle monuments. His ownership of property
there dated only from 1637.

In 1793 Sir Walter Scott saw the tomb of "Guenever" during
his visit either at the home of a Mr. Patrick Murray of Simprin,

or in the village of Meigle itself. Patrick Murray still resided in "Arthurstone," as he had named it; that name has occasioned ever since much useless searching for an Arthur monument there. Scott spent the night in merriment with a party of young bachelors. Next day or so he visited "Glammis," resident of the earls of Strathmore, and spent an "eerie night" in the castle. He seems not even to have seen the Guinevere monument or not to have paid attention to her tomb.

A far better observer was Alexander Campbell in 1802, who set out from Edinburgh northward to study the Highlands. At the confluence of the Isla and Tay rivers, near the village of Alyth, he wrote (1802), the Castle of Barryhill once stood. Its remains were still visible. This stronghold was said to have been the place of confinement of the "celebrated British Helen, *Vanora* who by some writers was called Wanor and also Guinevar, the wife of *King Arthur* of fabulous record." ("Helen" or "Elen" is the usual name of ancient Welsh queens.)

"A sepulchral monument, supposed to have been that of *Vanora,* is to be seen in the church-yard at Meigle" (Campbell 1802, vol. I, 297). Campbell's excellent account and eyewitness report went on to compare the many Roman and Pictish ruins thereabout with Tacitus and Boece. He left Meigle for Perth, passing through Shakespeare's Birnam Wood where he sadly saw few of the ancient trees still standing. Perth was the original "Bertha," he noted, where at the confluence of the Almond and the Tay rivers, the Roman dead from Agricola's victory were interred. When Campbell called Guinevere "Wanor," he followed Scottish tradition correctly. The Scottish *Lancelot of the Laik* of 1478 or 1490 had called her "Wanore" and "Vanore."

Robert Chambers from Edinburgh also reported at considerable length in 1827:

> A few miles above Cupar-Angus, the little parish town of Meigle is worthy of a visit, on account of some antique monuments in the churchyard, which the common people assert to denote the grave of Queen Vanora, the unworthy wife of King Arthur. . . . The tradition upon which the common-people

found their theory is very distinct, and the monuments which remain are unquestionably of such a character as might have marked the tomb of an early queen. (p. 378)

Chambers puts what else he learned in a long footnote (pp. 378–79), probably relegating it to small print because he considered it so unspeakable: Queen Vanora's lover was defeated. She removed to a hilltop called "Banna, near Meigle." Soon afterward she went hunting in the forest where she was "attacked and torn to pieces by dogs, which ate every part of her, except the right hand that had committed so many iniquities."

It is quite true that one of the sculptured stones now at Meigle actually depicts a human body being devoured by dogs. But Chambers continued that it struck him as peculiar that "if there was nothing of the queen left but her hand" why such pains would have "been taken to commemorate the place where that member was buried." The Meigle girls take great care not to walk on her grave for fear of not being able to "have any children." The enemies of Arthur much enjoyed, like the Anglo-Saxon translator Layamon, taunting him about a barren queen.

Modern scholarship, armed with the financial and moral support of the Spalding Club in 1856, supplied with the Bellenden translation of Hector Boece, and disposing of time and leisure for travel and observation, entered the Meigle monument question in 1856. That year John Stuart published his scholarly study *Sculptured Stones of Scotland,* which he compiled and edited for the distinguished gentlemen who were sponsoring him. Their Secretary Stuart pictured and described 150 Pictish sculptured stones, plus 40 fragments thereof. He found 75 such stones unaltered from prehistoric times and several others with later Christian crosses. Boece (1821) had noted that engraved images on the Pictish monuments, dragons, wolves, and other beasts, had been sculpted "to put the deides of nobil men in memore." Stuart reminds his sponsors that both Genesis 35:20 and Samuel record pillar stone memorials for illustrious dead.

The symbols carved on the stones, Stuart concluded, were

not Roman because *they are to be found only in Scotland.* They were also earlier than Christianity but sometimes modified to acknowledge the new, Christian faith. John Toland (1670–1722) had claimed the same for Irish (Pictish) monuments. Even so, the crosses in Scotland are unique, unlike such in Wales and Ireland. Only a few similar symbols, such as mirror, comb, and scissors, are found, either in the Catacombs in Rome, or in Greece as emblems of priestesses (found by Lord Aberdeen prior to 1818), or on Princess Anna's monument of 1543 on the island of Iona. Stuart (1867, xiii–xiv) concluded:

> The only influence which remains seems to be that most of the symbols were peculiar to a people on the north-east coast of Scotland, and were used by them at least partly for sepulchral monuments.

As for the Guinevere, or Guanora, monument itself, Boece had stated that separate "stones" formed it, as they did many such monuments inside eastern Scotland. Guanora's monument was by far the most "elaborate and remarkable" of any such sepulcher.

Boece had certainly heard a version of Arthur's last stand at Camlan, which brought about the king's death. Then many nobles, both men and women, and Queen Guanora first of all, were taken prisoner. They and a large plunder fell to the share of the Picts. The battle had been fought, Boece had read, in England on the banks of the Humber River. The Picts journeyed back into northeastern Scotland, or Lancelot's Angus, with their captives and booty. They lodged the queen and prisoners not in Dunbar Castle east of Edinburgh, but at "Dunbarre, now Barry Hill," two or three miles from Meigle. The queen was interred at Meigle in a grave that the "local women abhor." They will not even look at it. A hundred years later (1987), they are proud of it.

Chroniclers disagree as to all this and including Lancelot. Some have him miss the battle of Camlan because he was in France (being translated, probably from Old French), or because he wanted to rescue a sex-starved Guinevere and take her home to Angus. Some agree with the historian from Glasgow Joannes

Major, that Lancelot had been killed at the first of the several separate engagements called the Battle of Camlan, and his body was sent home to Angus, Scotland, for burial or was being escorted by Arthur on the way there. This would bolster O. G. S. Crawford's finding, that Modred caught Arthur as he attempted to cross Hadrian's Wall into the Highlands. The Camboglanna Fort above its deep river that protects it on the two sides of a triangle, facing southwest and southeast, would have been Arthur's logical crossing point. Once north of the Wall he could have made straight for Stirling by forced march.

John Stuart is much obliged to Henry Sinclair for the first and only close description of Guanora's monument, and for one made, as Stuart emphasizes, "little more than forty years after the publication of Boece's History." Sinclair was also the first to connect her stones with a Lord Macbeth at Glamis Castle. What he saw was Guanora's Monument at Meigle, Stuart concluded, "without a doubt" (p. 23). There Stuart found a description of the monument written hardly more than forty years after the publication of Boece's Chronicle, and yet Boece's tradition is not given, but a different eyewitness observation that links the stones to their commissioner, who was—like Macbeth—a Thane of Glamis Castle. Thus from a concordance of opinions Stuart theorized: a cross formed the upper part of her sculptured stone; Sinclair said her monument consisted of two stones; then the one cross probably formed an apex; below the cross was a "goddess" drawn in a cart; and below the "goddess" were horsemen, dogs, hawks, and serpents (which remain in broken pieces of stone).*

Before looking at the Guanora Monument as it stands in Meigle today (1989), we should also consider the observations of Stuart Glennie (1869). This genial scholar's *Arthurian Localities* has given great impetus to historians of Dark Age Britain. The Pictish memorials, he stated firmly, come from a separate territory inside Great Britain, and this well-defined territory and the ancient Picts who once dwelt there in virtual isolation are now being recognized by historians. King Arthur made close allies of them

---

*Stuart (1867) refers his reader to his plates LXXVI, #6; LXXVI, #1; 72, 77, 93, 127—and in that order. Stone crosses are on plates 53, 54, and 55.

from his own separate and distinct territory in what is now called Borders or Lowlands or southern Scotland (south of the Glasgow-Edinburgh, or Clyde-Forth line).

Anyone who wishes to verify this hypothesis, adds Glennie, is welcome to travel into Scotland and observe the geography for himself. He will probably also conclude that the natural terrain has shaped the country and must have dictated its history in the days before easy and rapid communication other than by beacons, birds, runners, and word of mouth.

The literatures from this ancient land are considered treasures by the whole world and have been so considered for long centuries since the introduction of writing and translations: (1) the Arthurian corpus, which is the largest single body of literature in the world, and (2) the works of Fingal and Ossian, which also testify to the living traditions of the Pictish peoples (Stuart thought them and theirs a "kindred, Celtic race and language"). The titanism and "passion" of these bodies of literature mark them as both Celtic and foreign, as unique, but also as strange and, therefore, Pictish, as does the "piercing regret" that stabs the heart for Guinevere, for the British Arthur, for Lancelot, for Arthur's half-sister Morgan le Fay, for the Lady of the Lake, but most of all, for the great Celtic religious leader who is still familiarly known as "Merlin."

Scotland and the Pictish Alba, or Albanach, were also the motherlands of the Pictish peoples, identifiably "white" as their women were white armed, white browed, as their mountains were white with snow, as their priestesses were Guanhu-mara, White Goddess. Their mythology differs from many others: It is topographical. The land they died preserving century after century was the eastern coasts of Ireland and Scotland. The Picts were a sea people. They had fled there from overseas. They had no choice but to resist and cling to this last, rich, and northern motherland.

Therefore, Glennie, whose Arthurian geography is the most extensive ever made of those realms, had to visit Guanora's grave in Meigle and had to study her monument. People commonly reported to him, said Glennie (1869, 38), that Guinevere was "drawn" and quartered by horses. They told me, he said, she had been devoured by wild beasts. But Archdeacon Sinclair of Glasgow, in his rare manuscript of the year 1560, clearly states that he saw Guinevere depicted as a goddess: "Ane goddess in ane caert and twa hors drawand her." He went on record, as a clergyman, to that effect.

Glennie went himself to this scene of Guinevere's last resting place. He looked, said Glennie, and frankly had *no sense of hideous catastrophe,* but saw depicted by the sculptors "something less rude, some nobler version of her story." Thus art is beholden to the beholder's eye.

Stuart Glennie arrived in Meigle toward the close of autumn, he testified, along the wide valley of Strathmore and past the wheat fields in stubble. It was sunny and warm there in the lee of the Siddaw Hills. Nobody could imagine that the cold North Sea was just over the brow. The countryside wafted about its own memories of King Duncan, the murderous Macbeth and his heir Banquo. On either side he saw this rich farming country that had welcomed back its own Pictish Queen Guinevere, and built for her a sculpted memorial that outlasts contumely and time itself. He measured with his eye the grain stacked high in the neighboring barns. He watched the yellow leaves drop softly to earth in Guanora's own churchyard, "through the sunny air; and beneath the lofty range of the snow-capped Grampians, lay the dying year in the beauty of ineffable repose" (p. 38). The great queen slumbered there softly and in peace.

Like other travelers, Glennie had come to Meigle's little churchyard via Cupar Angus, which still treasures Arthur's standing stone, past the estate called Arthurstone, past the neighboring farm called Arthur's Fold, and below the rock on the north hill of Dunbarrow, another Arthur's Seat less spectacular than the Edinburgh volcano so-called Arthur's Seat.

Let us make a new attempt henceforth, Glennie requested of travelers to Meigle, of authors, and of scholars. Can we not be more generous? Before 1850 all our work *in re* King Arthur was "analytic and destructive." After 1850 let it now become "synthetic and reconstructive" (p. 1). Can we not be less prejudiced? Let us now commence looking at all the evidence: popular records, folk memories, local traditions, legends, and romances.

They will lead us where we have up until now failed to go: into the real history.

The old "Arthur-land" was always southern Scotland, *if we could only admit it*. But future scholarship, all the new discoveries concerning Arthur and Queen Guinevere, lie buried here in the North. Modred and Guanora beckon from there, from northern Scotland.

Scotland in its northern region, or Highlands, predicted Glennie, will become a New Hellas as has happened before whenever poetry launched a renaissance. Homer's *Iliad* and *Odyssey* inspired classical Greece. The Pictish sculptured stones, which tell the story of the Arthurian heroes, but especially that of Queen Guinevere, will eventually launch a renaissance of Celtic peoples from this homeland they conquered and held after intermarriage with the Picts. Their art is dynamic, said Glennie:

> And, if I am right . . . the country in which . . . Celtic legends had . . . their historical origin, . . . in which, particularly, the Arthurian traditions have been shown . . . to have originated, at least . . . to have now their most numerous, and complete, their most scenically various, and romantic topographical records, will become a New Hellas. (p. 124)

Thus Strathmore, Cupar Angus, the Tay River, Guanora's Grave in the Meigle churchyard, and Modred's Castle on Barry Hill near Alyth together constitute King Lancelot's realm of the White Land, *Albanak, Alba,* or *Albany*.

From Glennie's list of Arthurian localities in this Eastern Division, which is Strathmore, Scotland, we understand that Queen Guinevere probably was escorted to Modred's fortress on Barry Hill after the rout of Camlan. And she was probably joined there by her brother, Bedevere. In any event, she would not have returned to her own birthplace at Stirling because it had not been governed by native Picts since her betrothal to King Arthur. Dunbarre and Meigle were, on the contrary, secure seats of Pictish lords, her heirs and Modred's. Furthermore, Dunbarre was also very probably the holy house to which the False Guinevere had been exiled, for her safety also, at the wedding of her twin sister. Twins usually argue endlessly, for fun if not seriously, over which takes precedence because of having been delivered first. The Queen Guinevere was most certainly recognized as her father's legitimate child because she first saw the daylight, or emerged first from the birth canal. Finally, both Guineveres (the sick and the well) were in reality loved, honored, protected, and carefully guarded by the Picts because theirs was a matriarchal society.

The 1970 edition of *Fodor's Scotland* contained a small reference to Queen Guinevere's monument in Meigle, adding the usual injunction about young women not treading on her grave so as not to become barren and that Guinevere was an evil, adulterous woman. Subsequent years must have discontinued even this unpleasant allusion. In any case, it had been altogether deleted from the 1987 *Fodor's Scotland.* By these years Glennie's hopeful projections had not come to pass. Oblivion had set in even more darkly.

In 1987 during summer research in Scotland I remembered the name *Meigle,* looked on a map and drove from Callender to Cupar Angus, thence to Meigle.

At the green gate of Mrs. Eileen Eaton my party was granted permission to accompany her across to the churchyard. The lady unlocked the door to a small museum there in the churchyard. She said the women of Meigle with their small personal savings had finally managed to place Queen Guinevere's funeral monument inside a building where it would be protected from the elements, especially rain and mold that over the centuries had eroded the lovely sculptures. She showed us other priceless sculptured stones stacked up outside, under the eaves, completely at the mercy of the elements.

Nothing had prepared us for the beauty of Guanora's Monument. The color strikes the viewer first and the immense lofty size of the sculptured stone. The huge cross encircled with bosses draws the eye, which has delighted during the first minutes in the soft, rose-colored, grainy-textured stone, like red desert sandstone in the American West that reverts to sand itself when heavy rain falls on it.

Guanora's pink stone rises as the eye looks upward to the wonderful, queenly cross, and the viewer's head lifts up and up to grasp it all, and up until the head goes over backward with the cross following as it appears to rise and plane through the air. Sculpture has a terribly strong physical effect on the viewer when it is great art. Guanora's Monument is art so great the viewers are left speechless.

We prowled about under the great stone. Mrs. Eaton spoke to us all the time, ceaselessly, in her lilting, high-pitched, sweet Highland voice. As a trained linguist I noted her intonation and wished I had paper to reproduce these traces of Pictland in international phonetic symbols, but the symbols on Guanora's Monument cried louder with the story of Queen Guinevere's life. "I am here," they said. "I am here."

These symbols must end her story, which otherwise has no proper ending. The texts claim Gawain died on the beach, then presumably at Arthur's return from an overseas expedition. He surely did not return to the Saxon-held Dover Beach but rather to a harbor in the Lowlands of Scotland. Gawain too had died before the rout of Camlan if his ghost emerged to warn the king not to fight another day. Lancelot had not gone to Gaul, had not betrayed the queen, and must also have died before Camlan occurred, as Scots long ago chronicled. Arthur died or was dying as he was transported by ship to the Grail Castle.

If the queen's monument were not in Meigle, one would have concluded that she spent her last years of life at the Grail Castle, which was a nunnery, and an Isle of Women (Isle of Man) between Scotland and Ireland. But the monument at Meigle is her sepulchral stone and one of the greatest, most thrilling works of sculpture the eye could ever behold. It is her Monument, say eye and heart. It looks right. It was commissioned by a Lord Macbeth for a Pictish queen he adored too, and she was in life a great White Priestess called "goddess."

Today the queen's names are missing on her Monument. Otherwise they would read something like this:

| Ganhumara | Guanhumara | Gwaynour |
| Gaynore | Guanora | Gwenhwyfar |

Geneviere	Guenevvar	Vanora
Genevre	Guenhera	Vennevaria
Genievre	Guenuara	Wanders
Genouer	Guinever	Wenhaver
Ginevra	Guinevere	Wennevereia
Goneoure	Gunnore	

Hector Boece may have been right after all. He said the queen was returned safely to the Highlands and, after Modred's death, was entrusted to the custody and care of the Scottish king named Rion-Eugenius, who was Modred's ally. Boece does not say whether this King Eugenius was the same King Rion of the Moray Firth, or the Urien to whom the heiress Guinevere had originally been betrothed.

Guanora's Monument is rich in symbolism, adorned with incised or deeply sculptured pictures. They need a study by themselves, for they may give us the solution to her life and her last days.

CHAPTER XII

The Guinevere Monument
at Meigle

This . . . points to the village of Meigle where
there is an outstanding collection of Pictish stones,
the largest of which has a figure surrounded by
four lions. I call it the *Guinevere Stone.*

—DAVID MACLEAN EATON,
*"Was Queen Guinevere
Buried in Scotland?"*

OUR KNOWLEDGE OF THE ANCIENT PEOPLES OF BRITAIN NEEDS BOTH COR-
rection and expansion, implied contemporary American author
and editor Barry Fell. The Celts, as he discussed (1976, 232ff.),
venerated a "Mother-of-Heroes," whose name was *Byanu,* a
name perhaps modified to *Guanhumara.*

The Celts generally held two divinities above all others,
the sun god Bel "and the great Mother Goddess, the goddess
may not be the second but the first," added Fell. He continued:

If I am correct in assigning the era of Celtic incursion into America to around 800 B.C., then we must admit that by this period the European Celts had transferred to the male of the human species the honor that had formerly been accorded to the female (p. 234).

After that date, he concluded, woman became the mother, not of *her* children, but of *his* children. This would explain why Julius Caesar in his *Gallic Wars* dared not enslave Celtic women, and why, after the men had died in battle, he proceeded to the slaughter of all survivors.

During Guinevere's day in northeastern Scotland, women still retained some vestiges of power and respect that remained from their ancient matriarchy. In Ireland also, some used that last power to escape bondage by entering the priesthood.

A career in the priesthood was still available in Scotland as an alternative to literal motherhood. Like her near contemporaries Saint Bridget in Ireland, and Saint Geneviève in Paris, Guinevere chose lifelong virginity and the priesthood. After a brief period as queen of France, Queen Radégonde of France also entered the Christian Church as a priestess. Furthermore, she was Queen Guinevere's contemporary.

Both scholars Squire and O'Rahilly agree with Fell that the syllables *Anu, Ana,* and *Danu, Byanu,* and *Guanhu* refer to individuals so-named as a "universal mother" (Squire 1975, 50–51). These names correspond to that of Ireland's earth goddess, another Demeter, who earlier in Greece and Rome was also mother of the gods, guarantor of agricultural prosperity, and consort of *Bilé* or *Bel,* god of the Underworld. When Guinevere is recognized not only as King Arthur's honored consort whose priestly powers must constantly be tested and corroborated by one ceremony of public testing after another, from season to season according to the calendar of dead of winter, sowing, reaping, and another winter, then her life story ceases to be mawkish and pornographic. Then it becomes awesome. The contemporary Irish scholar O'Rahilly (1946) supports the conclusions of both Fell and Squire.

The Irish syllable *án,* or *Án,* as the case may be, in a lady's name is also identical, formally and otherwise, with the Latin name of the Roman god *Jānus.* Thus O'Rahilly sends us back to Charles Mills Gayley (1911) of the University of California who has been for almost a century young Americans' guide to classical myths in literature and art. His original companion text to the study of fifth-year, or freshman Latin in college, was first published in 1893 in seven American cities as well as in London. The god Jānus, says Gayley, is far older than classical Rome. He goes back to the days of the ancient, migratory Celts of Italy.

A name with the syllable *án* has to do with a *going,* a passageway, perhaps a door from one interior to another, from our world to Queen Guinevere's Grail Castle of the Copper Mountain. The god Jānus and the priestess Guanhumara face both ways: here and there. She and he would be represented in art like the bearded acolyte Lancelot, as facing both ways, as being two-faced, alive and dead, born and reborn. The door of the Jānus temple in Rome faced east (birth) and west (death). Lancelot crossed the Sword Bridge on the last day of the old year and entered Guinevere's temple during that winter night; for the New Year commenced for the Celts also not in daylight but at the onset or fall of darkness—on November 1. At that moment New Year gifts were offered; Lancelot's offering was a blood communion.

The Jānus temple doors were closed only in times of peace. Guinevere's presence at the high altar on New Year's Night at the Grail Castle, therefore, also signified the commencement of a new war, the beginning of King Arthur's last deadly campaign. Both Gawain and Lancelot—for each sought the abducted Guinevere—would be among the first to die. Then King Arthur, at or as a result of Camlan, would die. Just prior to these tragic events Perceval formally became last King of the Grail Castle. His son, the Swan Knight Lohengrin, would migrate to the Continent. The High-Priestess Guinevere would be escorted safely home to the Pictish Dunbarre Castle near Meigle, Scotland. Her funeral monument is there, still cherished by the local people who must by now have venerated it for at least one thousand, or even fifteen hundred years.

As we know, the Christian Bishopric of the Isle of Man, which was the site of their Grail Castle and Lancelot's crossing of the Sword Bridge, was established by Saint Patrick in the year 447. King Arthur was born in c. 475. Lancelot's descent into Purgatory and his Christian Communion at night before Guinevere's *altar* (not her *bed*) seem to represent, or to occur as a result of the recapture and rechristianization of the Isle of Man by King Arthur, Queen Guinevere who freed his prisoners there, Gawain, Lancelot, and Perceval (Parzival). The Arthurian texts include *Parzival,* which has also recorded this; for as William Schofield said in 1906: Arthurian literature "is the glory of the Celtic race that originated it, the French (and Germans) that gave it shape, the English that adopted it as their own."

What we know of the early Celts, of King Arthur, and of his Queen Guinevere must also be gleaned from such facts, he said, as from their (lost) epics and romances, from their few inscriptions, from their prophecies such as Merlin's, from a study of their customs, from what remains of their languages in the order of their arrival into Western Europe and Great Britain, and only *in that order:* Picts, Britons, and Romans into the period of King Arthur (c. 475–542). Then arrive during his lifetime: Scots from Ireland, Angles from Denmark, and Anglo-Saxons from the northern shores of the North Sea and the Baltic. All northern Celts, said Dom Gougaud (1932), loved nature—fountains, trees, stones, and circles—as they loved their pale sun that gave so little warmth. They adorned their monuments with sun-flashing gold, silver, and copper. They also loved bright music, poetry, bright and beautiful and highly colored raiment, and also their fables, clever riddles, allegories, and witty triadic lore.

The mysterious Picts left only funeral inscriptions and king lists, but no literature unless they were the original authors of the Arthurian material, which is the largest body of literature in the world. Even before Heinrich Zimmer attempted to discover the origins of the Picts (by a system of elimination), an author in Scotland had attempted the same. In the years 1860–1862 John Francis Campbell, whose Gaelic name was Iain Òg Ìle (Young John of Islay) published four volumes of tales, which over the years he had collected in the Highlands of Scotland. These Gaelic romances were taken down in Gaelic as the scholar gained the confidence of shy natives and encouraged them to tell him their stories. Campbell (1860) points out that many of his narrators were illiterate themselves, and born of parents who as far back as anyone knew had always been illiterate. Furthermore, many of his narrators had never left Pictland or the Highlands. The tales they told had been passed down for ages. Their telling was the only entertainment enjoyed evenings by these isolated people.

Then Campbell undertook long journeys throughout the area lying below the Arctic Circle in search of the same stories elsewhere. He went from Spitzbergen in the west, to the North Cape, along the coasts of Norway, then through the Baltic and into the White Sea of Finland. His startling conclusions predate those of Zimmer and ourselves. Many key Gaelic words in the tales, he found, came from Sanskrit and point to the eastern origin of the Celtic nations (vol. I, lvii). Their love for horses and hounds "supports the theory that the Celts came from the east, and came overland; for horses would be prized by a wandering race" (lxxxiii). When they speak of giants, they simply mean "the nearest savage race at war with the race who tell the tales" (xciv). "Gold, silver, and copper abound in the giant's land" (xciv). "I believe there once was a small race of people in these islands, who are remembered as fairies, for the fairy belief is not confined to the Highlanders of Scotland" (xcv). "A Lapp is such a man" living in a fairy mound, "a conical green mound about four feet high." When he stepped through the roof of one such mound one day in the Hebrides, an old woman stuck her head out of the sods that constituted her roof and complained he had come through her ceiling; "the fairy was probably a Pict."

> Lord Reay's forester must surely have passed the night in [such] a Lapp cota on Ben Gilbric, in Suther-land, when Lapps were Picts; but when was that? (ci)*
> Fairies then milked deer, as Lapps do. They lived underground, like them. They worked at trades es-

*Lord Reay is at present (1990) the clan chief of the Clan MacKay.

pecially smith work and weaving. They had ham-
mers and anvils, and excelled in their use, but though
good weavers they had to steal wool and borrow
looms. Lapps do work in metal on their own account. . . .
Fairies had hoards of treasure—so have Lapps.
Fairies are conquered by Christian symbols. They
were probably Pagans, and, if so, they may have
existed when Christianity was introduced. (cii)

Thus the literature of illiterate peoples living in Scotland,
isolated a hundred years ago from the world, indicates, as has
done the Arthurian corpus, that the Picts were originally from
the far north of Europe, even that they came from Finland.

The dashing, mysterious Picts left the world a body of
sculpture incised on rose-colored monuments, which seem to be
funerary in character, that is to say, their monuments can be
understood, like ours, to name the dead. While similar stones
were gold-plated in Ireland for the gods and once stood around
in golden circles on the hilltops and are since long gone, some of
the sculptured memorials of the Picts remain still standing, perhaps not in their original cluster or group of statuary, but standing, at least. Neither are they after all these thousand years
pristine. Some have clearly been reworked. The eyes see that
without difficulty. They must have tempted younger sculptors.

What the eye also sees without difficulty is the Picts themselves, as they represent themselves on their monuments. They
look, indeed, like short people. They wear beards. They wear
hoods over their heads and necks. They ride very fast on horseback, sit on saddle cloths, hold snaffle bits, have no stirrups. They
ride alone, without crops also, like the ancient "horse whisper-
ers" of Scotland, who were once celebrated for their effortless,
whispered control of their mounts. The Picts there ride in threes,
and here in spirited cavalcades, horses and riders at one. Swift,
snappy hunting dogs leap alongside them.

These must certainly be the same Caledonians whom
Agricola defeated but could not conquer because they sped away
at fast trots into their green mounds and the Caledonian High-

lands of central Scotland. They mostly haunted the mountains, appeared like the original "white dwarfs" of the Scottish Grampians, and quickly disappeared.

That's why their contemporary Saint Gildas said c. 500 that the Picts came out like white grubs from their burrows every spring. He thus also correctly identified them as *gnomes,* who are by definition dwarfs or hobbits living camouflaged nearby, in the ground or woodlands. The dwarfs themselves are still popularly said, whether in Norway, Germany, Denmark, Scotland, Switzerland, or the Netherlands, to reside high up on some fairly distant mountain peaks. Folklore has it right. Only look at the Pictish sculptured stones to see once real, live gnomes.

One can also remember what Chrétien de Troyes learned in Scotland about his greatest hero Lancelot (*The* Angus), who was a Pictish ruler. Chrétien said whenever Lancelot rode onto the field of honor, he caused all the men present to cross themselves. Those who were not yet Christian could use some pagan charm for self-protection, such as lift one foot off the ground, or lock the first two fingers, or wish on the moon over the right shoulder, or pray to the Roman goddess Fortune called "Lady Luck." Lancelot could suddenly leap and ride bareback standing on his horse. He could leap from astride his own mount and jump on his opponent's horse. He was hypoglycemic to the point of fainting away before lunch time. He was also strikingly different in his physical conformation: tremendously barrel-chested but short-legged. Throngs of people collected at the fords to see him pass. His charioteer was a dwarf identified finally by Chrétien as a prince.

When Lancelot was described by the authors of the *Prose Lancelot,* that is, when he rode into the ring to defend Queen Guinevere at her judicial trial—and even before that scene when he advanced into King Arthur's Camelot to accept her defense— he was dressed as are the Picts today on their sculptured stones. He wore leggings or well-tailored trews that fitted his lower body and legs tightly. He wore over them a closely adjusted tunic. Over that he sported a superbly woven plaid, which was voluminous and fastened by a metal penannular brooch, doubtless of solid gold, at one shoulder. Down the ages Scots have worn this wool plaid, which is large enough to wrap around the whole body for sleeping on the heather while campaigning. After heavy rain the plaid can be wrung out and worn again at once; it will be almost completely dry.

Twelfth-century writers also thought that the Picts had been small, bearded warriors widely celebrated for metalworking, that they had forged Perceval's sword, that they were Scythians in origin (whatever that meant), that they had come from overseas to settle the northeastern coasts of Ireland and Scotland, that although powerful physically they were short and dark, that they appeared and disappeared quickly, and that they spoke a totally foreign language. The Picts were believed likewise to have educated their royal children on the Isle of Man, which was their safe house and spiritual capital. There is more and more agreement now for this and that once there lived royal Picts.

The Picts resided along the Rhinns of Galloway or north coasts of the Solway Firth, especially up and down both banks of the Nith River, which gave these tribes their topographical name of *Niduari Picts.* Today that, too, is accepted. King Arthur was born there, theoretically at Caerlaverock and the Ford Perilous, and educated close by at Loch Arthur and near the much later Sweetheart Abbey. Arthurian chroniclers and other historians also believed that the Picts tattooed themselves all over their bodies. Scots still say that even today, when the Picts have disappeared into the general population. The *Prose Lancelot* disagreed, however, claiming only that Guinevere herself, the future Queen Guinevere, had a single (identificatory) tattoo on one hip. It is difficult to regard the Picts as negligible savages when one thinks of their feats and looks at their wonderful sculptures.

No modern scholars have had more clues, or been willing to offer any explanation at all, for the fourteen or so strange symbols that appear and reappear on the Pictish stones still being found in eastern Scotland, near where Queen Guinevere was born and to which land she retired after the rout of Camlan. Rev. Charles Rogers (1884) in Edinburgh made, on the contrary, a very interesting and positive contribution. The Picts, he said, were excellent stone masons, for their *brochs* at Abernethy and Brechin, which were Pictish capitals, became prototypes for the later Christian bell towers. To them, a round pebble meant the sun. Saint Columba sent a round pebble to a Pictish king, thus honoring the king and announcing his arrival as "messenger" (angel) of Christ. When one sees cup-marked stones, Rogers observed, one ought to realize that one circle means "sun," that two circles in union indicate "sun and moon." The Pictish crescent symbol, crossed by a zigzag line that ends in a flower (a floriated terminal)—and this combination is one of the commonest of Pictish symbols—means a crescent moon, rising if the terminals point left, and waning if they point toward the right. The commonly repeated symbols of comb and mirror, which Lancelot took to mean "Guinevere Priestess" at the fountain, meant "mermaid's tools," thought Rogers, which is to say, he continued, the divining symbols of a priestess. Thus Guinevere, too, resembles the little mermaid on the rock in Copenhagen harbor, a priestess who could by the use of her comb and mirror, predict the future. She would also have been figured by a serpent symbol, sacred even to ancient African priestesses who were queens of Egypt and who wore armlets of copper or brass coiled three times about the upper arm, weighing two or three pounds and ending with serpents' heads.

Properly, then, Guinevere returned to the Isle of Man when Lancelot was to be ordained at her altar. And properly he arrived for this ordeal after a year of isolation, deprivation, and final instruction; Perceval also passed from one instructor called "Uncle" to another such instructor, and this over a long period of time, *while his mother wept,* before his final ordination, also at the Grail Castle. At such a ceremony, Rogers suggests, Queen Guinevere probably wore garments of white lambs' fleeces, for even today Welsh people remember her when they look up at white, fleecy clouds—which they call Guinevere's clouds. On the windy Isle of Man she would have been very cozy in a white lambskin coat.

What were the Picts thinking of, however, when among their superbly chiseled zoomorphic figures they carved swimming, legless *elephants?* Or have elephants been seen where no elephants were intended? Rogers's question should have been: what did the Picts know about Asian elephants anyway, unless they themselves had once lived in Asia or migrated from the Asian steppes?

Both Malory and Tennyson associated Guinevere with the symbolism of the color green, which was worn by Druid neophytes. In Tennyson's poem "The Mermaid," he has the maid using a pearl comb (the ancient Romans imported their best and most lustrous white pearls from Britain), and singing on her throne in the sea. With silver feet (Druid priestesses always walked with bare feet, because their feet, which would lead warriors into battle, had been consecrated) the mermaid resided beside a "fountain of gold." Although a great sea snake from across the ocean (a Fomorian) loved her with great calm eyes, a king would wed her.

The color green, said Wentz in his book of 1911, symbolizes spring, love, and eternal youth; and Malory associated Guinevere and green with the month of May. But it is also the color of the initiate's final robe. Guinevere perhaps wore green as she left Carlisle with Kay and Arthur's warriors because that was the color of resurrection, of her own rebirth, and of the rebirth of King Arthur's realm.

Queen Guinevere was the High-Priestess King Arthur sought as his bride, one who could counter and overpower the Saxon priestess Camille. And Guinevere commanded the forces that at Dumbarton Rock defeated Camille and liberated Arthur from her magical spell. When white doves were carried before Queen Guinevere at her coronation, they could have symbolized her death-to-the-world and her virginal assumption of the High-priesthood. Doves were present at the baptism of Christ, and the descending dove was mentioned by each of the four Evangelists.

The interlace design found on Pictish monuments, and as seen in Irish manuscript illumination, Logan (c. 1830) thought, derived both of them from the more ancient tree alphabet when twigs were twisted together to send messages (in the Tristan and Isolde stories, the lovers float twisted twigs downstream to communicate with each other). Logan too posited that the frequently recurring crescent also symbolized the moon (goddess), "lady of the white bow." The Pictish crescent is often crossed by a left or

right zigzag ending in floriated terminals (or decorated arrow-
heads). The white bull symbolized Earth, as it did in Greek
Orphic chants. "That stones were erected to mark the burial
places of celebrated men is not to be disputed, and instances have
already been noticed" (Logan, p. 63).

"The erect cross-slabs are" (like Guinevere's Monument in
Meigle), said J. Allen Romilly (1904), "with a few unimportant
exceptions, peculiar to Scotland and the Isle of Man. They are
probably older than the free-standing crosses" or "the high
crosses of Ireland." He lists the best cross-slabs in Scotland, as
follows:

Northern Pictland	*Southern Pictland*
Shetland (1)	Forfarshire (9)
Caithness (1)	Perthshire, which
	includes Meigle (4)
Sutherland (2)	
Rossshire (4)	
Elginshire (2)	
Aberdeenshire (4)	
Kincardine (1)	

In Romilly's second lecture on Christian symbolism he admits
that these sculptured pink sandstones could date from the earlier
"Romano-British Period." "Our knowledge of Celtic Christian
symbolism is, however, derived almost entirely from a study of
the sepulchral monuments and sculptured stones" of the Picts.

In 1945 Francis Carney Diack formulated a complete but
probably untenable theory for the decipherment of Pictish symbols on the cross-slabs and other sculptured stones in Pictland.
The Picts, he decided, were not Irish Gaels but Gauls who spoke
an intermediary Gaelic. The Picts were tattooed completely, over
their whole bodies, for which reason they always went naked.
Their tattoos showed their rank and status, and their personal
symbols were sculptured on funeral monuments after their own-
ers' deaths:

It is no flight of fancy but actual fact that in looking at these "symbols" on our hoary lichen-covered stones we see the very figure that the Romans gazed at with wonder on the white skin of the Caledonians. (p. 28)

The comb and mirror were symbols of the Pictish matriarchy, he continued. The Pictish stones were actually sculptured on the Isle of Man and thence transported into eastern Scotland.

Pictish was, as [W. F.] Skene justly saw, simply the parent of . . . the Scottish Gaelic we know. . . . The Pictish inscriptions alone are sufficient to uphold it.

Before examining the Meigle Guinevere Monument now in light of what Arthurian literature has had to say about Guinevere herself, it seems important to note that the Picts were not, or were no longer, completely tattooed in Guinevere's day. The monument is not a copy of a person's tattoos. And second, the study of Guinevere's life shows us that her people were far more likely to have been non-Aryan than Gauls or Gaels.

Next we should understand or review what we remember concerning the doctrines of symbolism, which as a literary movement led by great authors and poets around 1850–1870 drew up an *ars poetica,* or the formal literary program called Symbolism. For example, a word is a symbol that means what you think it means. Liberty of thought is by this doctrine returned to each individual. By the same token, we are all allowed suddenly to recognize symbols in sculpture, and we may all know, each one of us, what each symbol means. An image appears on stone to remove it from the real, to distance it, and to increase its power.

This modern theory of symbolism differs little from the ancient courses and books on rhetoric (oratory) as taught and written by Quintilian in Rome (A.D. 35–99) and by Cicero. It also differs little from the medieval concept of art and of how to read a book in five stages of increasing difficulty. Christine de Pisan (c. 1364–c.1430), biographer to King Charles V of France, repeated this theorizing for us, and very concisely, in the fifteenth century: (1) literal, (2) figurative, (3) symbolical, (4) allegorical, and (5) anagogical.

Symbolism is, by definition, a sacral art. Symbols themselves were originally the property of the priesthood, as in Guinevere's case. Therefore she could have directed, as Arthurian texts recall, the sculptures she personally ordered for King Arthur's funeral monument. Arthurian texts say she did so. Lancelot saw his own father's monument, his grandfather's, and his own sculptures before Dolorous Gard, in the castle graveyard. On Saint Patrick's Isle adjacent to the Isle of Man, and almost touching its western shore, another graveyard lies beside the Church of Saint Germanus. There once probably stood the same cross-slabs that today impress everyone with their enigmatic symbols in northeastern Scotland. They may very well be the very ones Lancelot removed from the Grail Castle site after Merlin's death, before King Arthur's last campaign commenced overseas, at the time everyone knew the prophesied end of Arthur's world was drawing near.

Plate #75 from John Stuart's *Sculptured Stones of Scotland* shows the front of the cross-slab now standing in the Churchyard Museum building in the small village of Meigle, Scotland; it is locally called Guinevere's Monument (see pages 207, 208). The stone was placed in a museum room built by public subscription to house it safely.

Side I portrays its superb cross first of all, although the upper corners of the monument seem to have been cut away and many of the round bosses are now also missing. The bosses, which make the stone look like a cut-out metal plate riveted to the stone base, are arranged in sets of four and eight, as follows:

Seven bosses plus one in the center equals eight.
Four on each side of the center equals four plus
    four plus four plus four.
Eight around each half of the original, outer circle
    equals eight plus eight.

According to a very ancient Greek theory of numbers as taught at Delphi and by Pythagoreans, four, as the first square of the first even number, is the perfect number for a hero, who is four-square. Thus, we could have symbolized here four heroes of the Picts with a matriarchal queen like Guinevere as the central and only larger boss. This view, that the queen is centered here, could be reinforced immediately on viewing the reverse side of the monument.

The circular border, or wheel of time or sun revolving across the sky, surrounding the central Cross is called by art historians the Ring of Glory. As Joseph Anderson (1881, 1886) observed, this stone and its fellows, *are all we know about Scotland in early Christian times.* More anciently speaking, then, the central boss should be Christ, and the Ring of Glory should be the rolling sun, which wheels across the heavens. Or Christ is the *Sol Invictus,* the Unconquered Sun. But the equal-armed cross with its four fours also brings to mind the four initials of Christ's name:

I	N	R	I
Iesus	*Nazarenus*	*Rex*	*Iudaeorum*
(Jesus	the Nazarene,	King	of the Jews)

From the free use of Christian symbolism (which, by the way, was found or invented or devised during King Arthur's lifetime) we may then understand, if we wish to do, that the Holy Cross, or Holy Rood, is the Church Triumphant, and that the Stone of Scone symbolizes Christ's martyrdom. If that satisfies the viewer, then the Stone should contain some beast, such as a White Stag which kills some foe such as a Pagan Snake: Christ killing Satan. Then the circle, the Ring of Glory, could also represent the orb of earth inside which the Cross Triumphant (the Cross of Victory) brings to convert the Anchor of Hope. The Rood or Holy Rood does commonly represent the Church Triumphant. And King Arthur gave to Melrose Abbey and/or to Holyrood in Edinburgh a piece of the True Cross (Holy Rood).

Whatever religious symbolism the viewer wishes to accept or to devise must rise from individual religious belief; for even the ancient Picts themselves had been converted to a Christianity, which was Judaic and Oriental in ritual, character, symbolism, and doctrine—all anterior to those of the later Catholic and Roman Church, or Catharist or Protestant Churches.

Under the Cross on Side I descends a long central shaft that has also been partially defaced. Stewart Cruden's (1957) guidebook sees there three pairs of facing beasts, and on the left side of the shaft three climbing figures. The small top figure is kneeling. She (or he) draws up a second person in a muscular depiction that Cruden says is absolutely foreign to Christian art. In any event, the small kneeling figure suggests the act of assistance by a young woman to an older, larger person, also with the large thighs of a woman. One is free to describe Guinevere as a small woman who brings aid to another. To bring help to a person who appears to be naked and in need of saving stresses the dangers apparent from the coiled beasts on the right-hand side of the central shaft.

The central shaft at last becomes a part of what appeared at first glance to be an equal-armed Cross. Thus, there are portrayed two different Crosses. That discovery is pleasing.

The monument seems to have two tenons on either side, which would support the old observation that the cross-slabs once stood dovetailed together as in a screen or pyramid, the tenons fitting into mortises cut into an adjoining stone to receive them.

The reverse, or Side II of this Guinevere Monument, Stuart's Plate LXXIV, is so much more pictorial as to elicit the theory that this cross-slab is the picture book the Picts did not write, and/or their illustrated life of heroic Arthurian personages (pp. 207–208). So perhaps it truly is a Guinevere Monument.

The sculptures here are so much clearer, less reworked, than those on Side I that they prance forth at first sight led by the regal King Arthur himself in the top center of the finished stone page. He is *the king!* He rides relaxed on his larger steed, sits solidly at parade with his back straight, on his mount, a high-stepping stallion whose neck is gracefully curbed, with a brace of hunting dogs escorting him, but one step ahead, obedient to the rider's signal to speed away. Heads are raised to scan the countryside.

Wonderful horse. Wonderful dogs. Powerful, kingly rider.

Below the king, on the viewer's left, three horsemen ride abreast, like Gawain and his two brothers. Behind them, but wearing a Phrygian cap, comes Prince Modred, beloved of the Pictish chroniclers and heir to Arthur's throne. He is a sister's son or an aunt's son. His hand is already raised in public greeting. Only one small dog is their outrider, in contrast to Arthur's well-trained, alert flankers.

Before Arthur there stands a slim but little angel ("messenger"): Guinevere herself. Her arms are raised to high heaven in the *orans* position of prayer. She has her back turned to the viewer, or she has her eyes on heaven, rather than on our world. Her bare feet betray her as priestess. The High-Priestess of the Celts also walked barefooted as she preceded her forces into battle. Warriors who trod in her footsteps were automatically guaranteed an instant seat in Paradise. Guinevere's wings show clearly in the picture. They strain to form a halo around her face. Under the long (white linen) robe she wears, her body is thin, as can be seen by the tucks the sculptor has cut on either side of her spine. Because Guinevere was the High-Priestess King Arthur wed so she could obliterate Camille's magic, then Guinevere must be the virginal angel who united and saved his realm: Britons, Scots, and Picts.

As an inspector of ancient monuments, Cruden finds this equestrian group at the top of the stone artistically "superb." The top figure whom we have identified as King Arthur is cloaked, observes Cruden, and bearded. He carries a spear, and is girt with a sword. He sits on a saddlecloth. His horse is bridled. Two hounds stand before him, and above all there is an angel. A cavalcade is suggested below him—riders abreast and a single outrider following. Neither Cruden, nor anyone else before today apparently, thinks of these stone sculptures as a continuous story, much less as history.

This Side II is part of what the local residents, who much resent the art historians' lack of interpretations, call the Guinevere Monument. They claim this knowledge by authority of their "mothers" and "grandmothers" going back to King Arthur's day in that very spot. They express embarrassment and considerable annoyance at British scholars, who come there and dare to contradict them and continue to treat them with absolute contempt. Only American and French visitors, they claim, will look at their Guinevere Monument with awe and reverence for the sculpting and speak kind words to the local women. This is a woman's monument, they say. It is the gravestone of "our own Queen Guinevere." We know because we have always known it. Her grave mound, and they point, is up over there beside the church door. It is our pennies that have saved her stone. This was our great queen.

But when the eye arrives at the central subject on Side II, identified by Cruden as Daniel in the Lion's Den, we come to the crux. This central figure is a chastened man with outturned feet planted solidly apart, outraised hands, standing ready and dealing appropriately with four lions. On closer inspection we then see that each creature is licking the hero, however. Each lion holds a paw raised to touch him, not necessarily a jaw open to eat him. So Daniel has been divinely delivered from four lions much as Lancelot was delivered from two. The long tunic on Lancelot, if one will oblige and think of "Daniel" as Lancelot, would make him no longer a warrior but the ordained priest he so ardently longed to become.

Below Lancelot is the Centaur, who commonly symbolizes in archaic, Christian terms the dual nature of Christ just as the Cup of Agony represents the Passion, and Guinevere's turtle doves symbolize the Presentation, and the Chariot of Fire depicts the Ascension.

The Centaur in Arthurian terms and letters would be their great teacher and prelate Merlin, teacher of Morgan, Lancelot, Gawain, Perceval, and the Lady of the Lake, just as the Greek Centaur Chiron taught medicine to Aesculapius, navigation to the Argonauts, courting to Peleus, and warfare to Achilles. Chiron brought gifts to the wedding of Peleus and Thetis: branches of trees from Mt. Pelion and flowers from the mountain meadows of Thessaly. The Centaur seems even more likely to be Merlin because he holds two axes in his hands. Arthurian texts identify any rider with an ax in his hand as a king, like King Mark of Cornwall in Scotland, as he was seen once by Lancelot.

The drama occurring in the bottom picture challenges the imagination because the beast whose snout is being held by the dragon is hard to identify. Is it an ox or a wolf? Cruden opted for the former notion, seeing a dragon holding "a horned beast by the nose." If the beast is horned, then he represents the Grail Castle and, possibly, Saint Luke.

In his wonderful book on the lost language of Symbolism, Harold Bayley (1952) found countless printers' watermarks of oxen symbolizing service at the Grail Castle. Therefore, the dragon here could represent evil paganism devouring the patient, long-suffering Christian. The ox appears commonly crowned with light, or with the Light of the World. Or he bears the Cross of Light between his horns.

But even so, only Queen Guinevere here and her two white doves open the Gates of Heaven.

CHAPTER XIII

Queen Guinevere

Verde que to quiero verde.
Verde viento. Verdes ramas.
El barco sobre la mar
y el caballo en la montaña.
Con la sombra en la cintura
ella sueña en su baranda,
verde carne, pelo verde,
con ojos de fría plata.

(Green, how I want you green.
Green wind. Green branches.
The boat on the sea
and the horse in the mountain.
With the shadow on her waist
she dreams on her veranda,
flesh green, hair green,
with eyes of frigid silver.)
—FEDERICO GARCÍA LORCA,
"Romance Sonámbulo"

A MAJOR ERROR FOR THE PAST FIFTEEN HUNDRED YEARS OR THEREABOUTS
has been not to think of Arthur's birthplace as Tintagel—error

enough to cast him and Queen Guinevere into fairyland—but to think of them as medieval. Queen Guinevere belongs only to the ancient world. She was an ancient queen who lived before Saint Columba Christianized the Picts anew, and she died soon after the year 542.

As the most talked-about queen of the ancient world, she lived while several traces of matriarchal customs still survived and before the dawn of medieval theology according to which women were debased and sex starved, with an uncontrolled passion for intercourse. Critics have seen in her garden scene (where she reached forward, took Lancelot's face in her hands, and of her own accord kissed him tenderly) Guinevere's hideous lust—a panting, ugly desire for intercourse. This is a medieval view of womankind.

The ancient Pictish artist who sculpted the Guinevere Monument, Side II, received as his mandate from a Macbeth and/or Lady Macbeth to hand down to posterity with a bare chisel this Pictish queen's biography. No vestige of language would intervene between sculptor, sculptured cross-slab, and viewers twelve hundred and more years later. How did he solve the problem? Did he sculpt a lewd, lascivious woman?

He sculpted another Winged Victory, the little angel we see on the stone. She is very small next to King Arthur, the conquering hero on his war-horse. But like the angels who hovered protectingly over the cornices of Diana's temple in Ephesus, Asia Minor, Queen Guinevere is another Delphic, ancient, and Winged Victory. Her Gaelic name should have been *Argento Coxa,* White Foot. Her plain, unadorned white robe and her bare, white feet symbolize a prime function of hers, which was to ride out to battle with or before Arthur's warriors. She hesitated a little before leaving Carlisle and bemoaned her hard fate. But she went to war and was taken hostage. Queen Guinevere knew her fate beforehand, but she departed. In fact, she preceded King Arthur into battle—the only one to do so. She may be thought of as equal to him in deed and in courage.

As for Lancelot and her kiss in the garden, was that equally voluntary action on her part not like benediction? Lancelot was an acolyte. He was a minor priest even when he stormed Dolorous Gard and delivered it from its double-key enchantment. Queen Guinevere reached up for Lancelot's face because he deserved her blessing. Not only was his blood both royal and sainted, he was, like herself, a sacrificial offering. The hero by definition offers his life for others, and others in the hero's lifetime accept that offering and prepare to feel the measured, appropriate, and necessary guilt at his death. The Pictish Guinevere and the Pictish Lancelot were birds of a feather. When Guinevere kissed the youth, she thought, "Blessed is he that cometh in the name of the Lord."

The garden scene should be read while accompanied by the "Requiem Mass," which Amadeus Mozart wrote as he lay dying: *Benedictus qui venit in nomine domini.* No hero lives long. All deserve a lady's kiss.

The Guinevere Monument in its little museum at Meigle, Scotland, is hers because the sculptor represented all the figures as alive, except Guinevere alone. It is her funerary slab, a sculpture for the dead queen seen as an angel in heaven.

On her Monument, Guinevere is comprehended as King Arthur's queen, certainly, but also as High-Priestess like queens of Egypt and Crete before her and like the Queen-Priestesses of the Hittites in what is now Turkey. Guinevere's wings are upswept like the tousled locks of a priestess. Her hair is the wings that almost form her halo. That was a High-Priestess whom Lancelot approached so reverently in the garden. She was virginal. She saved him once from the river at Camelot. She directed him at the fountain. She helped him across the Sword Bridge. She ordered him to kill the son of the pagan priest Bademagus. She ordained him, or completed his initiation in a blood sacrifice at her altar. She survived him because she was very revered by the Picts. They commissioned, made, and set up her Monument at Meigle, Scotland, in the rich Pictish country of Strathmore. We have only to admire it and read its cryptic pictures. It is a biography in stone.

The purpose of biography is to satisfy our desire for the knowledge of the private history of personages known to have been public figures associated with even more public figures of great renown. Our curiosity is not an idle desire. Beneath it lies a deeper need to regulate our own minds. Life gives us a prospect of possibilities. Biography affords us advance warning of pitfalls, safe lessons in adversity, studied and considered views of what the future holds behind its closed doors. In life we often have little time in which to make our decisions. Biography helps us make them in advance, helps us to make our strategy and take our stand before the onset of history.

Both time and history, the modern theologian Paul Tillich (1961) used to say, belong to religion and the priesthood as its ultimate concerns. Religious symbols like those carved on the Guinevere Monument, he also thought, point beyond ourselves. Such symbols participate in a reality as it is accepted by a group of people, our ancient Picts in this case. The symbols have therefore long since acquired the power to open our horizons, extend the dimensions of our ordinary thought to re-create a new referent for our own lives. They contribute to the stilling of our anxiety and ultimate concern. We live before the inherent and constant terror of history on a personal and, for us Americans, also on an international, even global scale.

The terror of history results from a view that sees lives as lived under a meaningless succession of events that seem to occur randomly and that sweep nations out of control from one catastrophe to another, under one monstrously evil leader after another. History is unforeseeable and unpredictable. King Arthur therefore chose Guinevere as his queen. She was a virginal priestess holding a comb and a mirror, symbols of her ability to read the future. Wisely King Arthur took over the rule of Camelot and in one stroke cemented Briton, Pict, and Scot into one people and one nation: Scotland.

More than one Arthurian text has King Arthur speaking of himself, and Malory repeats it wonderfully, as suspended upside down on the wheel of time. That symbolizes the cyclical view of history, a common idea, said Heinrich Zimmer, in about 1891, by which man is seen hooked inside the "noose of time." Both Hinduism and Buddhism adopted this image of the wheel of existence or life: cause into cause into effect, chains in the world of *maya* (illusion), an endless transmigration of souls from one miserable existence to another.

The Guinevere Monument escapes hopelessness by apply-
ing the theory of linear time preferred by Judaism, Christianity,
and Islam. The present, concurred the *Kalevala,* is a time of evil
where evil breeds evil; but a time of suffering will end. The
priestess showed Lancelot brief glimpses of the Paradise, which
the Pictish sculptors knew she would inhabit.

Queen Guinevere was very far from being a sex symbol or
any participant in, or supervisor of, fertility, bountiful harvests,
or thanksgiving ceremonies. Nor did she bear children herself or
engage in sex. She was in last analysis a priestess of the dead. For
this reason she officiated in the far Western world close to Ireland, which has always represented to Europeans the sunset
world where dead heroes go, as medieval kings went to Iona for
burial. King Arthur went there, to Avalon, on the Isle of Man,
for death and burial ceremonies befitting royalty and outstanding heroism. Queen Guinevere had prepared his monument and
entombment, about which we know no more than that. A barge
with queens in attendance conveyed him thus far.

The *Prose Lancelot*'s authors decided that one of Lancelot's
earliest adventures took place at the Castle called Dolorous Gard.
After Lancelot's successful penetration and after his defeat of the
monstrous Ethiopian who defended its last hurdle, the hero entered the copper chamber. There he saw the copper priestess. He
took her two keys from her. He opened the copper pillar. It
quaked. Shrill copper tubes screeched and whistled. The double-
key enchantment was broken. The copper mistress had been
merely a copper image, we were informed. The castle's name was
changed to Joyous Gard.

It would seem that this particularly gripping adventure was
chronologically misplaced, that it followed Lancelot's passage
over the Sword Bridge and anticipated his final ceremony at
Queen Guinevere's altar. Lancelot broke the magical spell of
paganism. He, Gawain, Perceval, and King Arthur recaptured
Dolorous Gard and renamed it Joyous Gard. Why? Because it
was soon to house the treasured relic, or talisman, which was the
Holy Grail, symbol of Christianity triumphant.

Dolorous Gard must itself have been the Copper Mountain.
Lancelot was originally assigned this adventure so that he could

release Queen Guinevere from her imprisonment there. After he had accomplished his terrifying feat and when the ordeal was over, he was informed that Guinevere had not been imprisoned there. The parallel exists: inside the copper chamber Lancelot saw the copper mistress. After he put the key into the pillar, he concurred that it had been merely a mistress image, and not Queen Guinevere sheathed in copper. He had been blinded by her copper mirror, presumably. What could be the meaning of all this?

Queen Guinevere as High-Priestess of the metalworking Picts was their Mistress of the Copper Mountain. Lancelot saw her clad in ceremonial copper, or she was sheathed in gold or in the shiniest metal of all, the lost orichalcum (copper? brass?) of which only the ancients are said to know the secret, which died with them.

Homer's *Odyssey* speaks of prehistoric palaces with bronze walls and golden doors hung on silver posts. Such lay buried perhaps inside the funeral mounds of Achilles and Penthesilea on the Plain of Troy. Ingots of copper were being carried by strange red men to the Pharaohs of Egypt and Kings of Crete, and some such ingots have been recovered by archaeologists. The domes of Atreus in Mycenae, or at Orchomenos, were once lined with copper. Superb sculptures in gold have been found in the funeral mounds of the Asian steppes. Grave mounds of Amazon priestesses in southern Russia have yielded even more such treasures.

Copper (Kyprios, cyprum) is a prehistoric word used from at least 6000 B.C., known to the Chaldeans from 4500 B.C., to Egyptians from 2260 B.C., and on the island of Cyprus (Kyprios) from 2500 B.C. The world's largest deposit was (or is) at Isle Royale in upper Michigan where 500,000 tons of pure copper was mined between 1800 B.C. and 1000 B.C. Copper is the only metal found in large masses; it has been used in industry, engineering, shipbuilding (sheathing of vessels and in nails), and as ornament. Its alloys are brass and bronze. It is a reddish colored element, of a reddish orange or carnelian red color. It is ductile and malleable, conducts heat and electricity easily. Fairly large deposits of copper were found in Europe, in the Faroes and Shetland Islands, in

Cornwall and the Rhine River banks, in Scandinavia, Germany, and Finland, and in the Ural Mountains of Russia. Copper was certainly in Arthur's day a sacred ornament. Its red color, plus black and white, constituted the three sacred colors at religious ceremonies.

In her plain white robe the priestess Guinevere gained status in King Arthur's Court and earned her wings. There was virtue in her veil; for, as Tennyson wrote of her, she had a strange power of seeing in an "awful dream" her future reputation as evil adulteress. Her story is not only mythological but historical. The reality of her presence on earth strikes us as both psychological and metaphysical. We still have more names to call her by than any earthly woman who ever lived.

The Guinevere Monument represents an official memory of Queen Guinevere whose person was recovered by the Picts, or whose corpse was recovered by them, and taken to Barry Hill near Meigle. Thereabouts popular memory treasures her still as King Arthur's queen and theirs. To them she is forever his Guardian Angel, and their Stone Flower.

The few archival traces of Queen Guinevere that remain in what is now Wales declare her to have been a daughter of the Ogre King at Camelot, one of twins or one even of triplets, sister of Bedevere, and a foul, criminal adulteress. Lancelot came into her "bed"—which charge we have discarded as having been misunderstood for "worshiped at her altar."

Medieval romances such as the compilation called *Prose Lancelot* give her history from betrothal to incarceration on the Isle of Man. There she fulfills several functions, as foreign heiress, bride, crowned queen, warrior, peacemaker, priestess, and link between her indigenous people (the Picts) and the new conquerors of northwestern Britain (the Scots). By allying Lancelot with Arthur, by placating and steadying Gawain, and by enlisting Galehaut, Queen Guinevere has been reconsidered as diplomat rather than as adulteress fit to be devoured by dogs; and yet, so great is modern scholars' "dread" of powerful women that she is branded still as heinously guilty of sexual crime.

By far the most significant deed in her life was not adultery but her descent into hell; this ritual of katabasis marks her incontrovertibly as King Arthur's High-Priestess. It also distinguishes her from all the other great ladies of her Dark Age century and the medieval and modern centuries to come. Thus Archdeacon Sinclair perceptively saw that there was a Goddess in that Pictish Cart of Chrétien, and that she was Queen Guinevere, King Arthur's crowned and sanctified consort.

No person denies that King Arthur was, like Alexander the Great, so popular a subject for medieval fiction and folk memory that his legend has for the past fifteen hundred years dwarfed his history. Such has also been the case of his Queen Guinevere, we must now admit. But the mythological trappings that hide her face never branded her an adulteress. Far from it. Aristocratic medieval romances, the even more aristocratic fairy tale, and a recognizable and recoverable symbolic code continually identify Guinevere as the most awesome, overpowering personage in Arthurian literature. She appears to have been second to none.

In her ancient ritual of katabasis, at her altar, Queen Guinevere officiated as another Mistress of the Copper Mountain. Like all such protectors of underground nature she wore green. Her ancient forbears were black-haired, green-eyed goddesses before whose step the mountain walls opened, at whose feet rubies and emeralds dropped in showers of glittering treasures. Inside her gold-sheathed temple she officiated at her Grail Castle with its carbonate of copper pillars. Those pillars, even in ancient Russia, had been carved of solid malachite. They were copper pillars—but gem green in hue.

Queen Guinevere thus leads one backward in time, across the Baltic Sea and White Sea, over continents, into the royal palace at what was St. Petersburg, with its twin malachite pillars sent to the czar by his Russian Mistress of the Copper Mountain, from the Urals. But before that and more to the east there was the Copper Mountain called Anārak in Iran. Guinevere's mythological system may go back in time even to China circa 350–270 B.C., where it had already been recorded as some cosmological system:

Element	Function	Colors	Direction	Season	Symbol	Constellation
metal	outlasts wood	white green red	west	autumn	white tiger	Virgo

For Guinevere's story, the fairy tale—which has for eons of recorded time recovered the essentials of princely lore—and the medieval romance—which relates only princely adventures of heart and sword—unite in common accord. Both archaic, narrative modes not only meet as they delineate Guinevere's life, but share its high points mutually and duplicate its happenings. Guinevere's only children were those of Sleeping Beauty: Dawn and Day. Her Goddess Cart was driven by a Gnome, a Pictish prince, as was Lancelot's Cart in Chrétien de Troyes's celebrated romance, *Lancelot, Le Chevalier de la charette.* Her dwarf was another of the Seven-League Boots.

Guinevere was also the incomparably beautiful daughter of the Ogre King, Lord of the Underworld. The princess sprang from the Orcan, or Pictish, or Ogre race. She was foreign and a future priestess of the dead on the Isle of Man, that sepulchral isle. The princess was wed by the dominant male. As in the classical fairy tale called Sleeping Beauty, which was earlier than *La Belle au bois dormant* of Charles Perrault, the prince wooed her because of her vast domains that he needed to annex. She was, in terms of real estate, the richest heiress. Her property and this alliance, Arthur and the Ogres, constituted his kingdom. As for Guinevere, her destiny was to reign over the dead in the golden chamber, between malachite pillars, at the Castle of the Holy Grail.

In 1974 Pavel Bazhov and James Riordan published in London (Frederick Muller Ltd., Edgware Road) *The Mistress of the Copper Mountain: Tales of the Urals,* illus. (9 tales, 86 pp.). The Russian Maid or Mistress, who is the central figure of these fairy tales, is a priestess much like our Guinevere. She has black hair and green eyes. She speaks what is also in Russia a foreign tongue. She can turn men to stone, or she is a Medusa-style priestess residing on some high mountain top like Chomolungma or Anārak or Munsalvesche of the Holy Grail. The Malachite Maid's army were green lizards with girls' heads who served her inside dark mountain caverns where copper crystals glittered among gold nuggets and blue sapphires and wine red rubies. There those who took food from her fingers forgot their last, sad, earthly life and prepared for reincarnation. The Maid changed color from white for her diamond chamber, to green for her emerald, to copper from her altared chamber. She allowed the prince from St. Petersburg to take two carved malachite pillars for his royal palace. Certain maidens who were changelings joined the Mother Mistress at her Copper Mountain. Maiden and Mistress were often heard laughing gaily as they strolled happily, mother priestess and daughter, echoing through their mountain grottoes.

"Do not pursue gold," the Mistress warned. "It turns to dust." Her Grannie gave a Russian prince three feathers for his hat: quick wits, firm will, and a kind heart. A white feather, she said, was for cheer in daytime, a black feather for protection in the dark, and a red feather for pleasure when he went out into sunlight.

The Arthurian hero Perceval falls into a trance at the sight of these three sacred colors of the priesthood: black, white, and red. A hero who saw the Mistress dressed as the Blue Baba in a blue mist could with her gift buy his freedom, but he would never marry after having seen the Mistress.

Those stone carvers who were taken inside her mountain mines learned that the Stone Flower grew there inside a malachite chamber. It had terrible power every autumn at the Serpent Festival. The Serpent Hill was the Mistress's abandoned copper mine. There she wore the copper robe that Lancelot saw her wearing at Dolorous Gard. She reigned in a stone garden of tombs and live, stone trees. Golden serpents wove and twined about her. The sight of her whirling copper, glowing bees flying overhead, malachite bells on her trees, and tinkling stars in the midnight heavens sent any human viewer running from his earthly home forever more. There dancing fire maids worked hard to turn winter into summer. Minor maidens from the Copper Mountain knew how to call the Sunshine Stone into the hand, of its own accord.

Queen Guinevere is a heroine of the fairy tale as well as of the romance all across Europe, grant those persons who have studied the transformations of popular tales and their charmed migrations, as here, from the Urals into Finland and then across Scandinavia and Germany into Great Britain. The queen's principal adventure, which is her descent into hell, follows the prototypical, Otherworld Journey.

In Volumes I-III of his six-volume *Motif-Index of Folk-Literature* (Bloomington, 1932–36) Stith Thompson (Study 101) locates the Otherworld by its recurring topographical features. The Grail Castle also contains each human and geographical characteristic:

A Mountain, plus
A Beautiful Priestess
This is the Earthly Paradise
A Water Barrier discourages the timorous
A River bars the route
Mist hides the site
(The Sword Bridge is typically Celtic)
The Way is hard to find
The Path is perilous
The Entrance is guarded by fierce animals (lions)
    The Castle revolves
        It is golden or
        It is glass, but
        It has two pillars of
          silver,
          gold, or
          copper (malachite)

But whether the pillars of Guinevere's Grail Castle are of green malachite or of red copper, the metal copper always appears, say the folklorists, in Otherworld journeys. Its presence alone alerts us to a radical departure from here to another realm. The apple one is forbidden to taste if one wishes to return to earth, may be of copper. Or the castle is all of copper. Perhaps the horseman one meets is a copper guardsman or he is a copper statue stood at the gate. Or the trees in her garden are copper trees or her bow or her boat or its rudder is copper.

Only in Russia was the first such dwarf made of copper. There he was called a little copper man: *Medny dradka.* Then in Rune II of the *Kalevala* we meet him again: pygmies there *clad* all in copper.

The Ural-Altaic fairy tale of the Copper Mountain and its Mistress was presented as the ballet *The Stone Flower*, music by Sergey Prokofiev in 1954. The Mistress of the Copper Mountain was danced by Maya Plisetskaya. That day Guinevere's Copper Mountain at Gorre, Isle of Man, became the Russian mountain (*gorý*). That day Guinevere returned to her Russian original: *Khozyáka Médnoy Gorý.* Program notes of the ballet inform us that this classical dance brings before us not only the fantastic beauty of Nature but also the overwhelming mystery and loveliness of Woman. The eyes of the Mistress are gems of malachite. She is the stone flower.

From such eastern realms Queen Guinevere adopted her copper costume, her copper pillars, and her magical Otherworld powers as wizard and foreign priestess.

It is no wonder everybody remembers Queen Guinevere with awe. She was the precious princess of the vanished Ogre race. How strange it is this one, lone presence has survived.

SELECTED BIBLIOGRAPHY

The following list of books was drawn up for the interested reader with the thought that it might lead him or her to the more rare materials used in this book. Many texts were chosen because they are easily available now in the United States. Others, which are most rare and can only be read in libraries, are mentioned, as far as possible, by first date of publication. Publishers of the available modern books are not given since they can so easily be found, or brought up on the computer in any library.

Alcock, Leslie. "Experts Cross Swords over King Arthur." *The Sunday Telegraph.* Great Britain, March 5, 1989.

Allen, J. Romilly. *Celtic Art in Pagan and Christian Times,* illus. (London, 1904).

———. *Early Christian Monuments in Scotland* (Edinburgh, 1963; London, 1887).

———. *Early Christian Symbolism in Great Britain* (London, 1887).

———. *Early Christian Symbolism in Great Britain and Ireland.* The Rhind Lectures (London, 1885).

Anderson, Joseph. *Scotland in Early Christian Times* (Edinburgh, 1881).

———. *Scotland in Pagan Times* (Edinburgh, 1886).

Anderson, Marjorie O. *Kings and Kingship in Early Scotland* (Edinburgh and London, 1980).

Annals of Ulster, 4 vols., ed. by W. M. Hennessy and B. MacCarthy (Dublin, 1893, 1895, 1901).

Annals of Wales, *Trioedd Ynys Prydein,* tr. by Rachel Bromwich (Cardiff, 1961).

Anwyl, Professor. "Wales and the Britons of the North." *The Celtic Review* IV (April 1908): 125–51.

Arbois de Jubainville, Henry d'. *La Civilisation des Celtes* (Paris, 1899).

Ashe, Geoffrey. *The Landscape of King Arthur* (New York, 1988).

Bain, Robert. *Clans and Tartans of Scotland* (Glasgow and London, 1968).

Bannerman, John. "The Dál Riata and Northern Ireland in the Sixth and Seventh Centuries." In *Celtic Studies* (Glasgow and New York, 1968).

———. *Studies in the History of Dalriada* (Edinburgh, 1974).

Bayley, Harold. *The Lost Language of Symbolism,* 2 vols., illus. (New York, 1912, 1951, 1952).

Becker, Ernest J. *Comparative Studies of the Medieval Visions of Heaven and Hell* (Baltimore, 1899).

Bede. *Historia Ecclesiastica Gentis Anglorum* [Bede's Ecclesiastical History of the English People], ed. by Bertram Colgrave and R. A. B. Mynors (Oxford, 1969).

———. *Venerabilis Baedae Opera Historica,* 2 vols., ed. by C. Plummer (Oxford, 1896).

Bergin, Osborn. *Irish Bardic Poetry,* ed. by David Greene and Fergus Kelly (Dublin, 1970).

Blackmore, Richard, M. D. *Prince Arthur. An Heroick Poem in Ten Books* (London, 1695).

Boece, Hector. *The History and Chronicles of Scotland,* 2 vols., tr. from Latin by John Bellenden (Paris, 1575; reprint, Edinburgh, 1821).

Borodine, Myrrha. *La Femme et l'amour au XIIe siècle* (Paris, 1967).

Boyd, Lucinda. *The Irvines and Their Kin* (Chicago, 1908).

Breeze, David J. *The Northern Frontiers of Roman Britain* (London, 1982).

Burn, Alexander Robert. *Agricola and Roman Britain* (London, 1953).

Burton, John Hill. *The History of Scotland* (London and Edinburgh, 1873, 1905).

Campbell, Alexander. *A Journey from Edinburgh through parts of North Britain* (London, 1802).

Campbell, John Francis. *The Celtic Dragon Myth* (New York, 1973).

———. *Popular Tales of the West Highlands,* 4 vols. (Edinburgh and London, 1860).

Campbell, Rev. John Gregorson. *Superstitions of the Highlands & Islands of Scotland* (Glasgow, 1900).

———. *Waifs and Strays of Celtic Tradition.* Argyllshire Series V. of 1891 and 1895. Introduction by Alfred Nutt (reprint, New York, 1973).

Chadwick, Hector Munro. *Early Scotland* (Cambridge, 1949).

———. *The Heroic Age* (Cambridge, 1912).

Chadwick, Nora K. *Celtic Britain* (London, 1964).

Chambers, Sir Edmund K. *Arthur of Britain* (Cambridge, 1927; reprint, New York, 1964).

Chambers, Robert. *The Picture of Scotland*, 2 vols., illus. (Edinburgh, 1827).

Chateaubriand, Francois René Vicomte de. *Les Martyrs*. In *Oeuvres romanesques* (Paris, 1969).

Chrétien de Troyes. *Arthurian Romances*, tr. by W. W. Comfort. Introduction and Notes by D.D.R. Owen (London and New York, 1914–1975). See "Lancelot," p. 270 ff.

Christiansen, Reidar. *The Vikings in Gaelic Tradition* (Oslo, 1931).

Chronicles of the Picts, Chronicles of the Scots, and Other Early Memorials of Scottish History, ed. by William F. Skene (Edinburgh, 1867).

Crawford, O.G.S. "Arthur and His Battles." *Antiquity* 9 (1935): 277–91.

———. *The Topography of Roman Scotland North of the Antonine Wall* (Cambridge, 1949).

Cruden, Stewart. *The Early Christian and Pictish Monuments of Scotland*, illus. Her Majesty's Stationery Office (Edinburgh, 1957).

Curtin, Jeremiah. *Hero-Tales of Ireland* (Boston, 1894).

Darmesteter, James. *Sacred Books of the East* (Oxford, 1880; reprint, London, New York, 1902, ed. by Jastrow Morris).

Dean of Lismore's Book. A Selection of Ancient Gaelic Poetry from a Manuscript Collection Made by Sir James M'Gregor, Dean of Lismore, in the Beginning of the Sixteenth Century, ed. and tr. by Rev. Thomas M'Lauchlan. Introduction and Notes by William F. Skene (Edinburgh, Edmonston, and Douglas, 1862).

The Death of King Arthur, tr. by James Cable (London, 1971, 1975).

Deffontaines, Pierre. *Géographie et Réligions* (Paris, 1948).

Diack, Francis Carney. *The Inscriptions of Pictland* (Aberdeen, 1945).

Dickinson, William Croft. *Scotland from the Earliest Times to 1603* (London, Edinburgh, 1961).

———, Gordon Donaldson, Isobel A. Milne. *A Source Book of Scottish History*, vol. I (Edinburgh, 1952).

Dillon, Myles. *The Cycles of the Kings* (London, 1946).

———. *Early Irish Literature* (Chicago, London, Toronto, 1948).

Diverre, A. H. *Arthurian Romance*, ed. by D.D.R. Owen (Edinburgh and London, 1973).

Dreyfus, Camille and André Berthelot, eds., *La Grande Encyclopédie* (Paris, 1886–1902). "Finlande," by E. Beauvois.

Duke, John Alexander. *The Columban Church* (Oxford, 1932; reprint, Edinburgh, 1957).

Duke of Argyle. *The House of Argyll and the Collateral Branches of the Clan Campbell from the Year 420 to the Present (1871)* (Glasgow, 1871; reprint, Morgantown, West Virginia, 1983).

Durning, William and Mary. *A Guide to Irish Roots* (La Mesa, Calif., 1986).

Eaton, David MacLean. "Was Queen Guinevere Buried in Scotland?" *Epigraphic Society Occasional Publications,* ed. by Barry Fell, vol. 18, 1989.

Eban, Abba. "Wisdom Lies in the Outcome, So Close Ranks on Terror." *Los Angeles Times.* August 6, 1989, V, 5.

Eliade, Mircéa. *Cosmos and History: The Myth of the Eternal Return,* tr. by Willard R. Trask (New York, 1959).

Evans, Emyr Estyn. *Irish Folk Ways* (London, 1957, 1961).

Fell, Barry. *America B.C.* (New York, 1976).

Flasket, John. *Certayne Matters Concerning the Realme of Scotland* (London, 1603).

Fontenelle, Bernard de. "Histoire des Oracles." In *Oeuvres de Monsieur Fontenelle* (Amsterdam, 1764).

Frappier, Joseph. *Chrétien de Troyes* (Paris, 1957).

Froissart, Sir John. *The Chronicles of England, France, and Spain.* H. P. Dunster's condensation of the Thomas Johnes translation. Introduction by Charles W. Dunn (New York, 1961).

Gayley, Charles Mills. *The Classic Myths in English Literature and in Art* (Boston, New York, Chicago, London, Atlanta, Dallas, Columbus, San Francisco, 1893, 1911).

Geoffrey of Monmouth. *Historia regum Britanniae,* ed. by Acton Griscom and Robert Ellis Jones (New York, London, and Toronto, 1929).

Gerald of Wales. *The Journey through Wales and the Description of Wales,* tr. by Lewis Thorpe (London, 1978).

Gildas. *The Ruin of Britain and Other Documents,* ed. by John Morris and Michael Winterbottom (London, 1978).

Glennie, Stuart. *Arthurian Localities* (Edinburgh, 1869).

Goodrich, Norma Lorre. "Concerning La Morte Aymeri de Narbonne." University of Maryland Publication, 1968, pp. 3–9.

———. "The Dream of Panurge." *Etudes Rabelaisiennes,* Geneva, 1967, VII, pp. 93–103.

———. "The *Vita Nuova.* A Dante Profile." University of Southern California Publication, 1967.

———. *The Ways of Love. Eleven Romances from Medieval France* (Boston and London, 1964, 1965).

Gougaud, Dom Louis. *Christianity in Celtic Lands,* tr. from the author's Ms. by Maud Joynt (London, 1932).

Grant, Isobel Frances. *Highland Folk Ways* (London and Boston, 1961).

Mrs. Grant of Laggan (Anne MacVicar). *Letters from the Mountains* (Boston, 1796, 1819; reprint, London, 1845).

Gray, Thomas. *The Correspondence of Thomas Gray,* 3 vols., ed. by Paget Toynbee and Leonard Whibley (Oxford, 1935).

Green, Miranda. *The Gods of the Celts* (Gloucester and Totowa, 1986).

Heber, Reginald. *The Poetical Works of Reginald Heber, Late Lord Bishop of Calcutta,* illus. Introduction by M. A. Wolfe Howe (Philadelphia, 1870).

Heinrich von dem Türlin. *Diu Crone,* tr. as *The Crown* by J. W. Thomas (University of Nebraska, 1989).

Henderson, Isobel. *The Picts* (London, 1967).

Henry of Saltrey. *Tractatus de Purgatorio Sancti Patricii.* See Marie de France.

Holinshed, Raphael. *Chronicles of England, Scotland, and Ireland* (London, 1577).

Huddleston, Robert, ed. *History of the Druids* (Edinburgh, 1814).

Hughes, Kathleen. *Celtic Britain in the Early Middle Ages* (London, 1980).

Hyde, President Douglas. *A Literary History of Ireland,* ed. by Briano O Cuív (London and New York, 1899; reprint, 1967).

Irving, David. *The History of Scottish Poetry,* ed. by John Aitken Carlyle (Edinburgh, Edmonston, and Douglas, 1861).

Jackson, Kenneth Hurlston. *The Gaelic Notes in the Book of Deer* (Cambridge, 1972).

Jones, William Lewis. *King Arthur in History and Legend* (Cambridge, 1933).

Joyce, Patrick Weston. *Atlas and Cyclopedia of Ireland,* Part I (New York, 1914).

———. *A Concise History of Ireland* (Dublin, 1837).

———. *Irish Names of Places* (Dublin, 1869).

———. *A Reading Book in Irish History* (London, Dublin, New York, and Bombay, 1901).

———. *A Social History of Ancient Ireland* (Dublin, 1903, 1920).

Kalevala. The Land of Heroes, 2 vols., tr. by W. F. Kirby. Introduction by J.B.C. Grundy (London and New York, 1907–74).

Keating, Rev. Geoffrey. *Foras feasa,* vol. 3 (New York, 1866).

Kennedy, Patrick. *Legendary Fictions of the Irish Celts* (London, 1866).

Ker, William Paton. *The Dark Ages* (New York, 1958).

Knight, Charles. *William Shakspere. A Biography* (London, 1843; New York, 1971).

"Lancelot of the Laik." EETS, Original Series #6. Introduction by Rev. U. W. Skeat (London, 1865).

Larminie, William. *West Irish Folk-Tales and Romances.* The Camden Library (London, 1893).

Layamon. See Wace.

Le Livre de Lancelot del Lac, vols I, II, and III from *The Vulgate Version of the Arthurian Romances,* ed. by H. O. Sommer (Washington, 1910). Or see *Romans de la Table Ronde,* ed. and tr. by Paulin Paris in 5 volumes (Paris, 1868–77). Alternate title: *The Prose Lancelot.* The *Lancelot,* recte *Lanzelet,* 2 vols., was edited by W.J.A. Jonckbloet (The Hague, 1846–49).

Logan, James. *The Scottish Gael, or Celtic Manners* (Hartford, n.d., but c. 1830).

Lot, Ferdinand. *Etude sur le Lancelot en prose* (Paris, 1918, 1954).

Mabinogion, The, tr. by Gwyn and Thomas Jones (London and New York, 1949).

MacDougall, Rev. James. *Folk Tales and Fairy Lore.* Introduction by George Calder (Edinburgh, 1910; reprint, New York, 1977).

————. *Waifs and Strays of Celtic Tradition.* Argyllshire Series #31. Introduction by Alfred Nutt (London, 1891; reprint, New York, 1973).

Maclean, Magnus. *The Literature of the Celts* (London, Glasgow, and Bombay, 1926).

————. *The Literature of the Highlands* (London, Glasgow, and Dublin, 1904).

Maclehose, Alexander. *Historic Haunts of Scotland,* illus. (London, 1936).

Mâle, Emile. *La Fin du paganisme en Gaule* (Paris, 1950).

Mallet, Paul Henri. *Northern Antiquities . . . Ancient Scandinavians,* ed. by I. A. Blackwell, tr. by Bishop Percy (London, 1873).

————. *Northern Antiquities,* ed. by Burton Feldman (New York and London, 1979).

Malory, Sir Thomas. *Le Morte d'Arthur,* 2 vols. Preface by Sir John Rhŷs (London and New York, 1906–61).

Mann, John C. and David J. Breeze. "Ptolemy, Tacitus and the tribes of North Britain," *Proceedings of the Society of Antiquaries of Scotland* 117 (1988): 85–91.

Marie de France. *The "Espurgatoire Saint Patriz" of Marie de France, with a Text of the Latin Original,* ed. by T. Atkinson Jenkins (Chicago, 1903). See also her romances: *Lais,* ed. by Alfred Ewert (Oxford, 1976).

Maspero, Sir Gaston. *Histoire ancienne des peuples de l'Orient classique,* 3 vols. (Paris, 1895–99).

McCallum, Hugh and John. *Poems of Ossian, Orrann, Ulin, and Other Bards Who Flourished in the Same Age* (Montrose, 1816).

McKerracher, Archie. "The Round Table Was at Stenhousemuir." *The SCOTS Magazine* 131, #5 (August 1989): 505–13.

McPherson, Joseph McKenzie. *Primitive Beliefs in the North-East of Scotland* (New York, 1929; reprint, 1977).

Mercurius Caledonius. Comprising the Affairs now in Agitation in Scotland: with a Survey of Forraign Intelligence. From Monday Dec. 31 to Tuesday,. Jan. 8th, 1661 (Edinburgh, 1661).

Mertz, Henriette. "Keftiu in Bearing Copper," from her *Atlantis* (Chicago, 1976): chapter V.

Meyer, Kuno. *Learning in Ireland in the Fifth Century and the Transmission of Letters* (Dublin, 1913).

————. *Selections from Ancient Irish Poetry* (London, 1911).

Miller, Helen Hill. *Realms of Arthur* (New York, 1969).

Miller, Stuart, J. K. St. Joseph, John Clarke, John Davidson, Anne S. Robertson. *The Roman Occupation of South-West Scotland* (Glasgow, 1952).

Moore, A. W. *A History of the Isle of Man,* 2 vols. (London, 1900; reprint, Manx Museum and Trust, 1977).

Northern Annals, The (lost). These Annals seem to have been last used in the thirteenth century. See entry #2168 in *A Bibliography of English History to 1485* by Charles Gross. Ed. by Edgar R. Graves (Oxford, 1975). See also Kathleen Hughes and Robert L. G. Ritchie.

Nutt, Alfred. *Ossian and the Ossianic Literature* (London, 1910).

"The Occult in Language and Literature," ed. by Hermine Riffaterre. *New York Literary Forum.* 1980.

O'Connor, Frank. *A Backward Look* (London, Melbourne, and Toronto, 1967).

O'Conor (of Belanagare), Charles. *Dissertations on the History of Ireland, etc.* (Dublin, 1753, 1766, 1812).

O'Faoláin, Sean. *The Silver Branch* (London, 1938 or New York, 1938).

O'Looney, Brian. "On ancient historic tales in the Irish Language" (Dublin, 1876).

Olrik, Axel. *The Heroic Legends of Denmark.* Scandinavian Monographs, Vol. IV, tr. by Lee M. Hollander (New York, 1919; reprint, 1976).

O'Rahilly, Thomas Francis. *Early Irish History and Mythology* (Dublin, 1946).

Orkneyinga Saga, tr. by Hermann Pálsson and Paul Edwards (New York, 1981).

Ó Suilleabháin, Séan. *A Handbook of Irish Folklore.* Introduction by Séamus Ó Duilearga (Dublin, 1942; reprint, Detroit, 1970).

Owen, D. D. R. *The Vision of Hell* (Edinburgh and London, 1970).

The Oxford Book of Welsh Verse, ed. by Thomas Parry (Oxford, 1962).

Paris, Gaston Bruno Paulin. *Histoire poetique de Charlemagne* (Paris, 1865).

Parzival. See Wolfram.

Pastoreau, Michel. "Armoiries et devises des chevaliers de la Table Ronde. Etude sur l'imagination emblématique à la fin du Moyen Age." *Le Finistère Autrefois* 3 (1980): 29–127.

Patch, H. R. *The Other World, According to Descriptions in Medieval Literature* (Cambridge, Mass., 1950).

Pennants, Thomas. *A Tour in Scotland* (London, 1776).

Percy, Thomas, Bishop of Dromore. *Reliques of Ancient English Poetry* (London and/or New York, 1802).

Pirenne, Henri. *Economic and Social History of Medieval Europe,* tr. (London, 1936, New York, 1937).

———, Gustave Cohen, and Henri Focillon. *Histoire du moyen âge,* 8 vols. (Paris, 1933).

The Poems of Ossian, tr. by James Macpherson, ed. by William Sharp (Edinburgh, 1926).

The Poetical Romances of Tristan, in French, in Anglo-Norman, and in Greek, composed in the Twelfth and Thirteenth Centuries, 2 vols., ed. by Francisque Michel (London, 1835).

Prose Lancelot. See *The Vulgate Version of the Arthurian Romances,* 7 vols., ed. by H.O. Sommer (Washington, 1908–16).

Quillet, Jeannine. *Les Clefs du pouvoir au moyen âge* (Paris, 1972).

Rees, Alwyn and Brinley Rees. *Celtic Heritage. Ancient Tradition in Ireland and Wales* (London, 1961).

Reliquae Celticae, 2 vols., coll. by Rev. Alexander Cameron, ed. by Alexander Mac-Bain and Rev. John Kennedy (Inverness, 1892–94).

Rhŷs, Sir John. *Celtic Britain* (London, 1882).

———. *Celtic Heathendom* (London, 1888).

———. *Studies in the Arthurian Legend* (Oxford, 1891).

——— and David Brynmor Jones. *The Welsh People* (London, 1900).

Ripley, William Zebina. *The Races of Europe: A Sociological Study.* Lowell Institute Lectures (Boston and New York, 1899).

Ritchie, Robert L. G. *Chrétien de Troyes and Scotland* (Oxford, 1952).

Roddy, Kevin. "The Descent into Hell: Medieval Literature and Medieval Myth" (Loyola University, New Orleans, 1975).

———. "Structuralism and the Harrowing of Hell" (Loyola University, New Orleans, 1975).

Rogers, Rev. Charles. *Social Life in Scotland,* 3 vols. (Edinburgh, 1884).

Romans de la Table Ronde, 5 vols., ed. by Paulin Paris (Paris, 1868–77).

Saxo Grammaticus. *The Nine Books of Danish History,* 2 vols., tr. by Oliver Elton, ed. by Rasmus B. Anderson and J. W. Buel. Preface by Frederick York Powell (London, Copenhagen, etc., n.d.).

Schofield, William Henry. *English Literature from the Norman Conquest to Chaucer* (New York, 1906).

Scott, R. D. *The Thumb of Knowledge in Legends of Finn, Sigurd, and Taliesin* (New York, 1930).

Scott, Sir Walter. *Complete Poetical Works,* ed. by Horace E. Scudder (Boston and New York, 1900).

———. *Minstrelsy of the Scottish Border* (Ed. of 1802, 1803).

Selections from Ancient Irish Poetry, tr. by Kuno Meyer (London, 1911).

Simpson, W. Douglas. *The Ancient Stones of Scotland* (London, 1965, 1968).

———. *Portrait of the Highlands,* illus. (London, 1969).

Skene, William Forbes. *Celtic Scotland,* 3 vols. (Edinburgh, 1956).

———. *Chronicles of the Picts and Scots* (Edinburgh, 1867).

Smart, J. S. *James Macpherson* (London, 1905).

Smyth, Alfred P. *Warlords and Holy Men. Scotland A.D. 80–1000.* (The New History of Scotland) (London, 1984).

Squire, Charles. *The Mythology of the British Islands* (London, 1905; reprint, Hollywood, 1975).

Stenton, Sir Frank Merry. *Anglo-Saxon England* (Oxford, 1943).

Stuart, Dr. John. *Sculptured Stones of Scotland,* 2 vols. (Aberdeen, 1856–67).

Stubb, W. *Select Charters* (Oxford, 1890).

Symons, Arthur. *The Symbolist Movement in Literature* (London, 1908).

Tennyson, Alfred. *The Poetical Works of Alfred Tennyson, Poet Laureate* (Boston and New York, n.d.).

Thomas, Charles. "The Interpretation of the Pictish Symbols." *The Archaeological Journal* 120 (1963): 31–97.

The Tibetan Book of the Dead (Bardo Thödol), ed. by W. Y. Evans-Wentz. Forewords by C. G. Jung, Lāma Anagarika Govinda, and Sir John Woodroffe (Oxford, 1949, 1959, 1960).

Tillich, Paul. "The Meaning and Justification of Religious Symbols." In *Religious Experience and Truth*, ed. by Sidney Hook (New York, 1961), pp. 3–5.

Toland, John (1670–1722). *A Critical History of the Celtic Religion and Learning as containing an Account of the Druids, as the Priests and Judges* (London, n.d.).

———. *Le Nazaréen* (London, 1777).

Treharne, Reginald F. *The Glastonbury Legends* (London, 1967).

Triads, The Welsh. *Trioedd Ynys Prydein*, ed. and tr. with commentary and introduction by Rachel Bromwich (Cardiff, 1961, 1979).

Turgot, Bishop of St. Andrews. *The Life of St. Margaret, Queen of Scotland*, ed. by William Forbes-Leith, S. J. (Edinburgh, 1896).

Vulgate Cycle of Arthurian Romances, 7 vols., ed. by Oskar H. Sommer (Washington, 1908–16).

Wace and Layamon. *Arthurian Chronicles*, tr. by Eugene Mason. Introduction by Gwyn Jones (London, Toronto, and New York, 1912–77).

Wainwright, F. T. *The Problem of the Picts* (Edinburgh, 1965).

Walsh, Maurice N., M.D. "A Possible Cryptomnesic Influence in the Development of Freud's Psychoanalytic Thought." *The Psychoanalytic Forum* II, 4 (Winter 1967).

Ware, Sir James. *The Antiquities and History of Ireland* (London and Dublin, 1705, 1714; reprint, London, 1871).

Webster, Graham. *Celtic Religion in Roman Britain* (Great Britain, 1986).

Webster, Kenneth G. T. *Guinevere: A Study of Her Abductions* (Milton, Mass., 1951).

Weinraub, Eugene J. *Chrétien's Jewish Grail* (Chapel Hill, 1975).

Wentz, W. Y. Evans. *The Fairy-Faith in Celtic Countries* (London, New York, Toronto, and Melbourne, 1911).

Weston, Jessie Laidlaw. *Lancelot* (London, 1901).

White, John, *The Meeting of Science and Spirit* (New York, 1990).

Williams, J. E. Caerwyn. *Literature in Celtic Countries* (Cardiff, 1971).

Windisch, Ernst. *Buddha's Geburt und die Lehre von der Seelenwanderung* (Leipzig, 1908).

———. *A Concise Irish Grammar*, tr. by Norman Moore (Cambridge, 1882).

———. *Kurzgefasste Irische Grammatik mit Lesestücken* (Leipzig, 1879).

———. *Māra und Buddha* (Leipzig, 1895).

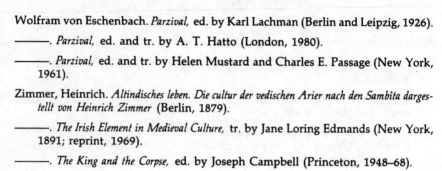

Wolfram von Eschenbach. *Parzival,* ed. by Karl Lachman (Berlin and Leipzig, 1926).

———. *Parzival,* ed. and tr. by A. T. Hatto (London, 1980).

———. *Parzival,* ed. and tr. by Helen Mustard and Charles E. Passage (New York, 1961).

Zimmer, Heinrich. *Altindisches leben. Die cultur der vedischen Arier nach den Sambita dargestellt von Heinrich Zimmer* (Berlin, 1879).

———. *The Irish Element in Medieval Culture,* tr. by Jane Loring Edmands (New York, 1891; reprint, 1969).

———. *The King and the Corpse,* ed. by Joseph Campbell (Princeton, 1948–68).

INDEX